D1286529

ISBN: 978-1-63385-324-9

Cover design by Rust Dyer, Digidyer Productions

Photo: Jini Vail at Château Regagnac by John Lester Vail, Sr.

Published by
Word Association Publishers
205 Fifth Avenue
Tarentum, Pennsylvania 15084

www.wordassociation.com
1.800.827.7903

'Coiffe Tourangeaux' is the traditional bonnet worn by women of Touraine. The above hand-embroidered wild roses are the remains of a family heirloom 'coiffe' made by Mado Renaud's maternal grandmother in the 1880's. The roses were originally sewn onto her bouffant white organdy bonnet, easily recognizable as typically 'Toourangeaux'. Each area of France is favored with a uniquely-shaped 'coiffe'.

Summering in France's Loire Valley

A Decade of Art, Cuisine, Music & History

Jini Jones Vail

"Carpe diem..." Horace

Jini Jona Vail

WORD ASSOCIATION PUBLISHERS
www.wordassociation.com
1.800.827.7903

Dedication

This book is dedicated to my loving husband, John Lester Vail, Sr. for designing and building my very own woman cave/library as an environment conducive to writing.

And to my ever true, son, Rusty, (Richard Hemenway Dyer III), who accompanied me on so many of these adventures and with his skill as a film producer, created footage to remember them.

Table of Contents

Foreword

FOR MY LOIRE STORY I write mostly in the present tense to show the action as it was taking place in the space of the decade (1987-1996). Naturally there have been changes in France, in America and around the world since that decade, so I urge you to follow the storyline in the context in which it took place in those years, unless otherwise noted.

I feel a compelling urge to share my experience in 'La Belle France' particularly, my decade of summers (1987-1996) centered in the Loire Valley and beyond. The Loire River, the longest in France, rises in the Cevennes region of the Massif Central (the central highlands), then flows 634 miles to empty into the Atlantic Ocean at Saint-Nazaire, situated at the south end of the Brittany peninsula. It is no longer navigable as it was for hundreds of years. Flooding, silt and shifting sand over the years have prevented shipping. Much to my surprise, there are nuclear power plants along the river, although I have only seen one as I followed the path of the Loire on the way from Tours to Sancerre. For the most part, the Loire flows quietly through peaceful landscapes. Along its banks are beautiful châteaux you will visit with me in this tome and taste the wines from famous vineyards such as Vouvray and Sancerre.

One summer I chose to follow the Seine River. It flows north of the Loire, on a somewhat parallel course, and is the third longest river in France, 485 miles, having found its source near Dijon in northeastern Burgundy between Paris and the German border. Unlike its sister, the Loire, the Seine is mostly navigable. The portion of the Seine that

I followed begins in Paris and continues west, zigzagging through Normandy to empty into the English Channel at Le Havre. The Seine is famous for passing under the bridges of Paris and for romantic river cruises. The mighty Seine beckoned me to visit the places where the Impressionists (Monet and Renoir) and Post-Impressionists (Van Gogh and Gauguin) painted; where my English ancestors: William the Conqueror, King Henry II, his son, King Richard I, as well as my French ancestors: King Louis VII and his first wife, Queen Aliénor (Eleanor) of Aquitaine lived, fought and died (for the most part). N.B. Queen Aliénor's second husband was Henry II of England.

The Loire River Valley is named the "Garden of France" and the "Valley of the Kings" both of which, gardens and kings, are prime tourist attractions. Around the turn of the 21st century the city of Tours, formerly a Gallo-Roman settlement, is a University town, with a population of about 134,000 and remains the predominant city in the province of Touraine. Tours is a short 1 ½ hour ride on the fast train (TGV) heading southwest of Paris.

My summers along the Loire began when I was a graduate student/ tourist in Tours thirty years ago. I was stretching to update my patchy French, barely able to distinguish one château from another, never mind the crisscrossing history surrounding them. I did not know a soul in France after a hiatus of 25 years away from her shores. Happily, as the summers went on, I made progress in being able to pinpoint the history of each château and to forge new friendships. In so doing I felt a growing attachment to the area. Each year I returned with renewed enthusiasm, adding to the foundations initiated the first summer, 1987.

A prime reason for my return trips was genealogical in nature. I already knew that my family roots stretched well beyond my maternal great-grandmother of some 29 generations ago, Aliénor of Aquitaine, Queen of France, later Queen of England. My search expanded to the family of Aliénor including her first husband, King Louis VII of France and their children, plus her second husband, King Henry II of England and their offspring. I sought places of interest pertaining to ancestors even as far back as Emperor Charlemagne, Fulk Nerra III, and William the Conqueror. The first of them drew me on a trip over the Pyrénées as a part of the Pilgrimage to Santiago de Compostela taken by Queen Aliénor's father, William X, Duke of Aquitaine.

My mother's cousin spent thirty years in pursuit of our family tree. He verified and later published his findings the tried and true method in the 1930's and 40's by traveling to France and England sorting through ancient records. At the outset of my visits to the Loire Valley I knew almost nothing of Aliénor's life, where she was born, lived or died. This would change significantly as my appetite for knowledge of her and my other forbears deepened.

I have been a Francophile since birth. You might say I 'inherited' it from my parents. My father, Lewis Rawson Jones, majored in French at Colgate University, and my mother, Anne Elizabeth Aulls Jones attended Syracuse University until the 1929 financial crash. She enjoyed delving into the cultural side of all things French.

I sailed to France in 1958 (my first trip) as an exchange student with the Experiment in International Living, spending four months with the Weber family in Belfort, 'Territoire de Belfort', near Strasbourg. The following summer, after graduation from Sweet Briar College with a BA in French Literature in my pocket, I returned to Europe with my parents, making the grand tour beginning and ending, you guessed right, in France.

After returning home I moved to New York City where I used my facility in French to land a super job, finding my niche as a travel writer at Air France, Public Relations, 666 Fifth Avenue.

Then came the intervening years of marriage, children and divorce. By natural progression, following the interwoven threads of my interests in art, architecture, cuisine, history and music, I recaptured my lost love, France. At age 49, in 1986, I turned to the reshaping of my new life in my favored field, French. Decision: I would become a French teacher.

I wholeheartedly encourage those of you on the threshold of choice, even in your middle years, to follow your heart. It is at once a looming precipice and a window into a new and fulfilling life. My friends told me they could never go back to school, let alone graduate school, at my age, nor could they contemplate so many hours of study. They intoned: "The whole process would require too much self-discipline." To their objections I answered, " It's never too late." My son, Rusty, gently, but firmly, pointed out, "Mom, if it's what you want, make it a priority." I have proceeded on these two premises, and they have not failed me.

Sixty-three graduate credits and ten summers in France later, combined with serving sixteen years on the "State of Connecticut Governor's Advisory Commission on American and Francophone Cultural Affairs" as well as Vice President of the Alliance Française of Northwestern Connecticut in charge of programs, I carried on with verve. Yes, these years of French immersion have been richly rewarding, fascinating and positive!

The decade beginning 1987 was a sweet time in my life during which I could concentrate on my beloved France. I entered Southern Connecticut State University (SCSU) as a graduate student. The first year I carried a full load of classes required for certification to teach High School French in Connecticut. For the next four years I not only continued my grad courses, but I taught French full time.

My younger daughter, Amy, was completing her final year at the same university. She encouraged me in every way, recommended the best professors, showed me short cuts in the registering process, walked me around the huge campus pointing out the best route from class to class and, most important of all, she divulged the best-kept secret between commuter students, i.e. how to choose the best professors, where to find the closest, safest parking.

I know many of you are thinking you wouldn't want to return to college with your offspring even under the best of circumstances. Well, I'm here to say it can work beautifully and create a stronger bond between the generations. Best of all, in this great experiment in generation mingling, Amy and I shared precious "together time."

In January 1987 with my certification completed, and an 'A' average under my belt, I found a job, no small feat at this particular time when French teaching jobs were at a premium. I know I had Divine help, as it must have been the only High School French position open mid- year!

My first return trip to France since the 1960's was during the summer of that certification year. SCSU offered a month-long study course at-+ the University of Touraine, "Institut de Touraine". I grabbed the chance to brush up on my 25-year gap to resume my studies in Tours, home of "the purest of the pure" French accents in the Loire Valley.

Needless to say, it was the beginning of many such summers of study and travel, always with Tours as my hub and with side trips far and wide. All of the adventures of which I write happened to me during this period. I kept a journal, took hundreds of photos I stuffed into a yearly album along with 'realia' to enhance my new teaching career. I shipped back to the US cartons of books, CDs of favorite French singers, and posters galore to decorate my classroom. I don't believe I missed any new publications on Queen Aliénor of Aquitaine. I made every effort while in France to follow in her footsteps.

I maintained correspondence with my new French friends during the winters. Also, by February each year I sent letters of inquiry for the next summer, requesting information on upcoming events as well as the dates of the annual "Semaines Musicales" (summer concert series) held in Tours featuring Russian violist, Yuri Bashmet. Many say he is the most famous violist in the world.

The French government helps teachers and Francophiles to make it fun to travel and teach by proclaiming a famous personage or event to be the focus of the year. The most memorable was the bicentennial of the French Revolution in 1989. This choice was a boon. It gave me a pivot point on which to concentrate my preparations for travel and juicy food for thought to share with my students.

In short, my winter preparation for the next trip afforded me a means of getting through the often difficult and trying school year. I have often said that as a teacher, in September one enters a narrow tunnel of concentration and does not emerge until the final grades are penned into the grade book in June. In this way I worked out a plan of action that I followed each year with great success. My light at the end of the tunnel was my return to the Loire Valley with the prospect of new adventures awaiting me there.

When my classes in Tours ended each summer, my son, Rusty, or a close friend, joined me for personal travel time that could be as long as three weeks. You will meet Rusty as we make our first visit by personal invitation to the Château de Rochambeau, our pilgrimage to Santiago de Compostela, to Cathar country and to the far reaches of Brittany. You will also meet my friend Judith on the Luberon trip and another friend, Antoinette, will follow in the footsteps of the French Impressionists in Normandy. For each sojourn we rented a car and headed out, usually on a specific quest to explore an out-of-the-way location, not on the normal tourist agenda.

I have filled the chapters of this book with the many delicious ways I spent my days in Touraine and surrounding regions. It is a goal of mine to share these adventures and serendipities with my reader as I availed myself of all the possibilities that came my way. For example, Joan of Arc is a recurring theme that I encounter in Chapter One, and I follow where her story leads as I wend my way through French history.

The first chapter is a sample of an actual day in my life as a grad student in 1988, living at the home of Lucien and Mado Renaud in central Tours. The first summer of 1987 our SCSU study group was housed in a University dorm, and a later summer study was spent at the University of Bourgogne at Dijon, once again, based in a dorm. Before the end of first summer in Tours my new friend and classmate, Rita, and I realized that to make the most of our time in France we must be totally immersed in the language day and night. Therefore, we looked for a home stay for the next summer of 1988. And we hit the Jackpot! That is when we found the Lucien and Mado Renaud family. Living as members of the Renaud household would mark the beginning of all the magic.

In the true sense of the word, even the summers when I no longer attended the month of classes, I never ceased to be a student. I found time to observe people, time to relax over a glass of wine with friends after a concert, and time to research Queen Aliénor in ancient archives. Often the best days were spent with the Renauds making forays into the countryside, either on regular jaunts to buy eggs, wine or melons from their favorite farmers, or full-day trips to show me a beautiful Romanesque church with fading frescoes.

Mado and I enjoying each other's company around the Renaud family dinner table. We frequently gather here at the end of each adventure. Her cuisine and her warmth draw us closer together each summer. We are still in close communication in 2019.

Chapter One

A Day in the life of a Grad Student

At the close of my first summer's study in Tours, France, I met Mado and Lucien Renaud who board students of all ages from a variety of countries. It is now my second summer in Tours, and I am well into the second week at the Renaud household. I invite you to walk with me through a decade of summers as I savor the art, cuisine, music and history of this multifaceted country that I love so much.

Tempest in the Garden

My alarm doesn't even have a chance to ring as I am awakened by confusion and startled voices from the walled garden below my window. I am living with a friendly, vivacious, extended family. We students at Mado's have one thing in common for sure. We are all studying French at various levels. I am getting to know them as I am renting a fine room on the 'premier étage' (2nd floor) for the summer. Mado and Lucien, her husband, are outside below. It must be close to 5:30 AM. Day is just dawning over the gray slate roofs opposite the back of the garden. The usual song of the mourning dove is interrupted.

It has been a busy time 'chez la famille' Renaud — when isn't it? Michael, the ex-husband of their daughter, Maryse's, has been visiting from Switzerland. This morning he plans to depart on a trip to Brittany with Maryse and their three sons, Martin, Gilles and François. Something must have gone awry. Generally, early morning departures are accomplished noiselessly while the rest of the household sleeps.

Michael is exclaiming to his son: "C'est incroyable!" (I do not believe it!) "Je ne comprends pas" (I don't understand). While struggling to make sense of this, I think to myself, it will be over soon, whatever the problem, and I can get back to sleep. There is no reason to run to the window. "Just relax, Jini", I say out loud to myself.

Michael and Martin seem to have left the garden and have taken the narrow path out to the street behind the house. It is quiet. About fifteen minutes into my reverie they return from the opposite direction quite agitated. Michael is saying he will take his bicycle and go look for it. I'm awake again, more curious than before. Maryse's aggravated voice rises from the courtyard. "Well, where is it? We are all packed and ready to go and no car!" Ah ha! The car is missing -I'm finally getting the gist. No wonder the rumpus. Calmly Lucien speaks: "I'll go call the police."

At that moment Michael can be heard re-entering the garden saying he found the car! It seems it is parked two streets over, not at all in the spot he recalled leaving it! "Ooh là là!" The tempest in the teapot is resolved; the vacationers can leave after all. Everyone can be heard kissing and saying their goodbyes and safe travel with apologies all around. As for me, having heard all this from my feather pillow 'en haut' (upstairs), I pull my Air France sleep mask over my eyes and go back to sleep.

Morning Routine and Off to class

After another hour's sleep, my alarm wakes me up in time to shower and get dressed for classes. Speaking of showering, I must confess I am still not used to the typical French bathroom arrangement. The toilet is in a separate room — a good idea that greatly eases wait time in a large household such as this. The difficulty, however, lies in the 'salle de bain', the bathroom. They have no provision for taking a shower in the American sense of the word. Thus, the awkward part is managing the hand-held shower apparatus in one hand while lathering your hair and holding the shampoo with the other, and all this in the usual American standing position. If the bathroom is cold, you freeze on one side while spraying on the other. The worst part, since the French never seem to realize the advantage of having a shower curtain, is that one invariably creates a pool of water on the floor every time, despite heroic efforts. But I am improving!

This morning I decide I need a few extra minutes to prepare for a quiz on the subjunctive mode, so I will skip the shower routine. Instead I drench my permanented locks under the spigot in my room to restore the curl and spend a few moments of study at the small desk in front of the open French windows. At 8:15 I descend the circular staircase to the dining room to find the table set up for 'petit déjeuner' (breakfast). As usual Lucien has already been out to buy the freshly baked 'baguettes' and "Le Figaro" newspaper.

In the center of the table is a new bouquet of gladiolas. Mado tells me that Lucien, now retired, keeps her supplied with flowers that he buys Wednesdays and Saturdays at the open-air market on Boulevard Béranger. The table is set for four. This summer I share the table with three other students: Margaret, a junior at the University of Alabama, and Floriana and Luana, both high school students from Sicily. Margaret attends the Institut, and the two young Sicilians are studying at the 'Lycée' Balzac (high school).

I am the last to arrive for breakfast. I pour my steaming 'café au lait' into my cereal-sized bowl and spread my 'tartine' (sliced baguette) with fresh Normandy butter made sinfully rich by Mado's homemade 'confiture cassis' (black currant jam). The Renauds, being the purists that they are, collected the berries themselves when last in Ardeche. In my daily breakfast routine, I retain only one American habit, orange juice, which I seem to need to aid in galloping down my vitamins. It needs to be stated here that the French are lacking in only one gastronomic item - freshly squeezed or even frozen, o.j. They have what they call 'sirop', a sweet-tasting syrup, which, when added to a ton of H2O only renders a faint fake flavor of orange. Mado buys the latter only as a favor to me; I have learned to stomach it.

Margaret is going on a field trip this afternoon to visit two châteaux, Blois and Chambord, as well as the cathedrals of Châteaudun and Chartres. Floriana and Luana are preparing for a 'soirée' at a local restaurant with their Italian friends. For me it is a fairly ordinary day of classes. But it is close to the 14 juillet (Bastille Day), and there is an air of excitement as everyone finalizes his or her long holiday weekend plans. I will tell you of my evening plans shortly.

My classes begin at 8:45. Margaret and I leave at 8:30 for our brief, brisk walk to the Institut. I don my belly pack and my backpack laden with texts, grammar books, workbooks, notebooks and dictionary, and off we go. After closing the heavy front door, we walk down the front steps that are lined with taller-than-I-am hollyhocks. We turn left toward the gate, passing the open kitchen doors where we see Lucien reading the paper and Mado watering plants.

We say our 'bonne journée' (have a good day), open and close the tall steel gate and head left onto the sand 'sentier' (pathway) toward the Boulevard Béranger. From there it is only 15 minutes to school. As we near the Institut we see students converging on the courtyard inside the archway. At the main building I leave Margaret and enter a marble foyer to climb the formal marble steps to the 'premier étage' where my class meets for the morning's 'Langue française' class. Some of my classmates are in the hallway outside the room; others are standing on the balcony. I go into the room to put my bag on the chair in the front row where I usually sit. My prof's desk is on a raised dais directly in front of me.

A breathtakingly beautiful crystal chandelier hangs from an elaborately decorated ceiling of sculpted plaster. At the rear of the room is an 18th century marble fireplace below a lustrous antique mirror. In blatant contrast to the luxury of our surroundings are our long wooden student desks and simple chairs. Giving onto twin balconies overlooking the quiet garden are tall French doors that I open to let in the cool morning breezes.

Not all of the classrooms are so ornate, only those of the upper level classes like mine (I am in the eighth level this year). I feel privileged that my eighth-degree classes draw these once formal 'salons of this 'hôtel particulier' (historic home). Further explanation is due here: this sort of 'hôtel' is not a hotel as we know it in America. Instead, the term describes an elegant home of a wealthy city dweller in times gone by. For instance, in Tours, on that very first day of my very first trip here, I was taken on a walking tour of the old city. The tour guide pointed out the Hôtel Gouin. Naturally one of the students commented that it looked like a nice place to stay. The guide very tactfully answered that it was the mansion of a wealthy 15th century man that had been turned into a museum. He explained that the word 'hôtel' meant a 'lodging' during the Middle Ages and had gradually evolved to refer to the sumptuous residence of someone close to the king. But by the end of the 15th century the word hôtel was used in more general terms to indicate any elegant home.

This explanation is getting lengthy, but I've gone this far, so I must take it to its conclusion, and besides it is fascinating. To continue, in the past they began to refer to the king's officer who lived in this fancy house as the 'Maître d'hôtel'. This begins to ring a bell, yes? Well this officer was in charge of everything having to do with the owner's table or food. Thus, we have the zigzag evolution of some words of French derivation which English-speakers use all the time. Now, if you are forming a picture of the Institut as an elegant Renaissance edifice and my classroom as one of the formal salons, you are right!

My Major Prof, M. Delande, and Fellow Students

Our prof comes into the hallway carrying his worn leather briefcase, bulging with our 'dictées' (dictations) and compositions. He has the ever-present cigarette in his hand and a warm smile on his face. M. Delande is well-liked among the students and teaching staff. He has taught here for many years. In the winter he joins the faculty at the main campus University of Tours where he is a professor of French literature par excellence.

At the ringing of the bell we find our chairs at the long tables. The class is made up of a variety of students from many countries. There is a dapper nautical type, slightly my senior, a real French scholar from Virginia — his name is Dan; and myself, a 'débutante' (still wet behind the ears) French teacher from Connecticut ever seeking to ameliorate my facility in that most romantic of all languages while hoping to unlock the key to the true French character.

For one and a half hours we grind through the technical side of the French language, then take our test on the subjunctive. Mr. Delande's tests are always a challenge. After that we proceed to translate together an article he has brought in from today's Le Monde about President Mitterrand's Premier Ministre', Mme. Edith Cresson, and her unpopular views on immigration. She's very controversial and outspoken. Many French people with whom I have spoken distrust her, including women — such a shame since she is the first female to hold such a high position in the French government. The rumors about her include her 'relationship' with President Mitterrand, never mind that she might have earned this high post on her own merit. Professor Delande is encouraging us to assimilate the nuances of the language along with the inside lingo known mostly to native speakers.

At 10:15 the bell announces 'la pause' (the break). Everyone exits onto a balcony to talk or smoke, or to go downstairs and into to the courtyard below to rendezvous with a comrade for a munchie, or like M. Delande, to make a beeline for the only cafe in close proximity. The café is a well-kept secret, not frequented by the students, still unfamiliar with the area. Only a few profs who have been at the university for years and who rely on the caffeine boost of freshly brewed Arabic coffee and a string of "Gitane" cigarettes, rush to the café. The interval is supposed to be only 15 minutes, but our prof never returns before 10:45. Do the French ever rush? Not often, and I like it that way

'La Pause': Firm up Plans for the Evening

On the other hand, I make good use of my 'pause' to hurry over to the 'Bibliothèque' (library) with my colleague Dan to speak to Françoise, the librarian. She is Dan's hostess in Tours. She and her husband, Jacques, also a prof here, have invited me to join them and their student/boarder for an opera this evening at the 'Château de Loches'. Each summer an opera is produced at Loches on the ramparts. This year it is "Jeanne d'Arc au Bucher" (Joan of Arc at the Stake), by Arthur Honegger.

I need to know where and when to meet them later on. Plans are quickly made, and we have just enough time to return to class. It has been a wonderful opportunity knowing Dan and through him, Françoise and Jacques. They have invited me to dine with them on previous occasions this summer in their charming apartment overlooking the Loire River. Since Françoise grew up in the Basque area of southwestern France, her cuisine is totally different from that of the Loire Valley. Her 'tarte basquaise' is a whole chapter in itself.

Language Lab: Mlle. Gautier

Back to my studies for now. Dan and I settle into our booth seats in the 'labo' (language laboratory) and put on our headsets. Our 'labo' teacher, Mlle. Gautier, is new this year. She has recently graduated from the University of Tours. Everyone knows that Tours is not only the hopping off point for visiting 'châteaux', but even more important to all of us students is the fact that it is here that the purest French is spoken. Mlle. Gauthier's accent-free speech rings as clear as a bell as we endeavor to imitate her every syllable. She is blonde and quite chic in her mini body-clinging skirt.

Our task this hour is responding to complicated questions in both the positive and the negative, present and past tenses, replacing the direct and indirect objects, singular and plural, masculine and feminine, with the correct pronouns, of which there are many choices. When answering quickly my tongue frequently stumbles over the proper word order, and I am left hanging, my mind racing over the many possibilities. No time to think it out. I must react instinctively and correctly. My answers are recorded. My prof listens in when I least expect it and corrects my errors. It is intense!

Back at the House for Lunch

Before I have time to check my watch, the bell rings to end the morning session. Since Margaret has special lunch plans, I walk home alone. My head is fairly spinning for the first few moments as I try to sort out the grammar lessons I have just been taught.

Soon I relax and feel how much warmer it is now. The sun is already quite hot as I wait for the light to change at Boulevard Béranger. I move into the shade as the small Renaults and Peugeots race past. In the median the market is still going strong under the shade of the large trees. I am thinking of buying a nice leather bag for my daughter, Amy, one of these days. I pass by the leather stall on my route, glance at the prices, but decide to wait until I have an opportunity to compare prices at some stores on the Rue National, the main shopping street.

As I near our gate I begin the one-handed search in my belly pack for the large iron key. Opening the lock, I hear Figaro, the Renauds' English Sheep Dog, announcing my arrival. I pass the kitchen door, inhaling an appetizing whiff of what is to come. Since the day is already steamy, we shall be eating lunch in the dining room where it is always quite comfortable. I have about fifteen minutes to go up to my room, shuffle my books for my afternoon classes, splash water on my face and check to see if I have any mail. Glorious of days! I have a wondrously long letter from my older daughter, Heather. Before I can finish her epistle, I hear the loud and clear voice of Mado happily beckoning 'A table' (Come to the table). No one hesitates. What gourmet treat awaits us today?

Lucien is already 'à table' when I sit down across from him in my usual place. At Mado's table one's place is easily recognizable, if one is a regular, that is. She has made several linen napkin holders, each one from a different Provençale fabric. At the end of the meal one places one's neatly folded napkin back in its own special holder. The French love ritual! Soon Mado comes in with a large oval platter heaping with our first course. It is a 'salade macédoine de légumes à la sauce mayonnaise' (cold Macedonian mixed vegetable salad with homemade mustard mayonnaise), a cool and refreshing mix of peas, carrots, corn and 'crevettes' (tiny shrimp) in a homemade mustard mayonnaise on a bed of luscious, buttery bib lettuce. It is a sight to behold. You know the French build their dishes much like they construct their famous gardens; that is to say, color-balanced and painstaking symmetrical.

We devour the first course while talking over the morning's events at school, the mail we received on our return, and our Bastille Day holiday weekend plans.

After mopping up my top plate with consistently crunchy-on-the-outside-soft-on-the-inside French bread, Mado clears our 'entrée' (first course) plates and brings in the main course. The running order of the typical meal in France as opposed to ours in the US: In France, both at home and in restaurants, they start with what they call the 'entrée'. In French this literally means the entrance or opening. Makes sense, 'non'? Just to confuse the gourmet traveler, we Americans call this first course the appetizer while on stateside menus we persist in calling the main course the 'entrée'. 'Vive la différence'! The oohs and aahs fill the dining room as Mado serves the 'saumon à la sauce oseille' (poached salmon in a sorrel sauce) with her made-from-scratch 'pommes frites' (French fries).

Lucien grows his own sorrel every year. This particular summer, as we were feasting one night at the garden table, I asked him about the herbs he grew. He pointed behind my chair to an amazingly abundant patch of sorrel that was obviously the source of many of Mado's savory sauces and soups. Another special thing about French cooking is their ready supply of fresh ingredients, either from their own gardens or from the nearby twice-weekly open markets. I know you are saying, yes, but we all have access to fresh ingredients. Yes, we do, to a degree. But, when I say fresh I mean freshly harvested at the point of ripeness close to the sale site. In France, fortunately, they still boast of fresh fruits and vegetables grown close to home and sold close to home.

By now everyone at the dinner (at noon) table is used to my ensuing questions on the sauces and their ingredients. Ever since my second meal chez Renaud I bring my journal to the table in order to faithfully record every tasty delight. This day is no exception. There is usually just enough time between courses for me to fill in the menu and annotate a recipe or two. I suppose it's my way of savoring these lovely meals in hopes of enjoying them again at a later date when I am far away, caught up in my fast-paced life in Connecticut.

Luana, in her hesitating French, tells us of an incident that just occurred in Sicily. There is current agitation in Palermo, and, since her father calls her everyday just at lunchtime, we are kept abreast of the latest news. Then the conversation shifts to the story of the two Loires, euphemistically two Loire rivers, that Lucien tells us when we ask him why we do not see people swimming in the Loire. He tells us there is really very little activity on the river nowadays compared to the heavy commerce that used to stimulate boat traffic in the past. First, he tells us that the river is far shallower than it used to be. As a result, there are islands that are growing here and there as well as areas of 'sables mouvants' (quicksand).

There has been the discovery of a subterranean stream which runs directly below the one we see. Lucien recounts the instance of a man who went into the river to swim and was pulled under by a strong current into the lower river. Fortunately, he re-surfaced downstream, alive. The man told the story of being swept deep below the usual depth of the Loire as though into a deep cave where he was able to catch a breath of air before being thrust upwards once again into the mainstream and, finally, to the surface. Now, I must add that I have never read of this phenomenon nor heard of it from any other source. If the dangers of the Loire are real, it seems strange that I have never seen a sign of warning to swimmers. Certainly, tourists and other passers-by are unaware of the Loire's hidden perils!

Meanwhile the salmon has virtually melted in my mouth, and we have found our way down to the third in our stack of plates in front of us. Our next course, 'la salade verte' (green salad) is a mainstay in the French diet. I have read that eating a green salad after a main dish greatly facilitates digestion. Of course, back in the good US of A, we do just the opposite, again, and for no stated reason. Although I have never observed Mado prepare a salad, I do recall watching my original French 'Maman', Mme. Weber, in Belfort near Alsace, (my first host family, my first trip to France with the Experiment in International Living years ago) as she meticulously washed and shook dry the fresh bib lettuce leaves, tore them into bite-sized pieces, then tossed them into a glass bowl in which she had already stirred the family vinaigrette. This performed-twice-daily French family ritual of salad making appears incredibly simple, is always savory, and ever elusive to the rest of us! Actually, in those early years I used to come home to my apartment in New York City and try to reproduce this simple-looking salad dressing, but, alas, was rarely successful in capturing that special French flavor that I craved. Chalk up another one for the French 'je ne sais quo'.

Lest I forget, the ensuing course is the cheese offering. While we Americans are relegated to our limited choice of over-processed Velveeta, American white squares, Vermont cheddar or an occasional under ripe Brie or Camembert, Mado is tempted daily by an array of over 365 regional cheeses. Oh, yum! She has chosen one of my favorites, Roay, medium 'parfum' (flavor), soft and delicious when spread on a morsel of bread. I do think one has to acquire a taste for many of the French cheeses since there is nothing that remotely resembles them in our cuisine. When I take my first bite of the Roay, the flavor fairly explodes in my mouth, with its woodsy, earthy essence. If you like cheese, it's worth the trip from anywhere! We also sample the Pont L'Évêque, a semi-hard, fermented cheese from Normandy, which is rich in cream, and another very special Cantal which our hosts' daughter brought from her region of Auvergne this week.

Dessert today arrives on the familiar footed compote. It is overflowing with the summer's bounty of fresh fruit. Lucien has just picked the white peaches from their tree this morning. They can only be described as dripping good! I have observed that the French eat lots of fresh fruit, something we neglect all too often for reasons aforementioned. Mado always serves a bountiful supply of apricots and nectarines as well as fresh cherries. We know that she and her countrywomen are capable of making some of the most sumptuous of desserts, but their everyday habit is to close their meal with fresh fruit, usually in season, locally or South of France-grown. I believe this is one of the secrets of their slender, healthy bodies. It is also very French to sit around the table for a couple of hours at a time, relaxing, savoring their food and exchanging ideas. The benefits of these gastronomic-centered habits are obviously healthy.

Wine for lunch? Visit to the Renaud's Viticulteur

You are probably wondering about now what happened to the ubiquitous French wine that supposedly accompanies every meal in 'Hexagon', an oft-used term referring to six-sided outline of France. Chez Renaud is no exception. Lucien and Mado make their regular forays into the country every four weeks or so to purchase wine by the cask, often from a vintner friend. Lucien then pours it into label-less wine bottles and stows it all in the 'cave' (cool, dry basement).

Earlier this week I was invited on one such trip to the 'viticulteur' (grape-grower/wine maker), M. Angelliaume, in Cravant-les-Coteaux, in the Chinon region south of Tours. There we were treated to a wine -tasting with the scintillating grape-grower himself. It appears that I have landed in the middle of Chinon's best-known wine-growing village, Cravant-les-Coteaux. Its gentle south-facing slopes with lime stone subsoil are just right for the growing of the fine cabernet franc grapes from which Chinon's famous red wines are produced. In fact, the red wines bottled there were so delicious I made the supreme, self-rewarding sacrifice of bringing some home with me. Meanwhile, I turn down Lucien's offer of wine with lunch, as I need to be attentive in class this afternoon!

Back to Class: M. Frizzy's History Lesson

By now, happily sated on 'la cuisine française' and fascinating conversation, I glance at my watch to see that I have only a few minutes to brush my teeth and head out for afternoon classes which begin at 2:30. The beginning French students are free for the afternoon. However, in my case, the eighth level always has a full schedule until at least 5:30, sometimes even 6:30 if there is a special 'conférencier' (lecturer).

I find my way to M. Frizy's classroom in one of the annex buildings. The class is already in session. His subject is 'Civilisation'; he is lecturing on events leading up to the French Revolution. I could easily write a chapter on his manner of lecturing, his unique way of illustrating details, his pointed sense of humor, how fast he speaks. At any rate, it is not long before he is hanging up newspaper clippings of the Storming of the Bastille in chronological order. He has strung up a clothesline from the door to a hook on the opposite wall without skipping a beat. Now he gets out clothespins and with each picture comes an in-depth news commentary leading up to the capture of the Bastille and the impaling of its captain's head on a pike. Ugh! French history can be very gory. Suddenly M. Frizy falls on the floor with a loud thud imitating the fallen defender of the prison. Manet's fallen toreador flashes before my eyes.

To a foreigner like myself, it is a lively, enlightening way of putting us right into the fray. His gesticulations are so French! His facial expressions so typical of the way I have come to expect the ever-fascinating race of former Gauls to relate a happening. The eyebrows undulate, the lips protrude in exaggeration, and the cheeks puff out regularly, expelling an audible 'puup'! These 'gallicismes', ancient Gaul-like habits of speech, give the spectator a moment to digest the info just spouted forth. Very effective. It has always gotten my attention!

Inspired by Professor Frizy's oration, I am beginning to grasp what really happened in 1789 and why. He definitely piques my interest for further study. I am late leaving class as some of us linger to listen to the postmortems. I ask his opinion regarding an article I recently was given by Jim, my school librarian at home, on the possibility of hallucinogenic spores in rye bread causing overreactions on the part of the revolutionaries. That's food for thought! At 4:20 I pull myself away, knowing I need a little time to prepare for my opera outing this evening.

On my way home, I stop by 'la poste' (post office) to buy some airmail stamps and some boxes for mailing home my literary purchases. When I reach the house luckily the shower is free. I'll give the hand-held procedure another shot. I decide to wear my blue and white packable polyester-looks-like-silk dress and my new French blue strap heels to match. We are going to dine at a restaurant in Loches prior to the opera. In France one always 'dines' rather than 'eats'. Perhaps it is borrowing a phrase from the English, but the food and the method are decidedly French.

Heading to Loches for Dinner and Opera

It is a lovely evening, still quite warm and sunny, when Dan, Françoise and Jacques pick me up. It takes us the better part of an hour to reach the château town. I have already visited Loches and its château on an Institut excursion, so I recognize the towering stonewalls of the outer 'enceinte' (exterior walls) as we enter the 'old town'. When you become an inveterate château-hopper later in this book you learn to follow the signs pointing to 'la vieille ville' (the old city). That is where all the action is in French towns. We find a place to park near their favorite restaurant. Our friends have reserved a table for us on the terrace where we install ourselves for a rather early dinner. As most French restaurants do not start serving before 7:30 PM, we are among the early birds. So, we should have plenty of time for a leisurely repast; the performance starts at dusk. When I mention dusk, I should not assume that we all have the same time frame in mind. At home, dusk in summer is around 9PM or earlier. In France in July it's more like 10PM or later! Another reason to adore France in the summer!

It will be a long evening counting the ride back, but I love the anticipation of a protracted dinner 'à la française' with good friends followed by excellent classical music in such a unique setting. The combination has me all aglow even before our 'Kir aperitifs' (French wine cocktail served before dinner) arrive. In case you are not clued into this drink, still exotic to Americans, it is what I call 'typique de la région' of Burgundy, yet very much 'à la mode' in the Loire Valley. It is traditionally served in a tall fluted glass gently curving in at the top. Some call this shape a tulip glass. The ingredients are zingers! It is usually made in these proportions: 3/4 White Burgundian Aligote wine and 1/4 'crème de cassis' (black currant liqueur). If you are in a really festive mood, order a 'Kir Royale' spiked with champagne instead of white wine.

It's so interesting hearing about Dan's career. Currently he is teaching French aboard a navy vessel which berths in Annapolis, Maryland, between cruises. Quite a unique post for a French teacher, 'n'est-ce pas'? Apparently, he has plenty of free time between cruises or he wouldn't be in Tours at the University planning to visit friends in Spain after our study session is finished. He is such a good conversationalist, and he does so enjoy, as do I, searching for the meanings and derivations of new words. This evening is such a good workout for our French skills. Dan and I relish the opportunity to spend the evening 'ensemble' in the company of Françoise and Jacques. It broadens one's scope so much to talk with a variety of people to accustom one's ear to as many native speakers as possible, not to mention how knowledgeable they are regarding our surroundings and the opera for this evening.

After dinner we move the car up the hill inside the walls to a space closer to the castle keep. Then we join the 'mélomanes' (music lovers) wending their way up to the bleachers erected at the base of the inner walls. It was the English King Henri II, second husband of Queen Aliénor, my ancestor, who fortified this castle by building these tall, thick fortifications in the late 12h century. This is the background for the remarkable set that faces our seats tonight. The stage is built out from and attached to the ancient walls of Château Loches; quite a feat in itself. As darkness descends, I notice a few clouds over the horizon past the castle towers.

"Jeanne au Bucher": The Opera

All is well; the stars are beaming, and the opera orchestra tunes up. I read in the program about Honegger (1892-1955) with whom I am not familiar. Although he was Swiss, he lived most of his life in Paris. He was a prolific composer in various genres of music. His "Jeanne d'Arc au Bucher" was composed in 1935; he called it an operatic oratorio. It is broadly dramatic in form and is presented with a full orchestra, boys' choir, a bevy of operatic soloists, as well as actors. The lines are partly spoken and partly sung.

The action takes place in Joan's last hours at the stake, with flashbacks of her trumped-up trial. It ends with her pleading for her life as the fire is set at her feet. The libretto was written by French poet, Paul Claudel.

I know the story of Joan of Arc rather well, as I have studied it here, and I incorporate it in play form in my high school French classes in Connecticut. Since my first trip to France, it seems that wherever I go, to nearby towns, cathedrals and châteaux, there is a recurring theme – plaques and statues of Jeanne d' Arc. It is at the castle of Chinon where she introduces herself to the 'dauphin' (son of the King), Charles. In a later account in this memoire, I find her in Paris, Reims and Rouen. For example, every Sunday morning in Tours I pass the forge where Jeanne, the Maid, had her armor fitted on Rue Colbert. Tonight, I find her right here at Loches Château where she came with the dauphin looking for support to have him crowned and to oust the English. I am thrilled to be here tonight watching her story unfold in operatic form.

The Movable Opera

After Jeanne's eventual capture and trial, the sky over Loches which must have been amassing clouds unnoticed while we were caught up in the plot, opened up to spill rain all around in buckets!

The conductor calmly announces that we should proceed down the hill to the cathedral where they will finish the performance. He instructs us to follow the orchestra through the narrow streets to allow them time to hurry on ahead protecting their instruments as best they can. They will re-organize in the 'choeur' (choir section) of the church. The drama was at a crescendo point in the story anyway. Now the excitement builds. Our moveable opera is processing through the medieval streets where Jeanne herself has walked. It is pouring now. We hold our programs over our heads. It is little protection.

Soon we are ensconced in the church, and 'Jeanne d'Arc' is singing her 'adieux' (farewells) at the burning stake. The climax takes on a mystical quality in this sacred environment while Jeanne stands in the pulpit bravely battling the invisible flames and praising God. We are all moist and steamy in the heightened collective humidity we brought into this place. The extended applause echoes our appreciation. I am almost glad it rained. I think the plot was intensified by our own hardship.

Thus ends our evening at Loches. We look back at the floodlit castle's heavy fortification as we leave in the waning drizzle. It was an inspiring event. I feel close to Jeanne and her untenable predicament. She met her death in 1453. Shortly afterward her cause was accomplished. The French finally repulsed the English. The close of the Hundred Years War marked the end of a very long struggle between the French and the English that began, in my opinion, in the 1100's. It was more like a Three Hundred Years War.

I love the sense of history that meets me face-to-face in the most unlikely places in France. It is to be uncovered everyday here in the Loire Valley. I'm only too happy to assuage my curiosity again and again. Tonight. I filled in many blanks in the giant puzzle of Jeanne's life. There will be more on Jeanne in later chapters when I will stand beside her: at the large equestrian statue in Chinon and feel the chill up and down my back before the remnants of the great fireplace there where she first met Charles, the dauphin; pass by the forge where she was fitted for her armor in Tours; step onto the spot where she stood at Château Blois; share her successes at Beaugency and Orléans; sit in the Cathedral of Reims where King Charles VII is finally crowned; and lastly follow her to the central square in Rouen where the British martyred her. On that precious place of her unimagined suffering now stands an incongruous 'non-sequitur', wildly contemporary, ugly monument. A simple brass plaque in the cobblestone would be more appropriate for the valiant Maid of Orléans. With the exception of the crowning at Reims, these locations are interwoven with the flow of the mighty Loire. Lastly, in the middle of Paris, dominating the 'Place des Pyramides', near the Tuileries Gardens, stands a triumphal statue of Jeanne astride her horse, both saint and stead bathed in brilliant gold leaf.

'Bonne Nuit' to a Memorable Evening

We discuss all these things in the car on our return to Tours. It was a moving production; on that we agree. Dan and I are most grateful to Françoise and Jacques for tonight's unique, musical experience dramatized by the sudden thunderstorm. As my colleague, Dan, walks me down the narrow 'sentier' to Mado's gate, he reminds me that tomorrow we are having our class photograph. I hope no one awakens as I enter, and that no one awakens me at the screech of dawn as they did this morning! What a glorious full day this has been! The student/ tourist, would-be-historian is very tired indeed. I'll write in my journal tomorrow. Happily, 'bonne nuit'.

Chapter Two

Château Hopping

"If you have seen one French château you have seen them all,"
exclaims the bored American traveler. I say: "Not so fast. If you
love history and you adore art, architecture and gardens, you
can never see enough châteaux!"

I BEGIN MY CHÂTEAU QUEST in the first few days of my return
summer to study in Tours. You see, I am not here just to study French
language and literature but all that goes with it. In a word, I thirst for
ALL things French as I did in Connecticut when my friend, Sue, and I
combed our state for every sign of French influence. We then compiled
a small book on the subject. It seems I am doing it now in France!

My first summer I was billeted in a University of Touraine dorm
with my group from Southern Connecticut State University (SCSU).
Beginning with the second summer I was fortunate to find Mado
Renaud and no longer needed to lodge in an impersonal dorm. Mado
has become a lifelong friend. She and her family housed me for the
greater part of my delicious decade of summers in the Loire Valley.

There will be no holding me back after many years at home bringing
up children and all that goes with it. I intend to make tracks and my m.o.
(modus operandi) is to soak up everything in my sight, my hearing, my
touch and on my palate, that is a part of French culture. I plan to savor
all of it with gusto.

Walking Tour of Tours

The University offers day trips to the châteaux. I sign up for every trip, every lecture that comes my way. My American study buddy, Rita, also housed at the Renauds, and I start out with a guided walking visit of old Tours. I find it is a city of deep historical background. It is 'de rigueur' (a must) that we start here before launching out on the château circuit. We take up the pen and pad eager to learn about the city.

We learn that the 732 Battle of Tours under the leadership of Charles Martel halted the advance of the Muslims, leaving Europe under Christian control. The Arab advance forces were pushed back as they had been before when they crossed the Mediterranean into Spain, into France even into Vienna, Austria.

We are shown the center of old Tours, Place Plumereau, a huge open square ringed with late 15th century half-timbered Burgher houses. Plumereau is the center of nightlife here in Tours. The square lights up every night at dusk with a medieval flare. Not far away, the guide points out the location where Joan of Arc had her armor measured and forged. We visit the Musée des Beaux Arts with its beautifully manicured floral beds and the nearby spacious Botanical Garden. We come to know the open markets near the center of town as well. We welcome the in-depth descriptions of what Rita and I refer to with growing familiarity as 'our town'.

When we are not in class Rita and I tour many royal residences in the Loire Valley. We are in the Valley of the Kings, are we not? The weather is super-hot and humid on our free afternoons. Despite the lack of air-conditioning on our tour bus, as well as in these famous old castles, we carry on from room to room learning as much as we can. We use bandanas to tie up our tresses and to soak up the perspiration that drips through our hair and down our necks. We stand on one foot and then the other, listening intently to the guides spouting the history that attends each royal dwelling.

The challenge is to sort out the more than 30 châteaux, castles and palaces that we visit without boring the reader to death. I will choose those that have impressed me the most. Each château has a history relating to the King in power, his Queen, their family, (the question of inheritance never fails to create a squabble), lovers and mistresses when they appear on the château scene, and how the King deals with his ever-encroaching enemies.

The evolution of architectural style interests me very much as well as the interior decor that becomes more refined over time. Gardens tend to become focal points as the owners spend less time defending their properties, leaving them time and funds to enjoy the sweeter side of life.

Also, we must keep in mind that each inhabitant of these fabulous houses adopts certain architectural devices according to the era. After all, rulers want to leave their mark on history. That, they have accomplished, since we are still enchanted with these châteaux. Some still attract visitors after 1,000 years. There are some 10,000 châteaux in France. We are not daunted by any aforementioned hurdles.

Why have so many kings chosen to live here? The climate is mild; the land fertile; it is a not a bad journey by horse or carriage from the center of government in Paris, or Versailles. Unlike today, the Loire was navigable, and the river afforded an easy route into the center of the Valley. Boats brought in people and supplies needed for the building of such formidable fortresses. The accessibility of 'tuffaut' (limestone) was essential for the building of these permanent houses. The extensive forests of the region were a necessary benefit. Do not forget that when the building was finished the Kings and their retinues utilized the forests for a favorite pastime— hunting.

A brief timeline of the châteaux we visit in the Loire Valley:

High Middle Ages 11th – 13th c.

Late Middle Ages 14th – 15th c.

French Renaissance Apex 16th c.

Many of these châteaux were built on ancient foundations dating as far back as the 800s when the 'château fort' (fortified castle) was the style. The main reason to build a fortress was to protect one's family and greater surroundings from armed invasion.

The construction of the 'château fort' includes a surrounding high stone wall, even a double stone wall as at **Carcassonne** in SW France, a single entrance with a drawbridge, and 'machicolis' (large holes over the entranceway) through which cauldrons of hot oil or large rocks could be launched onto the heads of invaders. There were deep moats surrounding the exterior walls and often a series of inner walls as well. Once inside there was an open bailey, then an inner bailey separated from the outer one by another tall wall or walls. A bailey is an inner space, protected from invasion. There may be one bailey or more, depending on the contour of the land and the size of the fortification.

At the very center is a tall building called the keep where the King lived with his family. This was the most highly defended part of the castle where the royals could find sanctuary.

In the late Middle Ages, the true 'château fort' of the early Middle Ages became obsolete with the discovery of explosives such as gunpowder and canon shot. Gradually the double thick walls, moats and drawbridges became a thing of the past. As a high school teacher of French in Connecticut, I asked my students to research the classic 'château fort', including the French terms for all the sections of a medieval fortress. Rita and I visit perfect examples of this early fortification. Even into the Middle Ages it was still advisable to build one's castle in a defensible high place beside the Loire and other rivers in the area, namely the Vienne, the Indre and the Cher.

This brings to mind another important feature that we see in most of the châteaux on our list. It is the requisite water feature for most, if not all, the major châteaux. If the builders did not build overlooking a river, then they brought in water to enliven and enrich the beauty of the land surrounding their palaces such as **Versailles** and **Vaux-le- Vicomte**, both near the Seine River, but whose builders channeled the river and small streams into ponds and even lakes onto their properties for their own pleasure. We have not changed that much over the centuries, have we? We may not be royal, but we are drawn to build homes and vacation retreats near water.

Chinon

The jumping off point for our château study is one of the oldest structures still standing, **Chinon**. From the heights of the plateau where it stands, it commands a splendid view of the Vienne River, a tributary of the Loire, and the bridge that was built by its well-known 12th century owner, Henry II Plantagenet, King of England, second husband of Queen Aliénor d'Aquitaine, both in my ancestral upline. On three sides of the plateau are rocky outcroppings, and on the fourth a deep ditch stands guard, making invasion all but impossible. Henry preferred hunting for large game and Aliénor favored hawking for smaller game in the surrounding forest. Perhaps, their sense of safety when in residence at Chinon was the overarching reason Henry and Aliénor called this their favorite abode.

In the late 12th century English King Henry II rebuilt the fortified castle of Theobald I, Count of Blois, dating back to 954. He constructed the bones of the present-day version of Castle Chinon over the original site of a Gallic 'oppidum' (an ancient, fortified, Roman town). Henry held sway here for many years. He died here in 1189, and his son, Richard Lionheart, also King of England, died near here in 1199 after an unforeseen deadly crossbow wound at Chalus. In 1205 Henry's last son, John Lackland, King of England, lost Château Chinon to Philippe-Auguste, the Capetien King of France who had long lusted to take over Henry's holdings.

It was at Château Chinon in 1429, in the great room in front of the still standing fireplace, that Joan of Arc recognized Charles, Dauphin of France, who was 'in cognito' in a crowd. This was the turning point Joan needed to convince the Dauphin that she was to be the one to fend off his foes and take him to Reims Cathedral to be crowned Charles

VII, King of France. It is moving to stand on that same spot where Joan, Maid of Orléans, stood that day so long ago, not to mention my personal connection with Henry, Aliénor, and their sons, Richard and John, who once called this home.

Sometime after our self-guided tour of the ruins of Chinon, I read there is now the museum of Joan of Arc installed here. The good news is that at the beginning of the 21st century, the royal apartments facing the best view of the Vienne River and much of the rest of the 1312 foot by 230-foot, three section footprint of the once grandiose château, is undergoing renovations amounting to 14.5 million Euros!

The three sections Rita and I see are mostly in shambles in 1988. On the far right to the south, as we look up from the bridge, is the Fort St.-Georges; on the far left, the north side, is the Fort du Coudray; and in the middle is the Château du Milieu. The Fort du St.-Georges was built by Henry II and held a chapel dedicated to the patron Saint of England. The Château du Coudray was built by French King Louis-Philippe II in the early 13th century, and the middle section was constructed in the 13th and 14th century. The notable round tower that soars above the center of the medieval fortress guards the fragile-looking bridge linking the Coudray and Milieu sections. On the far right, south side, is the14th century bell tower that strikes the hour when we are here. It rises up from the ruins in working order.

When I return a few weeks later to take in the famous annual Chinon Medieval Fair I can hear the ancient clock tolling over the din of the festival. I notice the necessary drawbridge guarding the entrance, the massive thick towers at the corners and the super thick walls. I cannot resist considering the important history pertaining to Joan of Arc that unfolded here at Chinon, while today the streets are peopled by the real-life actors portraying their ancient forebears who once walked the narrow streets centuries earlier. What more could a château have to hold the interest of the 21st century scholar?

In my play, **Conversations with Queen Aliénor d'Aquitaine**, she and I meet in locations of particular importance to us both. During one of these meetings with my 12th century great grandmother of 29 generations in the past, we meet here after she has just returned from an invigorating morning of hawking in the forest near Chinon. I get my first one-on-one description of what it was like to be an avid hawker in Aliénor's time. She even introduced me to her favorite white peregrine falcon. All this is shared between us in lively conversation.

Moving on to our next château on the list, please note that we find recurring royalty, place names, rivers, venues and events that become interfaced from château to château. I will try to distinguish them, one from the other, so as not to be confusing. That is part of the challenge of *Summering in France's Loire Valley*.

Chaumont

Chaumont-sur-Loire is our next destination. It is perched high above the lovely Loire River. Our bus lets us off at the bottom of the hill so, as we trudge up the access road, the sight before us is like the image of castles of our childhood storybooks. At first glimpse we see the tall, twin, cylindrical, towers with dunce cap shaped, slate roofs guarding the drawbridge. We cross the wooden bridge into the courtyard. Next impression: this fortress is fully restored and well maintained.

The Count of Blois built the original castle here in 995. We never would have guessed this beautiful, gleaming fortress was totally demolished by French King Louis XI in 1455 to punish the owner, Pierre d'Amboise, for sedition. Later the King forgave him, and Amboise was allowed to re-build with the aid of his sovereign. With some changes for the better the job was well completed in 1475. Bizarre bit of history. These names recur in our next visits.

We are able to keep up with the guide's spiel in French as she continues. In 1530 a new name takes center stage: French Queen, Catherine de Medici, widow of King Henri II of France, not to be confused with our story of Château Chinon's Henry II, King of England, but living in what we now call France. Oh, oh, now the plot thickens. It is the way of royals between France and England. You see, when my ancestor, Queen

Aliénor, (wife of Henry II of England) divorced her first husband, King Louis VII of France, she wed soon–to–be-King of England, Henry II. He was of the family Plantagenet. He was also Count of Anjou (therefore an Angevin) and Duke of Aquitaine, both titles in France thanks to his French wife, Aliénor. I promise these main characters will be sorted out as we go along.

Our new subject, Catherine de Medici, was born in Italy, the daughter of Lorenzo de Medici of the infamous, powerful Medici line. At the age of fourteen she married King Henri II of France. Her husband was the son of King François Ier who had spent time in Italy during the Renaissance and brought many new, enlightening ideas in the arts to France. Her life with Henri was not a happy one however; he preferred to heap honors on his mistress, Diane de Poitiers, who wielded power over Catherine. Following a horrible, lingering death as a result of a failed joust, Henri II of France died in 1559, leaving Catherine with their large family (10 children). Catherine, who often was derided for consulting an astrologer, was told of the ill-fated future of three of her sons. Although she became one of the most powerful women in France, she was stout and unbecoming of countenance.

The reign of Catherine as Regent and her sons was fraught with civil and religious unrest in France. Three sons became Kings of France: François II, (1544-1566); Charles IX (1550-1574); Henri III (1551-1589). Her son Louis became Duke of Orléans died shortly after his birth, and two of her daughters became Queens and one a Duchess. Of her three frail sons, François, Charles, and Henri, she wielded power over her last and youngest son, Henri III, whose weak character gave in to her over and over until his death.

Rita and I learn that in 1559, upon the death of Catherine's husband, Henri II, Diane de Poitiers inherited the gracious Château Chenonceau where she had been residing. Unhappy with this course of events, Catherine forced her husband's paramour to trade Chenonceau for Chaumont. Amazing stuff, I would say. There is much more to this story, but I leave it to you to pursue it.

In 1750 the Château Chaumont passed to Jacques – Donatien Le Ray, considered by the French as one of the fathers of the American Revolution as he loved America so much. Thereafter, Chaumont passed to Mme. De Stael, daughter of King Louis XVI's Swiss chief of finance; she was also a well-known writer and political activist. In 1840 the château was classified as a 'Monument Historique'. The exquisite 16th century! Medici tapestries from Chaumont, now at Cleveland Museum of Art, are emblematic of the period of 'eternity in the country'. They had been cut and pieced to fit the room in the Catherine de Medici Tower, where she is said to have spent time with her astrologer.

Architecturally, the oldest section, the outer west façade of Chaumont, retains its military appearance. The other two façades, though still slightly military, show the influence of the Renaissance. Rita comments on the perfection of the spiral staircase. I love climbing this staircase and peering out the window slits as I ascend.

One can easily find links to the past owners of Chaumont in the monograms that still exist throughout the house. For example, there are intertwined C's for Charles d'Amboise, and one can readily recognize the entwined D's and images of Diane (the Huntress) de Poitiers for whom she is named, throughout the residence. Just inside the drawbridge are the initials of King Louis XII and Anne ode Bretagne in a field of fleur de lys and ermine.

The north wing was demolished by an owner who wanted to restore the view it blocked. Catherine's Council room is paved with Renaissance Majolica tiles made in Palermo, Italy.

Loches

If you recall my visit to the castle of **Loches** and the Honegger Opera I attended there, its history goes back to early Celtic days. It is well placed on a promontory of the river Indre, a tributary of the Loire. Some call Loches 'the acropolis' for that reason. The writer, Alfred de Vigny, was born here (1797). He was a famous French novelist and poet in the romantic style.

During the 11th – 13th century the château Loches fell under the control of the English, that being the Counts of Anjou. For this change of hands, we turn again to the family of English King Henry II and his wife, Aliénor d'Aquitaine, who took over Loches in the 12th century. The walls were reinforced under Henry's rule, well before the third crusade of 1189-1192 led by his son, King Richard I, Lionheart.

Unfortunately, Richard was held captive in Austria (Holy Roman Empire) while returning from the crusade. He had set out on the journey to Jerusalem with French King Philippe-Auguste, but the latter returned ahead of Richard to wrest more land from Richard while he was away from his kingdom, and his lands were in the hands of his ineffective younger brother, John. While en route home, Richard was imprisoned by the Holy Roman Emperor and as a result, was unable to protect his domain.

When Richard was released, he headed to Loches to re-capture it from Philippe in a mere four hours. Some years later, after Richard's untimely demise in 1199, Philippe re-took the castle in a year's siege. In 1249 Loches was purchased by French King Louis IX. It remained a royal residence thereafter.

Here is a familiar name of another person with a connection to Loches: Joan of Arc. She came to Loches to meet with the 'Dauphin' (the King's son) Charles after her amazing victory at Orléans and prior to crowning him as King Charles VII at Reims. After a fashion, a tourist like myself, becomes familiar with these royal rituals. These sidebars of concurrent history, dear reader, are all by way of filling you in on the notes we gathered at Loches early on in this narrative.

Most of these fortified residences have deep 'donjons' (dungeons) where prisoners were kept. Loches was one of these. When these huge residences were unoccupied by kings and their families in later centuries, they may have been put to use as modern-day prisons. The term 'donjon' in French, does not always signify a place for prisoners. In the make-up of the early 'château fort', the term 'donjon' described the oversized tower or the innermost keep and had nothing to do with a prison. Ooh, là là! More mental notes to hold dear.

Chenonceau

To follow the thread of Catherine de Medici who, by persuasion, took over the Château **Chenonceau** for her own selfish reasons, Rita and I arrive here on a fine summer day to check out why it meant so much to the Queen. Our bus parks just outside 'le parc'. In French this term means anything from a large property with grassy, wooded areas in a city of the 20th century or a very large parkland of a ruler with ponds, gardens, grassy areas and extensive forested acres. We walk toward the château along a lovely 'allée'. (pathway for walking, riding horseback or in a horse drawn carriage between two matching lines of trimmed 'plane' trees, (the sycamore tree is commonly used ornamentally in France).

The first building we see is the tall imposing, very stout towered Keep. There are three stories of windows plus conical pointed roofs, making it appear daunting. It stands separate from the main edifice of Chenonceau. In fact, one cannot gain entrance to the main château without crossing a drawbridge, a carryover from feudal times. We know from the picture in our guidebook that the main building stretches from the near side of the Cher River to the opposite side but no longer connects with the far shore.

We walk past the Keep. It appears to be much older than the château itself. Then we follow our guide across the last walkway toward the main building. This is the first span over water, only visible from a side view in the drawing we now carry in hand. Next, we cross the narrow wooden drawbridge also over water. I count this bridge as the second span over the Cher River. Again, consulting the drawing, we count another five or six rounded spans over water under the main building, including the gallery.

Voilà! The château sits entirely over water with only the stalwart wooden drawbridge to connect the visitor to the near shore. Of course, in times of danger the drawbridge would be lifted and secured. Apparently, there are rooms over the spans with rounded underpinnings much like English King Henry's bridge at castle Chinon. This is really gorgeous! It may be for me the most ethereal of the châteaux!

The guide has some unpleasant remarks to add to what we already know about Catherine de Medici. While her husband, French King Henri II was alive, she was relegated to the quiet shadows. Following his death, she was made Regent, gaining much more power. She went about beautifying Chenonceau. For instance, the orderly balance of the 'allée', the matching gardens that capture our attention as we approach the Keep and admired them on either side, were her additions. Today, there is Catherine's garden on one side and Diane's garden on the opposite side of the entry. The gardens appear equal in size and beauty. Is this an indication that the two women are treated as equals? I fear both would object.

A note here about the difference between French and English gardens: The French gardens are almost without exception designed with balanced, well ordered beds of flowers in set patterns that are repeated in like designs, whereas English gardens have the reputation for being natural in design, almost wild. Flowers are planted in drifts, with no matching one on the opposite side. English gardens are more haphazard in appearance than their counterpart plantations on the east side of the English Channel. Here at Chenonceau presents a perfect example of French style gardens. So, we learn that Catherine has a softer side.

In her widowhood Catherine expressed her whimsical side as well. It was she who added the two and a half story enclosed gallery on top of the several bridge spans to avail herself of the glories of the sparkling waters beneath. As we step into the gallery here at Chenonceau we pause to gaze out of both sides of the broad interior span and spot a rowboat gliding silently underneath us. The guide says that during World War II the entire gallery where we are standing was filled with soldiers in hospital beds.

Still looking out over the water, I try to imagine the extravaganzas that Catherine held here for the court and nobles. She planned plays, banquets, masquerades, and torchlight dances. There was even a naval battle played out on the River Cher. Guests were dressed like satyrs and other characters of Greek legends. One on hand observer penned this: "Beautiful and virtuous ladies appeared half-naked." Sounds like the wild parties at Versailles under Sun King Louis XIV. Catherine pulled out all the stops and spent hundreds of thousands of French 'livres' (French coinage) for these 'soirées' (evening parties).

The floor of the Chenonceau gallery catches my eye. It is paved with large tiles of black and white that I recall as being out of place and not of the period, but I am wrong. This harlequin pattern floor appears in paintings including one of King Louis XIV by Regaud. And I recall a similar pattern of black and white floor tiles embellishing the semi-circular entry at the elegant Château Vaux-le-Vicomte outside Paris. Here at Chenonceau, as in most of the châteaux, there are few of the original owners' furnishings; some of course have been donated by family members over the years. We hesitate before a portrait of Catherine, imposing and dour as one might expect. I remark on seeing beautiful, important, flower arrangements in the foyers and bedchambers reminiscent of those that adorn the Metropolitan Museum of Art in New York City. They soften the simple lines and requisite dull limestone of these royal interiors.

I should mention here that most of these châteaux are built of the local limestone found in this section of France, the Loire Valley. For instance, a good example is at the Château de Rochambeau that I mention visiting in a later chapter. Count Michel de Rochambeau and Countess Madeleine de Rochambeau whom I had the good fortune to meet in 1993 when I was traveling with my son, Rusty Dyer, showed us the caves from which the stone was quarried to build their residence near Vendome.

On the subject of 'tuffaut', in the town of Lerné, near Chinon, I was visiting a new friend one day. I learned that the 'tuffaut' to build her home was quarried from under the house. I asked: "How can this be done without weakening the foundation of the building?" The fine lady who loved history told me that her family used the space for a generous size 'cave' (wine cellar) to store her husband's collection of fine wines. Very practical wouldn't you say? That same day when I was invited for lunch, Madame asked me to open the door of a large armoire in her living room. I did so and saw a door at the back of the large cabinet. She stepped inside the armoire, turned on a light and asked me to follow her as she descended a long stairway to their 'cave'. She proudly showed me the well-ordered stash of wines arranged from floor to ceiling. She picked an appropriate wine, and we drank it with our lunch on the 'terrasse' (patio). Likewise at the Rochambeau château in the Valley of the 'Little Loir' the quarry was not under the home, but across the driveway and was large enough to billet 150 of General Rochambeau's soldiers under King Louis XV.

Apart from convalescing soldiers, I see no real tragedies surrounding the history of Chenonceau. This is a nice change. Like in the château of Chambord, Chenonceau was built in the age of Catherine's father-in-law, the Valois King François 1er 'Premier' (the first), (1515-1547). It is therefore neither sitting on top of an ancient Celtic site nor a Roman oppidum.

As we prepare to depart from Chenonceau we are told that Catherine left this magnificent royal residence to her daughter-in-law, Queen Consort of France, Louise de Lorraine. After the murder of her husband (Catherine's last son), King Henri III, in 1589, Louise retired here to live out her life in peace and tranquility sacrificing her time and her treasure to help others. She put on white from head to toe, as was one of the royal customs of widowed queens. She wore it to the end of her days, a sign of fidelity to her husband's memory, and she became known as the "White Queen".

I think we can agree with the phrase given by Chenonceau historians: "Chenonceau is the "Château of Women: Diane, Catherine, and Louise."

Amboise

On another fine French summer morning when we have no classes Rita and I are outbound once again. We move on to **Amboise** this time; it is not far from Tours, just a short drive north along the Loire. Once again, we see that the château is perched high on a rocky bluff overlooking the Loire River. In the 11th century there were two fortified castles here; one on the lower level in the town and the other on the heights. The latter was enlarged under King Louis XI (1423-1483) but reached its zenith under Charles VIII who was born here in 1470. At age 22 he began a huge reconstruction of the edifice. His portrait reveals him as rather somber with a pronounced irregular line of his lips, as though painted a dark hue and his aquiline nose. What I remember most about him was his sad and unintended death at age 28 (1483). He had been playing tennis and ran into the house and cracked his skull on a low doorjamb and died. Le pauvre! (poor man).

The next event makes it easy to remember Amboise. Louis XII's interest in Italy was continued by his successor and cousin, François 1er (1494-1547). François was the French King who was associated with bringing the best of the arts from Italy to France. This action brought about the French Renaissance. Life under the rule of King François 1er was magnificent at Amboise. Festivities were arranged for his betrothal to Claude of France, for his departure to Italy and the birth of the dauphin. There were all manner of celebrations such as: beast fights, tournaments, balls and masquerades to name a few. In 1534 the king was shocked when a pamphlet was pinned to his door accusing him of abuse of the Papal Mass. But, according to our guide, as early as 1518 François was often busy elsewhere building the largest château of them all, Chambord.

King François may be even better remembered when in 1516 he invited Leonardo da Vinci to join him at Amboise. Da Vinci was installed in a small château, **Clos Lucé**, not far from Château Amboise. It is said that Leonardo brought the Mona Lisa and a few other paintings with him to Clos Lucé. The famous Italian painter continued his work here, mostly inventing machines that pre-date many contraptions we use today, predominantly military and airborne. I made a return visit to Clos Lucé ten years later and spent time looking at da Vinci's numerous drawings and models for his inventions preserved there.

On the terrace that surrounds the Château Amboise, is the exceptionally beautiful Chapel of Saint-Hubert (and Saint Christopher) with intricate carving. Built by Charles VIII, it had once been a part of the main building but was separated from it at a later date. The chapel architecture can be described as "a jewel of flamboyant gothic". After only four years in France living under the sponsorship of King François 1er, da Vinci died May 2, 1519 and is buried in this exquisite French chapel. This story featuring da Vinci in France working and dying here is a detail that I had not known until my first visit. As I stand in front of this chapel dedicated to the artist, I know that few realize that the Italian artist /inventor Leonardo da Vinci of Mona Lisa fame, lived out his last days in the Loire Valley.

Amboise was the site of many royal intrigues over the years, especially fierce in the 16th century connected to the battles between the Huguenots (French Protestants) and Catholics. In point of fact, Catherine de Medici, wife of Henri II (successor to François 1er), earned a bad reputation for her treatment of the French Huguenots. In 1560 after her husband's death (1559) the struggle between the Catholics and the Huguenots heated up. The latter decided it was a good time to attack since the King had died and his young teenage son, François II, had just taken over the throne. The Huguenots marched on Château Blois; the Catholics and the Count de Guise fled to Amboise since it was easier to defend. The Huguenots followed and pleaded with the young King François II for freedom of worship. Their pleas went unheard. Although Catherine tried to make peace between the two factions in order to keep the kingdom together, it was of no avail. In short, on March 15, 1560 the Huguenots planned to seize the King and force him to denounce the Catholic de Guise family. The antagonists were arrested as they reached

Amboise. Savage punishments were meted out to them over a period of days. The town, as we are told "ran red with blood".

There is a 'great room' at Amboise where the guide tells me that Catherine de Medici had been present with one of her young sons, for whom she was Regent. This son was François II. At any rate, Rita and I are told that Catherine and her son were forced to watch as many Huguenots were gathered forcibly on a large, outdoor balcony with heavy ropes knotted around their necks. They were then cast off the roof and murdered.

The balcony where she stood with her son and the condemned Protestant Huguenots is just below us within our view. History tells us that Catherine had witnessed cruel behavior in Italy at the Vatican well before moving to France. It does not make it any easier when the doomed are your citizens. There is a film on this period of the Wars of Religion in France called "La Reine Margot" (Queen Margot). She was Catherine's daughter, twice Queen: Queen of France and Queen of Navarre.

The battle between Catholics and Protestants went on for years. Thousands were massacred on St. Bartholomew's Day 1572. In an extant letter from Jeanne d'Albret, Queen of Navarre, Catherine was accused of "eating little children". Furthermore, when Jeanne came to Paris at a later date, she was suddenly taken ill and died. Catherine was accused of "killing her with poison gloves". Fake news? The press spreads ill words when they favor one side or the other. Please note that Catherine's life was not all bad. As a woman ruling alone, she tried her best to keep the peace and to be fair to all sides whenever possible, while keeping the law.

From the point of view of the architecture of Amboise, it reached its greatest size in the 16th century. Today what remains is beautiful but scant compared to its former outline. I am particularly attracted to the Tower of Minimes that props up one corner of the château and is unique in its use. It acts as a means of conveyance for horses to enter the château. It can be likened to the entrance to a parking garage in the

20th century. The builders of Amboise foresaw an expedient method of enabling horses, carriages, even pedestrians, to enter the elevated fortress via an enclosed spiral roadway. The main level of the château is much higher than the street in the lower town. This entrance ramp is an innovative addition and is one of a kind in my experience of château architecture. The tower that enfolds the ramp exhibits Italian influence as it rises above the town. Plus, it takes up less space than the usual sloping road to gain the upper level and makes it easy to defend the castle.

The Herault Tower on the south border of the château is purely gothic. Unfortunately, the Italian gardens are no longer in existence. This is a château showing High Gothic to Middle Ages to Renaissance influences.

Several wings and sections of the original château have been demolished. However, we are able to visit King Charles VIII apartments that do remain. There are two stories adorned with slender, pointed towers. On the first floor we admire the décor provided for King Louis-Philippe (1773-1850), a much later inhabitant. We see a portrait of his royal family dressed in the Empire style of the early 19th century. We notice the usual fine tapestries that adorn the walls, a guardroom with intricate vaulted ceiling, and several rooms furnished in the Gothic and Renaissance styles.

Meanwhile Rita and I are trying to deal gracefully with the extreme heat today. I have never been so hot. The perspiration drips down from the top of my head nearly drenching my hair. Rita says that July in France this year is almost unbearable, especially as we are now in an enclosed area where one might think of it as being cooler inside such an old building. Not so today. We are wearing tee shirts, skirts and fanny packs with our valuables around our waists AND we are carrying the large notebook-like brochures we picked up as we entered. It is the English version of the tour in case we miss some key points of the château as pronounced by our French-speaking tour guide. We pass through what is called the Hall of States where the Protestants were judged. Then they were hanged from the

"Conspirators' Balcony" already mentioned. This area is marked by a line of columns that march down the center of the large room. We are told they are a necessity as they are holding up the roof.

In 1630 the outer fortifications of Amboise were razed leaving less than half of the original great rooms, apartments and surrounding walls. This is according to a map we are shown. Amboise is currently maintained by the St-Louis Foundation that preserves French National Heritage.

We leave, regretting the loss of so much of the edifice over time. With Kings and Queens no longer in existence, the funds for upkeep of these gigantic properties is left to foundations or the French government. It is truly amazing that so many, however, still retain their original glory. For students of French history like Rita and myself, we are grateful that so many of these châteaux are so well maintained.

Blois

Our tour today also takes in the château of **Blois,** "La Perle de la Loire" (The Pearl of the Loire). It is but a short drive north of Amboise, still following the course of the Loire River. The powerful Counts of Blois have been on the main stage in France since the mighty Fulk Nerra III, (970-1040) Count of Anjou. We learn that many of the same characters from the last château have played a part in the history of Blois. As we descend from our tour bus, we find that the heat and humidity have increased if that is possible. To press on is our motto. 'Excelsior' (upward and onward)!

We assemble in the courtyard for an overall look at the different eras of changing architectural styles matching the royal owners' interests. Each King finds his way to leave his mark on history. We see it before us here in solid stonework. Louis XII who preceded King François 1er was crowned in 1498 and spent a good deal of time in Italy fighting for control of Naples. A popular ruler, he was called 'Father of the People".

As we enter Blois, Rita and I see a fine example of how King Louis XII wanted to be remembered. Our guide asks us to look above the archway to see the near life sized, finely carved likeness of King Louis

XII on horseback within an elaborate double arch with a background screen decorated with many fleur-de-lys, symbol of royalty. The king is, of course, wearing his crown. This is HIS château. He was born here (1498 – 1515). Early on he had his first marriage annulled and married 'Anne de Bretagne' (Anne of Brittany), the widow of King Charles VII. They had four stillborn sons and two daughters. Louis XII was followed by François 1er whom we know and Henri II whom we know as well from previous royal residences.

Although Louis XII was born here, this château goes back in time to the feudal period. We pass through the Chamber of the States General and into the tower of Foix and emerge into the 15th century section in no time, via the St. Charles Chapel. All around us we see the emblems of Louis (the porcupine) and Anne (the ermine). Their initials are intertwined throughout. The stained-glass window depicts Louis and Anne's betrothal. We welcome this kind of good news in a château's history. "It is about time," we say to each other as we examine the beautiful stained-glass window.

Our good spirits are soon dashed when we hear the terrible story of what happened on October 9, 1566 involving King Henri III, Catherine's youngest son. Our tour of Château Blois leads us to the Charles of Orléans Gallery in the Anne de Bretagne wing (1498 - 1501). "With triumphal arch doorways and Italianate arabesque ornamentation applied to the three Gothic pillars on the courtyard side and the use of galleries to link rooms," the François Ier wing shows early French Renaissance influences, all reminiscent of each owner's particular taste and era. We shall remember Catherine de Medici's secret cupboard for sure. It is made to look just like the rest of the ornate wall, but her special section opens much to the surprise of the visitors. Did she keep jewels or private papers here?

We linger during the guided tour of King Henri III's bedchamber on the second floor to discover that the Duc de Guise was murdered here by many of the King's men, stabbing him multiple times! The Duc de Guise, a man of superior size and strength, had risen in the midst of the mêlée to use his incredible stamina to put down some of the assassins and then sadly, to fall back and die. The Duc had been skillfully lured into a meeting with the King, had suspected danger, but did not back down. All this, a part of the Religious Wars.

Here is the final shocking part of the killing: King Henri III, knowing that his enemy, the Duc, lay dead in his room, appeared from behind the curtains where he had hidden. He barely looked down at the dead Duc and proceeded nonchalantly to find his mother, Catherine, and together they went into the chapel to pray. There was little or no emotion shown by either one. The death of the Duc de Guise marked the end of a long struggle between Queen Catherine de Medici and the Guises. Catherine had won for her sons and for her daughters and herself, all of whom were Kings and Queens of France. Some years later, Henri himself was murdered. Who needs to read fiction when history covers all sorts of dastardly deeds?

We walk slowly back into the huge courtyard where we are urged to pay close attention to the exterior stairway. It is indeed amazing. There are cut out openings between the buttresses and balconies at each level as it rises and turns back on itself. Did the Duc de Guise enter by this stairway? I believe this is one of those unique architectural features seen only here at Blois. Blois has been a stunning study, both in architecture and history.

Chambord

Back on our tour bus, we continue north along the Loire toward Château **Chambord**. It is located about halfway between Tours and Orléans. The Loire River is leading us to one of the most astonishing places I have ever seen, the Château Chambord.

I do not know much of the history of Chambord so Rita and I do a short study of maps and descriptions en route to our last stop for the day. We find that Chambord stands in a vast 'parc' surrounded by a 20-mile wall. It is built on what I would call an open flood plain. There are no drawbridges, no double thick walls, no keep, no machicolis, no huge, round towers. Chambord is the brainchild of King François 1er. Rita and I are up for it.

Beyond the breathtaking edifice is a private forest for the King to partake in his favorite sport, the hunt. As we drive in, I do not see the exterior wall. Oh, yes, the wall is not a tall one, and it is not far from the palace proper, foreshortened with cut off pillars at the corners.

We soon learn that everything here whirls around King François 1er even though his main residences remained Amboise and Blois. We know him already. He was the King who brought Leonardo from Italy. He is different from other kings. He is interested in the arts, not just a conquering military man. (Although at the young age of 21 he was already a winner on the battlefield, bringing Milan, Italy, under his sway). Perhaps Leonardo had a hand in the planning of this castle, built more for pleasure than for war. I was right, it is the largest of the Loire royal estates. According to the guidebook its footprint spans 21,829 square yards.

What a way to end our day of château hopping! Chambord is going to be the plum in the pudding, the star on top of the Christmas tree, the opera singer's high A! Never mind how hot it still is, we are ready to be awed and amazed. As we drive down the long avenue toward our goal a silence falls over the busload of graduate students of French. We have seen quite a few châteaux up to this point, but nothing like this. The closer we get, the more details come into view.

First, it is HUGE. Second, it is a sparkling white jewel in the sunlight. Chambord stands alone here in peaceful solitude. It is taller, and it is wider than any we have seen. It stands almost like a Cathedral to the Renaissance with its many steeples, chimneys and roof top ornaments in perfect whimsy-like symmetry. Take a breath; do not forget to breathe, beloved tourist!

Now, we get down to brass tacks. Like the Palace of Versailles (12 miles outside Paris), Chambord began as a hunting lodge (for the Duke of Orléans) that François razed so he could build an elegant château more suitable for a king like himself. François was attracted to the area, a corner of the well-known extensive Bois de Boulogne. It would be suitable hunt country for the King and his court. The building was begun in 1519 and was near to being completed in 1547. A few architects' names were associated with the design: Da Vinci, Il Boccadoro, and François de Pontbriant. The latter two had worked at Amboise and Blois.

No sooner had François begun the project than he returned from Italy under duress and decided that a king should live nearer his people. Chambord was never fully completed. However, there are 440 rooms, 365 windows, 13 main staircases and 70 back stairs. On the back of the post card I buy, it states there were 1,800 builders and workers on the job at Chambord for a total of 15 years. Then a strange change of heart occurred to the king. He preferred to live closer to Paris, in the château Fontainebleau for example. Oh my. I am sure this slowed down progress on his fanciful residence of Chambord. Not to worry as there is much to see all the same.

Let's explore some of the highlights of the interior. Really there is one that makes its mark here as being unique. It is the double staircase that rises spectacularly out of the ground floor. The staircase is a symbol of beauty with tongue in cheek in my view. It is constructed in such a way that a person coming down from above cannot run into, or even see, someone climbing up from the first floor. Is there a reason for this outlandish, complicated design? Could it simply be that a mistress could leave the house unnoticed while someone else she does not want to see or be seen by, ascends by the other side? It certainly could have been put to good use in the days of kings that followed François, for instance Louis XIV.

The double staircase can be described as two sets of stairs spiraling around each other from the ground floor to the roof terrace. It rises from the center of a cross, formed by the intersection of the four guardrooms on the ground floor. When mounting the stairs one can see François 1er's emblem, the salamander, that adorns the vaulting.

The stonework is pierced with many openings, so perhaps one could identify the person on the other side after all.

We are told that the King received some highborn visitors to his unfinished chef d'oeuvre. Charles V, a Holy Roman Emperor, proclaimed` "Chambord is a summary of Human Industry". François' near relatives did not show up very often except to hunt in the forest, even today inhabited by deer and boar. I am sure it would have been different if François and his court had spent more time at his new digs.

Naturally we take the opportunity to follow the unusual double twist staircase all the way up to the roof terrace. I must say, I did not notice anyone going down. From firsthand experience, I think the goal of secrecy was achieved after all. I had no idea that the roof terrace was one of the biggest attractions here. We hit it on a good day, as it is not always open to the public. Today we are in luck. Our guide tells us that the idea for this terrace was one borrowed from François' time in Italy. We walk out onto the broad, flat surface of the topmost part of the château just as the king must have so many times. The spires, dormer windows and sandcastle-like chimneys surround us and rise above us. The area up here is enormous. Everything is oversized here. Up here the first thing we notice is that there is a fine breeze as compared to the stagnant air in the stifling hot rooms below. No wonder the terrace is popular.

This is really my favorite part of the entire château. I love standing here in the breeze, not minding if my hair is blown every which way. I look over the broad expanse of 'le parc', even see the glassy lake that François has diverted from the Loire (not very distant). I can see the man-made moat that runs along two sides (barely visible from here), a carryover from feudal times. Also visible are the gardens in the distance, and even farther removed, is the forest where kings have hunted to their hearts' content so many years ago. I am in heaven up here on the roof terrace. I shall forget neither the breeze nor the view.

Feet on the ground again, we visit the main rooms, see tapestries and paintings galore. Then we hear a bittersweet story about 'la Grande

Mademoiselle'. Her real name: Anne-Marie-Louis d'Orléans, Duchesse de Montpensier. As cousin of King Louis XIV, she was the "wealthiest single princess in Europe during the reign of Louis XIV". She had fallen in love with the Duc de Lauzun (1633-1723) in 1666 (Lauzun, the father of a famous 18th century cavalry officer, also the called the Duc de Lauzun, who came to America with General Rochambeau in 1780 and plays a central role in my biography/military history: *Rochambeau, Washington's Ideal Lieutenant.*)

When Anne-Marie's father visited Chambord, Anne-Marie, showing modesty and humor, breathed heavily onto a mirror she was holding and traced his name (Duc de Lauzun) in the mist on the mirror. Such a unique way to reveal one's love. But it was not to be. Chambord at that time was under control of King Louis XIV as was the entire court. Therefore, Lauzun and Anne-Marie were obliged to request permission for their marriage from the king. In the end King Louis XIV, who originally gave his blessing to their upcoming marriage, rescinded his vow and sent Lauzun to prison. To free him Anne-Marie waited for him and pleaded with Louis, to no avail.

Finally, in 1682 King Louis said if she gives up two of her valuable properties to the crown, he will free Lauzun. She did, and he did. Yes, he freed Lauzun, but Louis kept the two lovers permanently apart. Anne-Marie then retreated in great sadness to her Palace of Luxembourg in Paris for the rest of her life. She is buried at St. Denis, necropolis of Royals, which I shall visit at a later date.

More history to add to that of Chambord regarding the famous French playwright, Molière. He made nine visits to Chambord between 1660 and 1695. He wrote the play "Monsieur de Pourceaugnac" in a few days while in residence here. At the first performance at the Château, King Louis XIV never smiled. (I read that he fell asleep). The composer of the accompanying music, Jean-Baptiste Lully, who was playing the part of the apothecary, suddenly took it upon himself to jump from the stage onto the harpsichord, smashing it. King Louis burst into laughter, and the play was deemed a success!

"Le Bourgeois Gentilhomme", another of Molière's plays, was presented at Chambord as well. Molière was trying to hide his anxiety over the fact that at the premiere he saw the King looking rather cool. Then, as a consequence, the whole court was not pleased with the way Molière treated them in the play. But the day was saved at the second performance when the King had a positive reaction and the courtiers quickly altered their response from deadly dull to delightfully droll. We know how that story goes. When the king is not pleased, no one is pleased. But when the king is happy, everyone follows suite. Some things never change.

Chambord has lent its name to a fine black raspberry liqueur by the same name. This liqueur found its inspiration in the Loire valley in the late 1600's. It was stocked and offered at Château Chambord during the time of King Louis XIV when the practice was to serve it during the meal, not following the meal as liqueurs are served today.

With this, Rita and I exit the ravishing Château de Chambord.

Villandry

Because of space constraints I will only mention three other châteaux briefly while recommending them highly for a visit. Villandry, known for its vast vegetable gardens planted à la française as one would plant flowers in rows and circles; Azay le Rideau, recognizable as a sparkling diamond surrounded by water; and Beauregard, sought out by historians like myself for the extensive collection of royal portraits.

The remaining châteaux I visited will pop up in the course of other chapters: The Louvre, Versailles, Fontainebleau, Château Nohand de George Sand, Vaux-le-Vicomte, and Chantilly and others.

In America we have very little resembling these breathtaking kingly homes. The homes of the Vanderbilts and the like in North Carolina and Newport, Rhode Island, historic homes of our Presidents are certainly beautiful. A tourist in America has to travel hundreds of miles between attractions. By comparison, the proximity of France's incredibly well-preserved Loire castles with their fine-tuned gardens, most within half an hour or an hour of each other, is one reason that makes touring in the Loire Valley so exciting.

I dare not bring this chapter of Château Hopping to a close without describing the wonderful welcome home for Rita and me after each château outing. Mado and Lucien are always at the house when we return, hot and tired after a day of touring but radiant in our newfound treasures of the day in the greater Loire Valley. We refresh ourselves with a nice, cool shower and dress for dinner to be served in the lush and lovely summer garden of the Renaud family.

Slowly we gather around the table with other students arriving from thither and yon. Two are away on a weekend trip to Mont St. Michel. We are the lucky ones who come to taste what Mado has prepared for us tonight. We hear the last 'A table' (Come to the table) rising from the kitchen, and soon we have a full table under the shade of the banana tree. Lucien opens a bottle of wine from a nearby vineyard. Mado comes out of the kitchen carrying the first course of cold white asparagus in a tasty Normandy butter sauce that we relish with crunchy baguettes to sop up the remains. Then she returns with a heaping platter of sweet breads in a tarragon sauce and crispy French fries. After much conversation of what everyone has done today along with a good helping of world news, Mado serves the salad course. It is 'salade verte' (green salad) tossed at the table with tonight's homemade vinaigrette over tender bib lettuce, my favorite. We tone down our conversation to savor the flavors. The meal is complete with an abundance of local fresh fruit, a regional, creamy cheese and a café crème.

This evening Rita and I will meet some friends for a concert featuring Russian violist Yuri Bashmet and his Moscow Soloists. It will be held in a local historic church within walking distance. We may not be kings and queens, but we know that at this congenial table Lucien and Mado do their utmost to spoil us in the finest French fashion of true friendship.

Chapter Three

Two Hundred Years and Counting: Celebrating the Bicentennial of the French Revolution

ANOTHER FALL AND EARLY WINTER of teaching have passed, and I am planning my next summer at my now well-established center of operations in Tours chez Mado. Only recently did I ring in the New Year, 1989. Once again, I find myself champing at the bit as I prepare to spend my next summer in dear old France. My plans start with the usual registration at the University of Touraine simultaneous with my letter to Mado making sure I could nail down my old room for yet another summer. Mado and I are becoming fast friends. It would be my third summer, and I am full of anticipation, as every summer thus far has brought me wonderful surprises and unanticipated discoveries. It will be a banner tourist season, it being the bicentennial of the French Revolution. Every issue of my French newspapers announces more celebrations. As a teacher of French, I am certainly in the right place. I would also continue my annual habit of writing to the French Government Tourist Office and the French Embassy, Cultural Services Section, both in New York City. In this way I will be apprised of the forthcoming summer music festivals, as well as any literary or historical events.

I determine early that to be in Paris, in the midst of all the bicentennial celebrations, is not my style. There will be too many people. The Champs Elysées, the main street in Paris, will be jammed with onlookers for "La Fête Internationale de la France" (Bastille Day) Parade on July 14th.

I have been reading that the preparations for the big day have been underway for months, even years. Jean-Paul Goude has been appointed Cultural Minister by President Mitterrand. Goude's name is pronounced in French like the beginning of the word 'gouey', with a 'd' at the end. His name sounds curiously like the anglicized version of Frenchman's pronunciation of the opposite of 'bad'. Goude is in charge of the monumental Bastille Day Parade. He has spent the previous year traveling around the world to all Francophone (French speaking) countries judging entries for the grand parade. It will follow the great axis road in Paris, made all the more splendid by Mitterrand during his two term (6 years per term) presidency. He was elected in 1981; he is in his second term when I arrive.

The parade will begin at President Mitterrand's newly-built Arche de la Défense (ultra-modern monument/office building), pass by the Arc de Triomphe (triumphal arch memorializing soldiers from Napoleonic Wars forward), continue down the length of the Avenue des Champs Elysées (named after the Elysian Fields of Greek mythology and is known as the most beautiful avenue in the world), ending at the Place de la Concorde (Square of Peace), where, not incidentally, shortly following 1789 and beyond, the tireless Guillotine stood busily beheading royals, nobles, priests and many more innocents during the French Revolution. In 1789 a French physician, Joseph-Ignace Guillotine penned the design of a machine to kill swiftly and avoid suffering. It was used in France until the death penalty was abolished in 1981.

Back to the planning of the Bastille Day parade. Jean- Paul Goude will eventually pick one marching/performing group or float, from each former colony of France to travel to Paris and take part in the enormous parade to beat all parades in this bicentennial year. Goude and Mitterrand promise that the festivities will have special meaning this year. They want the people of the world watching the 200-year celebration unfold on live TV hook-ups to be reminded why the French

Revolution was perpetrated and that its heritage is alive and well today. They plan to promote a theme extending far beyond the boundaries of France, the theme of "Les Droits de l'Homme" (The rights of Man) as expressed in the French Constitution.

Of particular note to Americans, this precious document stating everyman's right was adopted directly from The United States "Bill of Rights". This exchange of ideas was made possible through such statesmen as the Marquis de Lafayette, Thomas Jefferson, and Benjamin Franklin, who lived in each other's countries as diplomats for extended periods of time during these years of upheaval, first in America, and later, in France.

Every event will be televised live around the world. Having heard of the coverage by A & E, the Arts and Entertainment television network, I will have the full six-hour parade taped in my absence. So, hooray, I do not have to battle the crowds in Paris to see the spectacle. When I return home at the end of summer, I will have a front row seat in the serenity of my own home. My French students and I will also benefit from the in-depth commentary and overall magnificence that surely will attend the coverage.

Another aspect of world interest happening concurrently with all this revelry in Paris is that of the International Summit (G7) the seven leading industrialist countries of the world. French President François Mitterrand will be the host. What great planning on his part to further draw attention to himself, and his accomplishments over his last eight years in office. The big names in attendance are to be Le Président Bush (pronounced by the French as "booosh", sounding much like a can of Busch beer after the top is popped); English Prime Minister, Margaret Thatcher (pronounced very much like "that chair" by the French); and West German Chancellor Helmut Kohl. The summit goals are to discuss these looming topics: the evolution of the eastern bloc, (to include Human Rights, East-West relations in newly reunited Germany), terrorism, climate and the environment.

The leaders of the free world are to be feted and dined in the spirit of a new Europe, surrounded by the new 'look' (pronounced by the French like the word 'loo', the British bathroom) of Mitterrand's new Paris. The Arc of Defense, already mentioned, the Pyramid of the Louvre designed by Chinese architect IM Pei, and the new Opera of the Bastille, all of which are recent modern and controversial. All three were created by Mitterrand to be monuments to his glory. The Opera of the Bastille is thus named as it is constructed partially on the foundations of the old Bastille, symbol of the French Revolution. The greater part of the ancient foundations, pulled down shortly after the Revolution to build homes for the poor, are now outlined in white paint on the street in front of the new opera lest we forget.

I learned the names and locations of the former French colonies while working at the French Embassy, "Presse et Information" division, Fifth Avenue, New York City in the early 1960s. At that time most of us had never heard of these small Francophone countries; most were either in or near Africa and had recently gained their independence from France. Declared independent from France between 1956-58 were former colonies: Morocco, Tunisia and Guinea. Then, in 1960, also freed were the following small African countries: Cameroon, Senegal, Togo, Mali (now Sudan), Madagascar, Dahomey (now Benin), Niger, Upper Volta (now Burkina Faso), Ivory Coast, Chad, Central African Republic, Republic of Congo, Gabon, and Mauritania. In the far east of course, Vietnam and others. I am not sure how many former French Colonies around the world were represented in the parade in 1989. I cite the aforementioned African nations by way of demonstrating their ongoing influence in France, as well as the important role they will play in the bicentennial celebration.

This summer of 1989 these tiny independent states are to be recognized in the biggest fête in France's recent history. Each one would bring an example of what it does best and be seen by the entire world as its participants sashay down the Champs Elysées in their native costumes. They will be taking their place in the Free Former-French-

Colony-world; they will be prime examples of how the rights of man have been carried to even these faraway places. This statement was the 'hype' of Mitterrand and Goude.

Further into the parade plans, the word is that an African - American opera singer, Jesseye Norman, is volunteering to sing "La Marseillaise" (the French National Anthem), to culminate the gathering of all the floats from all these participating free countries as they group in formation, around the huge Place de la Concorde late in the evening of the 14th.

Jesseye Norman spent much of her youth in France, attended French schools, learning the language at a tender age. According to the newspapers, she learned every word of the French National Anthem by heart at the age of 6. This is truly a feat even for an adult, since the anthem is long and difficult with vocabulary not normally taught in American schools. I will be sad to miss this part of celebration for in person it will surely be mesmerizing!

By late spring, the suspense was building for Francophiles as to the extent of the celebrations. Who is celebrating, anyway? Is it only the 'people' of France, the ones who gained personal rights when the Bastille was stormed and the prisoners were set free? Is it simply everyone in France who celebrates with parades and dancing in the streets as they do every year? What would the aristocrats, the clergy and the descendants of royalty do when all of Paris is caught up in this enormous party? Are they the forgotten ones? How about Americans, do we have something to celebrate too?

On this subject I recall an incident over dinner in a château in deepest, darkest Southwest France, where I had my comeuppance when a 'royalist' (supporter of King Louis XVI and Queen Marie Antoinette) Frenchman astounded me by saying that his family does not to this day find anything to fête on July 14th. For them it is but a reminder of a sad day in their history and the unforgivable loss of their innocent King and Queen.

As an American, albeit one who has studied French history for decades, it had never occurred to me that all Frenchmen did not embrace the cause for freedom commemorated on July 14th each summer. In my chapter "The Little-Known Little Loir" you will read about a saintly, devout lady named Jehanne whom I meet at the abbey in Solesmes in the summer of 1993. I mention her here, as her story is relevant to the July 14 celebration.

Jehanne tells me that she convenes annually with her fellow royalists/monarchists in Paris at the Church of Saint Denis where King Louis XVI and Queen Marie Antoinette are buried. They congregate at the tombs of the royal couple to celebrate their birth dates and to lament their tragic death dates, while praying and plotting for the day when the monarchy will be restored in France. There are at least two present-day descendants of royal blood living in France and in Spain in 1989. This faction shuns the huge preparations for the bicentennial bash. Most likely, this particular year, 1989, some have planned a vacation to another country so as to extricate themselves from what would be for them a most unhappy occasion. Imagine their discomfort in watching all the preparations, sanctioned by their own government, going on for at least a year, readying for the biggest street party in 200 years!

It all depends on your point of view and on those with whom you choose to be on this day. In my case, up until this year I, too, celebrated, with professors, fellow students and ordinary people, and did not give it much thought. But now I am considering both sides. After all the books I have read about Marie Antoinette, I think I tend to favor her side. But, as I am often a mugwump on this subject, I will be celebrating this summer with the swell of tourists and loving all the history I am absorbing. I will leave it up to you to do your due diligence study to determine which side you will take.

In America's case, the major difference is that the colonist rebels did not have to go as far as killing the King of England to gain our freedom. First of all, he did not take up residence on our soil. King George III was never one of us. However, there was a formidable faction, the Tories, who remained monarchists and wanted to maintain English rule. Many Tories returned to England to save their skin.

By the end of June 1989, with preparations at an end and having celebrated the wedding of my eldest daughter, Heather, on June 24th, I arrive at Mado's to take up residence in my old room above her garden. I will have two weeks to get into my studies before the celebration on the 14th.

Not surprisingly, I decide to be far away from Paris and Tours, for that matter, in the southwest of France by then. A history teacher colleague from my US high school is coming to meet me here in Tours. We will take a train to Bordeaux and then rent a car, ending up in the medieval walled town of Carcassonne for Bastille Day. In the meantime, I am happy to pick up my routine as a summer grad student at the Institut, savoring the great meals Mado prepares so well. I look forward to stimulating, educational and humorous conversations with her husband Lucien, and their international students at the garden table.

This year my main Prof. is still M. DeLormes, the best-beloved teacher at the Institut. His specialty is French literature. On my schedule will be the usual broad-spectrum support courses: French language (syntax, dictation, discussion of current events and composition), oral expression, oral comprehension, language labs, literature, civilization, translation, art, film and music.

Naturally, it goes without saying that I will top off every night, including weekends, with heavy doses of homework! I love every moment but have to admit there are a few evenings when I am stumped on how to synopsize highly technical, intensely complicated, sometimes philosophical essays. This exercise is humdrum for the French students who practice the technique of summarizing since their youth. Their standardized testing always includes synopsizing subjects with which they are not familiar. American students, on the other hand, rarely are asked to beat our brains out in this practice. I find it most challenging.

The other brick wall for me this summer is oral comprehension. It is taken to a higher level by our prof, who, after lunch, in a top floor airless classroom, in the blistering heat of nearly 100 degrees, requires that we begin by listening to an audiotape of a two- or three-person radio interview. On the spot we are asked to transpose the audio to written word.

I recall one steamy afternoon in particular as we listen to a radio announcer interviewing a racecar driver. It was my first time discovering how difficult it is to sort out two voices, to figure out which is which, pick up the overlays while absorbing the gist of the conversation thus distinguishing what each is saying when they speak at once. Comprehending the technical lingo they use regarding racecar driving compounds the difficulty.

First, we listen to the entire interview. Then our prof plays a couple of sentences and stops the tape. We are to write down in French the exact dialogue. Then he replays the whole tape and asks questions on the content. I can recall being taken completely off guard by the extreme difficulty of this exercise, straining to grasp every syllable to the utmost of my ability. I realize then how helpful it is to watch one's lips and gestures in order to better comprehend the spoken language.

Luckily, I had purchased a Walkman and brought it with me this summer. After that horrific experience, I listen to my Walkman to improve my oral comprehension. In fact, I often fall asleep at night this summer listening to radio discussions on art and music or interviews with literary greats. It helps.

In one of my laboratory classes our prof, Caroline, plays French songs, sung by Edith Piaf, Jacques Brel, Georges Brassens or Yves Montand, and we are asked to follow much the same routine as in the radio interviews. Better yet, she also plays contemporary hit songs, first leaning and then singing all the words. But, reminder: comprehending songs is far easier than taped radio interviews. With music there is repetition and certain other aspects that one can anticipate, such as rhyme. Overall, by contrast, I adore the exercises with French songs.

In fact, I keep the copies of the lyrics in order to enhance my teaching in Connecticut.

Coming home for lunch is always a great way to break the intense concentration of our morning studies. I stuff my books and pads in my (sac à dos) backpack, trot down the winding marble stairway and head out into the sunshine for the ten-minute walk back to Mado's. Most of the students walk north toward the Loire to the University Cafeteria for lunch.

My first summer I lived in the University dorm and took most of my lunches at the cafeteria as well. The food was not bad, plenty of mystery meat in hearty sauces with loads of fresh fruit. I always love the abundance of small, ripe apricots grown in the south of France that were offered with most meals. But at Mado's, the fare is truly 'extraordinaire'!

On the day before my colleague and I leave for the south of France, July 13th, Mado prepares her gala Bastille Day lunch for us. As I walk down the little 'sentier' to her gate, I can hear the excitement in the garden. I insert my enormous iron key into the gate lock and enter with the giant sheep dog barking his welcome. Mado had spared nothing decorating for the event. The balcony from her room, surrounded with vine-covered wrought iron fencing, is festooned with French 'tricolore' (blue, white and red) crepe paper and open-up, fluff-out tricolor buntings.

The special table for the day was decorated in much the same way with blue, white and red cloth and napkins. It is set up under a flowering tree at the front of the garden, about ten steps from the kitchen. Mado has hung little French flags all over. But this is nothing compared to the meal that awaits us. She calls us to eat (À table), her melodic voice ringing out from the garden. It takes only a few minutes to rearrange my books, splashing refreshing cool water on my face upstairs. This year's summer students from Alabama and Japan, meet me at the table.

Lucien, Mado's husband of 40 years, takes his place at the head of the table. Mado appears from the kitchen dressed in blue, white and red, very chic, carrying a silver tray filled with champagne glasses. But the drinks were not pale gold fizzy ones, they were bleu, blanc et rouge in layers. I soon learn the color combination is patriotic for the occasion. Leave it to Mado to think of this. The 'rouge' (red) is grenadine; the 'blanc' (white) is 'Framboise' (white raspberry liqueur); and the 'bleu' (blue) is Curacao. We enjoy the festive drinks and toast one another with "Vive la France", "Vive la Révolution" and "Vive Mado et Lucien!"

Mado then disappears into the kitchen and returns momentarily, bearing a large platter of 'coeurs de palmier' vinaigrette (hearts of palm), our first course. The hearts of palm are meticulously arranged on the platter in a star shape with a mound of freshly grated celeriac smothered in an aromatic rémoulade sauce in the center. We devour this cooling dish savoring every bite. You can really work up an appetite doing heady work in a language lab all morning. Amidst lots of talk of how we were all going to spend our holiday weekend, Lucien slices the baguettes.

Then, Mado clears the first course By the way, she does not like people cruising through her kitchen or even assisting to clear or do dishes --- so we obediently hold our ground at the garden table. She next appears with a luscious-looking cold poached salmon covered in a tarragon sauce, surrounded with Bastille red cherry tomatoes decorated with fresh mint leaves. As you can imagine, it goes down easily with great relish and appreciation on our part.

Did I forget to mention that my habit at Mado's house has always been to bring a 'bloc' (pad) to the table every day on which to record the menu and occasional recipes? There is always much discussion about recipes and ingredients. I know Mado takes great pleasure in preparing these wonderfully fresh meals made totally from scratch in her smallish, but up-to-date kitchen. Nota Bene: There is no dishwasher other than herself either.

At an average meal of 6 or 7 courses, she uses a plate for everyone for each course. There are usually no less than 6 and often 8 people around the table at mealtime. You can figure how many plates she needs to fill, serve, clear and wash. I know that on the rare occasion when I have brought something into the kitchen after a meal, I can testify the dishes are stacked up to the ceiling. It is a daily miracle she performs twice a day. I am still in awe of her tireless energy and her indefatigable spirit of creativity in meal preparation and presentation. In the course of six weeks at her house, I never have seen the same thing served twice except the bread and the salad. And that's the truth!

On with the meal. We wait for the main course with great anticipation. It is 'lapin chasseur' (rabbit stew) with 'haricots verts' (thin French string beans), the pride and joy of the typical French chef.

Mado and Lucien had made one of their regular forays into the country the preceding day to pick up fresh rabbit for this occasion. It was perfectly cooked and served with the usual amount of bones. Our salad course follows, served on a new plate of course. It is prepared in their signature glass bowl with raised leaf pattern on smoked glass. The Butterhead lettuce is melt- in- your- mouth good 'comme toujours'!

I use my 'baguette' pieces to sop up the remaining vinaigrette made fresh every day. Salads are not usually adorned with anything, but served as plain lettuce, dressed with vinaigrette, thus the appellation, 'salade verte', (green salad). They mean it! All through the meal Lucien generously offers us the red wine from his wine 'cave'. Most of us refuse at lunch knowing we must return to classes clear-headed.

At last, the 'pièce de résistance', the dessert! For our special occasion Mado made a beautiful pear flan, Spanish recipe. The pear slices are carefully cut and arranged in concentric circles over a custard cream. Plus, she has saved, especially for me, an over-brimming bowl of her raspberries, harvested fresh this morning from her backyard. My dear friend, Mado, serves these for me every summer with my favorite 'fromage blanc'. This is a type of white, very light, farmers' cheese with sugar added to desired sweetness. The farmer's cheese is almost the consistency of yogurt and is a perfect complement for the tart berries. I revel in my special dish.

Every year, even if I arrive past the raspberry season, Mado remembers how much I adore fresh raspberries served in this fashion. I truly appreciate it! By now it is getting late. She brings in a plate of cheeses quickly followed by the compote of fresh apricots, cherries, peaches and bananas.

I run upstairs to brush my teeth and get my afternoon books. My walk back to school is quick; the air, by then is heavy with mid-afternoon summer heat. I savor the marvelous meal I have just consumed. It will be a little hard shifting gears back to lowly student after being treated like a queen. I will have to fight the heat and the aftereffects of the large meal I have just put away. Worst of all are the extra flights of creaky wooden spiral stairs to my fourth-floor afternoon literature classroom. And, did I mention? The Institut has no air-conditioning. The higher I climb, the hotter it gets.

The next morning my colleague, Jackie, who has just arrived from Connecticut, and I, are on the early train south to Bordeaux. We will change to another train headed for Pau at the foot of the Pyrenées Mountains. There we will pick up our rental car. We will avoid six hours on the autoroute. Avis has a special train/drive package that we find advantageous. It is another incredibly blistering afternoon in the South of France as we descend from the train to walk to the car rental office. No time to sightsee here. Soon we are off in our lovely sea-blue Citroën with maps in hand heading for Carcassonne where we plan to spend the big Bastille day in relative peace.

A few days prior to our departure, we asked Mado's daughter, Maryse, to help find us a hotel reservation for the weekend of the 14th as we had been unable to find one on our own. As she is in the hotel business, we were very grateful for her expertise. The hotel she chose was 'intra-muros' (within the walls) of the old town of Carcassonne. The old towns are always the preferred place to stay in France when touring since everything is within walking distance.

We have a few hours ride through the beautiful Languedoc region of south-western France. We test the car and our nerves, to see what all this talk is of driving as fast as the French, namely over 100 miles an hour, which we try on a quiet stretch of superhighway. People are still passing us at greater speeds. We give it up quickly for a conservative 80 mph and strictly confine ourselves to the far-right lane. The roads are strangely unpopulated for a holiday weekend; for that we are grateful.

Upon arrival at Carcassonne we are awestruck by the sight of this magnificent storybook town so often pictured in tour guides and so rarely seen by tourists who hop in and out of Paris. Driving in from the plain surrounding the ancient double-walled 'cité' (city), Carcassonne can be easily seen. Indomitable, it is perched on a plateau overlooking the river Aude. One soon discovers that rivers are important in France. Historic destinations are formed by the rivers that flow through and around them. Tours is a perfect case in point as the river Loire flows through the center of town. Countless towns in France are named and recognized by the river that dominates the town such as: Saint-Cyr-sur-Loire.

The founding of Carcassonne reckons back to 3400 BC and derives its name from a folk story of a woman called Carcas and the ringing of the bells after a siege. Thus 'Carcas sona' (Carcas rang). It once was a place where the Cathars lived (see my chapter on Cathar Catharsis) during the Albigensian Crusade. They were chased from Carcassonne by the Pope and the King's soldiers led by Simon de Montfort in the 1200s.

We drive up to the East entrance by the Narbonne Towers and park our car outside the walls, where a porter with a small vehicle from our hotel awaits us. It is the Hôtel de la Cité, a 4-star hotel with large rooms in the old-world tradition with medieval decor.

Carcassonne is the former seat of the Episcopal Palace. I love to step outside the hotel on the old town side and immediately be immersed in the hustle bustle of the medieval atmosphere of the 12th century Château Comtal, the gothic cathedral, and ancient stone fortifications, shops, and crowded narrow winding streets. Yet if I want just the opposite, I can explore within the hotel boundaries where it is peaceful and quiet.

The next morning Jackie and I do just that. We step out of the hotel in the opposite direction into the private garden overlooking the ramparts and the lower town far below. There we are served our café au lait and croissants on rattan chairs under rose arbors with not a trace of the tourist noise. I love it here.

On the afternoon of our arrival, we quickly settle in and after a rest, we begin exploration in the old town and then dress for dinner. As we leave our hotel to look for a resto, the bell captain tells us that the hotel will be temporarily closing its doors about 10:30PM to allow for the 'Son et Lumière' (Sound and Light Show) that will take place shortly thereafter. He requests that, before leaving however, we must close our room windows. I later discern the reason. I am surprised to hear all this, not having been forewarned that there would even be a Sound and Light show. But it is Bastille Day 1989. I guess they celebrate in a big way here at Carcassonne too! I dutifully run back upstairs to baton down the hatches.

After supper in an outdoor café, Jackie and I notice people beginning to leave the old town. We, too, head for the main gate. As we leave the inner city the crowd grows tighter and tighter but remains upbeat. We do not know exactly where we are headed but soon determine that the idea is to exit the walled cite and descend to the edge of the lower town on the plain that surrounds Carcassonne. When we reach the level city streets below, we are in a crush of humanity. The crowd slows to a stop. Whew! We turn around to look back up at the impressive fortress of Carcassonne we have just evacuated. By now it is pitch dark—not one light belies the many homes, hotels and restaurants we have just abandoned. All we can see are the foundation lamps that bathe the walls. There is a hush over us all as we wait to see what will happen.

It is midnight according to my colleague's illuminated wristwatch. Suddenly the entire medieval town is drenched in a fiery red light from end to end. Classical music comes from every direction. Everyone cheers from astonishment and wonder. Silence again reigns over the crowd as the show begins. It is a computerized laser light show with synchronized light and sound, the likes of which neither of us has ever witnessed. It is an historical program written especially to tell the story of Carcassonne at the time of the French Revolution.

The Sound and Light show is at once violent and sad. When the story becomes violent the lights reflect the sentiment, and the music swells; when the story turns sad, the music and the lights follow suit. The synchronized lights project the history of the town in realistic scenes across the walls via distinct colors. Music and lights tell the story of Carcassonne over the centuries, from vicious attacks to the fleeing of persecuted Cathar Christians.

By the finale, the tension builds with an orchestral crescendo and massive explosion of fireworks until I am mute with tears streaming down my face. I am so moved by the history we have just witnessed that I can barely speak. I do not even wish to speak. There is thundering applause. It is some time before the crowd stops, becomes silent, and starts the procession back up the hill to "la cité". Now I know why we were asked to close the windows of our hotel rooms. It was to keep out the smoke and sparks.

For me this was a wonderful way to celebrate Bastille Day, 200 years later. Yes, we encountered the crowd, but I have no complaints. The best part was that the Sound and Light Show was totally unanticipated. We must thank Maryse. I am also content in the fact that even as we are peacefully climbing towards our towering medieval castle hotel, in Paris the many floats from the huge parade are assembled in the Place de la Concorde (during the French Revolution, called the Square of the Revolution). At the center of the square is the 3300-year old pink granite, hieroglyphic-covered Obelisk of Luxor. Yes, today, it is a place of concord where 200 years ago chaos reigned, and a monarchy was tumbled. Yes, today the Place de la Concorde symbolizes unity between the 5th Republic and the people of the French world, freed colonies and all. Yes, this night 200 years later they all come together to parade, to lift a glass, and to dance the 'carmagnole', the dance of the people in the streets and in the bars during the French Revolution to the advancement of the rights of man.

In Paris, at the stroke of midnight, the sound would be turned on from the Place de la Concorde to the Arc de Triomphe. The throngs of thousands are holding their breath as Jesseye Norman's voice is heard simultaneously throughout the parade route. She stands at the base of the 75-foot obelisk with huge spotlights beamed on her billowing tricolor silk gown with long floating train. There is a lump in everyone's throat and a butterfly in each stomach. It's 200 years and who's counting? "Alions, enfants de la patrie......le jour de gloire est arrivé...." (Come, children of France...the glorious day is upon us!).

The next morning Jackie and I step out of the hotel onto the immense terrace planted with flowering trees and a gracious garden overlooking the ramparts and the lower town far below where we stood last night. It is quiet this morning. We are served our café au lait and croissants. It is easy to love it here.

It is hard to tear ourselves away from the most beautiful, best preserved, double-walled medieval city in France, but we did. We have Saturday and Sunday to make it back to Tours in our rented car. We made plans in advance so we could make the most of our time. Our destination today is between Toulouse and Limoges in the center of the Périgord region near the Dordogne River. We will avoid the large cities and take as many back roads as possible to get the feel of this part of Queen Aliénor's Aquitaine. We pass bastides, (fortified medieval towns), stop to stroll through their open air markets.

More specifically, we are headed for the Château de Regagnac. I discovered it in my research last winter in Karen Brown's book of "Country Bed and Breakfasts in France". I wrote the owners, M. and Mme. Serge Pardoux, saying we would be coming on the 15 July for one night. It was "de rigueur" (a must) to let them know if we wanted to have dinner that night. I wrote in response that dinner for two would be perfect.

We drive through Montpazier and then follow the signs for Regagnac, driving along beautiful country roads with little sign of civilization. If you are looking for a wonderful castle in the valley of the Dordogne River, one that is absolutely brimming with character, tucked far from the madding crowds, the Château de Regagnac is your dream come true. The road to the castle winds through a forest and finally deadens at the Château de Regagnac. Go through the gates and into the courtyard that extends to a bluff and offers a sensational view out to the forested hills.

Le Château de Regagnac is furnished in family antiques – although the decor is stunning, there is a homey ambience – nothing seems stuffy or ultra- formal. Some of the bedchambers are in the main part of the castle and others across the courtyard, but it does not matter which you reserve, they are all beautiful. The owner of the château, Serge Pardoux (now sadly he has passed away since my three visits), is a great collector---don't miss seeing his stunning collection of lead soldiers. Mme. Pardoux is a superb chef, and with advance reservation, will prepare a gourmet meal for us. We park our car in front of the charming L-shaped château with a tower.

We soon find M. Pardoux, the tall, elegant, handsome proprietor. He briefly shows us around and takes us to our rooms. A young man brings in our luggage. We approve of our lovely well-appointed rooms, both with canopy beds. The owner informs us that we will be sharing the dinner table tonight with a couple from Paris and a couple from Aix-les-Bains. I recall passing through Aix-les-Bains in eastern France years ago. The hills there rising on either side of the lake are breathtaking and reminded me back then of the hills and lakes of Steuben County, NY where I grew up.

Before settling in, M. Pardoux beckons us to follow him toward the kitchen, the heartbeat of their home. After introducing us to his wife, Mme. Véronique Pardoux, we are offered a peek into the kitchen where we meet the diminutive Arlette, maid and all-around helper at the château. Arlette has just entered via the garden door hefting in a huge wooden bowl of fresh mushrooms just picked on the property. Oh yes! Now it is really getting interesting. Madame proudly tells us that everything we eat while in their home is grown on their grounds. She adds that tonight we will be served a 10-course formal dinner and that our evening will commence at 8 PM on the terrace with champagne cocktails.

With introductions all made we return to our rooms in the main part of the château to organize and prepare for this magnificent gourmet meal we are about to enjoy. Fortunately, M. Pardoux speaks English, a great help for my colleague Jackie who knows very little French. I translate everything for her on the spot. I read that Monsieur is a collector of antique lead soldiers, so we look for this collection before we gather for cocktails. The collection is an important one and is housed in a fine display case in the owner's library.

We stroll through the well-groomed garden on our way to the terrace. Did you notice that terraces are BIG in France? In every sense of the word? The French love to eat outside, under trees, small or large spreading trees, under garden arches, on mountainsides, outside the back door, any place with a view. As we find the tables and chairs waiting for the six of us, we are amazed by the view! The broad stone terrace is elevated over the edge of a broad expanse of wooded hills that seem to go on forever. There is no sign of civilization for miles. We introduce ourselves to the other guests as they arrive and enjoy champagne in lovely flutes as the sun fades.

When the moon begins to rise, we are summoned to the dinner table. I had read that the château is furnished with family heirlooms. I follow the group into the dining room to find that the walls are decorated with a plethora of medieval weaponry of all kinds. At each end of the room stands a suit of armor. Most impressive. The multi-branch candelabras are lit on the long table surrounded by tall-back carved chairs. I am seated to the right of the gentleman from Paris, and Jackie sits next to his wife on the other side.

While waiting for the first course I strike up a conversation with the Parisian next to me. For some crazy reason I begin speaking of the Marquis de Lafayette who is well-known to most Americans as the bridge between France and the United States during the American Revolution. This dinner is years before I write my book on French General Rochambeau, in my estimation, an even better friend of ours during our revolution. But in my innocence, I rhapsodize about the Marquis de Lafayette.

After a patient silence on his part, my French dinner neighbor begs my pardon and lowers his voice to say that he hopes his wife does not hear me singing praises of the Marquis as she is a royalist/monarchist. That puts Lafayette at the far end of never in her mind. Oops! I do not expect this response and am non-plussed and abruptly silenced as I ponder his wife's beliefs (perhaps his, too). It is true that the Marquis espoused America's independent spirit of liberty from our British overlord in the 1770s and 1780s. True enough, but it never occurred to me that the French might despise him for it.

Let us not forget that Lafayette served as a member of King Louis XVI's national guard. He tried in vain to save the King and the Queen from the revolutionaries. And he was imprisoned by the same revolutionaries when he returned from America. Wasn't that enough? OK. Still, in the eyes of this Frenchman our hero was really a turncoat. I was thoroughly embarrassed and put in my place over a fragrant mushroom soup! I changed the subject in deference to my new acquaintance, and we managed to get through the evening in good spirits.

The menu for our ten-course dinner, thanks to Mme. Pardoux, is served by Arlette:

Tourrain des Jeunes Mariés
(Mushroom soup for young newlyweds)

Truite saumonisée, sauce

Chambord, feu de bois
(Salmonized/steelhead trout in Chambord sauce over a wood fire.)

Maigret grillé au feu de bois
(Grilled filet of duck over a wood fire)

Pommes sarladaises
(Sautéed apples from town of Sarlat)

Salade du jardin à l'huile de noix
(Garden salad dressed with walnut oil)

Plâteau de fromages
(Cheese platter)

Omelette Norvégienne
(Baked Alaska)

Fruits
(Assorted fruit from home orchard)

Vins
Saint Émilion (We visited this town and caves today.)
Sauvignon (local, dry, white wine)
Montbazilic (nearby vineyard)
Digestif Maison liqueur
(Homemade after dinner drink)

Café
(Demi-tasse)

Following this extravagant gourmet repast, we all sat in the comfort of the dimming light of the tall candles for the rest of the evening, enjoying each other's company until the wee hours.

The next morning, after an elegant breakfast, we reluctantly pack our things and bid our goodbyes and deep thanks for such a memorable stay with the Pardouxs. Ever on a quest, we head out for another part of Aliénor d'Aquitaine's Gascony. This area is connected with the story of the "Three Musketeers" (i.e. D'Artagnan) by Alexandre Dumas as well as the play "Cyrano de Bergerac" by Rostand. Gascony is usually described

Sumptuous table set for elegant ten-course dinner party
at the Château de Ribagnac

as being east and south of Bordeaux. Aquitaine includes Gascony, and Gascony includes much of the Basque land. Their language is related to ancient Occitan.

Our destination is a town with a castle well known to Queen Aliénor's son, King Richard I, Lionheart. We travel through Périgord to the Dordogne River region and the Castle of Beynac. Not long before his disturbing death, Richard took control of this castle that at the end of the 12th century lay on the border between lands held by his family, the English Plantagenets, and the French King, Philippe- Auguste, Richard's arch enemy.

Richard was in the process of replenishing his depleted treasury after being imprisoned by the Holy Roman Emperor for 2 ½ years following his crusade to the Holy Land, also a financial drain. I realize that is a mouthful of history, but as the 12th century was drawing to a close, Richard had to make up for lost time to keep his kingdom strong. Phillippe was literally knocking at his door, hungry to acquire more of Richard's holdings on the continent. It was a bitter fight.

Shortly before Richard's untimely death, he had been at Beynac and then detoured to the town of Chalus, not far to the east. He had heard of a treasure trove there that he sorely needed to acquire. It was the biggest mistake of his life, for he was hit by an arrow as he searched a field for the treasure. It is possible that the shooter of the crossbow did not know he had wounded the King of England. Unfortunately, in those times there was no way to save Richard as there is today. After several days of suffering he died from septicemia of the infected wound.

His mother, Queen Aliénor, rushed to his side from the Abbaye of Fontevraud in the Loire Valley to give him succor. He was yet alive but succumbed shortly after her arrival and is buried at Fontevraud with his father and mother. This history digression connects the Valley of the Loire with that of the Dordogne.

As Jackie and I explore the Château de Beynac we learn that a retired couple has recently purchased it and are going full tilt to restore it almost singlehandedly. The tour guide, probably a family member, points out the elderly owner as he pushes a large, heavy-laden simple wheelbarrow down from an upper level. He is covered with stone dust from hair to boots. We notice that he has but one helper of similar age doing the heavy work, and we are astounded that these two grey-haired men expect to accomplish such a lofty goal. Although the tower stands tall atop a rocky outcropping above the river Dordogne, much of the castle is truly in ruins. Never underestimate the power of slow and steady winning the race.

Next we stop in a bustling bastide town for a local dish of some fame, 'cassoulet'. This is a must in the Périgord region, as is 'foie gras' (goose liver), and I cannot wait to taste both. Our table is virtually in the street where on this July 14th holiday weekend we are fortunate to be seated to try the specialties of the region. We notice that most people here are French. That speaks well for our choice of restaurants.

Since I am writing this from my summer notes brought to light at home, I check to see how my go-to chef, Julia Child, describes 'cassoulet. She writes that the dish is as popular here in the southwest of France as our American baked beans are in Boston. The main ingredients are white beans, pork loin, shoulder of lamb and homemade sausage cakes. For the best melding of the beans, meat, onions, garlic and herbs, introduce to the mix, a homemade 'bouquet garni' (packet of dried herbs such as: parsley, bay leaf, and thyme for the basic bouquet – or one made of celery, garlic and fennel) in a small cloth bag tied tightly at the top. The flavors deepen when the dish is cooked off and on over as long as three days. Don't panic; it can be done if you crave the optimal result of a true French 'cassoulet'. The one we ingest here is a marvel, barely describable! Since I always brag that "I travel on my stomach wherever I go", I am in culinary heaven in the Dordogne this weekend.

Back down to earth, our long holiday weekend has been a delightful change of routine. This summer I am in the 9th degree level of study at the University, and classes resume early tomorrow morning with a full schedule. Jackie and I must make our way to the superhighway to head north to Tours before we utterly lose ourselves in this gastronomical dreamland of the Dordogne Valley.

Jackie and I are so glad we could spend this auspicious 200th anniversary of the French Revolution together in France. We learned a few things about French politics and even more about French cuisine. Travel always presents a forum for learning. We arrive just before midnight at Mado and Lucien's gate, opening up as quietly as possible while not exciting Figaro. Figaro knows me well by now, but a few of his loud barks would not be welcome at this hour. Jackie has a room across the hall from mine. We bed down quietly, and sleep follows quickly.

I have a few more weeks here in my beloved Loire Valley, and Jackie flies home in a week's time. We shall meet again in the fall when school begins in Connecticut.

Chapter Four

Paris to the Luberon of Provence:
Traveling in Style – My Doorstep to Paris Hotel

THIS SUMMER OF MY POST GRAD classes is over. I have accomplished sixty-three required grad credits during four summers and five school years of teaching and attending night classes. My concert-going pal, Judith, a math teacher, is traveling with me. We start as her son, who is doing limo driving for the summer in Connecticut, picks us up at my house, and we are off to JFK airport New York in style.

It is high time to give some details of my many flights across the Atlantic. Since I used to work in Public Relations at Air France on Fifth Avenue, New York, I am obviously prejudiced toward that airline and chose it every summer. The best fare was on an Air France: Travac Charter flight. The overseas flights going east to Europe usually leave about 7PM from JFK and arrive about six hours later, making it early morning in Paris. Our flight is as enjoyable as possible. Only on rare occasion did I end up after my meal next to a crying baby all night. This time Judith and I partake of a fine French dinner in flight. I keep the artistic menus each year. So, I know how well we ate, compared to the nothing they serve these days (25 years later). Sad, sad, sad. And ours is a charter flight, cheapest fare.

Here is our delicious menu: First course: smoked Norwegian Salmon; main course: sautéed lamb in a curry sauce, Basmati rice with Julienned vegetables; green salad and a cheese course; dessert: a Bavarian Cream cake, garnished with raspberry cookies, and topped off with Columbian coffee, not to mention our fill of Evian water straight from the French Alps. We watch a French film and sleep well until we begin the descent to Charles de Gaul Airport just outside Paris.

Judith and I do our happy dance all the way to our hotel near the Arc de Triomphe in the center of Paris! It will be a fantastic trip, and we both feel it in our bones. We are pleased with our four-star Hôtel Elysées Céramic on Avenue de Wagram, one of the spokes fanning out from the Arc de Triomphe. We have carefully planned our time to the best advantage of the plentiful history, art and music available in Paris. It is Judith's first visit.

6th Arrondissement: Concert, Oldest Church and Cinnamon

The second night we are off to a concert of organ and trumpet music at Saint-Julien-le-Pauvre church, (building commenced in 1170), may be the oldest church in Paris. We make our way to the Cathédrale de Notre-Dame since it is just across the Seine. After exploring the cathedral using our Michelin Green Guide, we cross the bridge that leads to the oldest church. It is in a tiny square with a garden and a huge tree. I tell Judith that this tree is touted as the oldest tree in Paris, c. 1600, and some of its huge branches are held up by large wooden crutches to keep them from breaking under their own weight.

I have been here before since my usual hotel in Paris faces the old church and Notre-Dame. I am very fond of this small, intimate Hôtel Esméralda and have stayed here several times. There is no elevator. I usually ask for the room with a balcony overlooking Notre-Dame. It is a lovely place to sit, and we admire the lights on Notre-Dame, its façade and rose window at night.

The woman who owns the hotel has a small dog. The first time I stayed there I asked her for a good restaurant for supper, and she recommended the one where we are headed tonight. She asked if she could accompany me since she was going there too. She brought her well-behaved dog, 'Cannelle' (Cinnamon), that sat on her lap throughout the entire meal. The lady shared every other bite with the canine. There is a children's book about this hotel. It is about a small girl who is on her way to visit Monet's Garden in Giverny. It is called: "Le Jardin de Monet" (Monet's Garden). The girl and her grandfather are pictured in my favorite room, both looking out the two windows at the oldest tree. Even Cannelle, is mentioned, along with their two cats Mona and Lisa. 'C'est mignon!' (It is darling!) We pass the tree, the church and my Hôtel Esméralda to find the same restaurant behind the church. I love this small jewel of a neighborhood.

After dinner, we cross the narrow 'rue' (street) and enter the old church. The concert venue is small, and every seat is filled. It is my first concert with two trumpets accompanied by organ and kettledrum. The group is known as "Les Trompettes de Versailles". They play early music by Vivaldi, Purcell, Bach, Marcello and Handel. The last piece is a triumph of Handel's "Water Music". The acoustics are excellent in this very small ancient church. The program is startlingly beautiful, and we are sorry to see it end.

The next day we start at the Arc de Triomphe and walk the length of the Champs Elysées to the Place de la Concorde. Please note: in the chapter "200 Years and Counting" where I also walked this famous street (in my mind's eye) at the Bicentennial Bastille Day parade from the Triompheto the Place la Concorde. Well, here I am again recalling that the American singer, Jesseye Norman, standing here in semi-darkness wearing her long flowing gown of 'bleue, blanc et rouge' (blue, white, and red) and sang the "Marseillaise". This is the spot. Chills run up and down my spine while absorbing the meaning of all that occurred here two hundred years ago in contrast to today's peaceful surroundings.

A Full Day of French Impressionism

Soon we arrive at the left bank "Musée d'Orsay" (Museum of the Orsay), a former railway station of huge architectural proportions. The station was built at the turn of the 20th c. 1900 and re-created as a museum in 1986. This is my first time here. I have been so curious to see it. It houses the largest collection of French Impressionists' work in the world, concentrating on the period between 1848 and 1914. Judith and I will have a whole day here. We shall need it. We both love art, so where to start?

We make a plan to meet about lunchtime at the rooftop deck outside the restaurant. The building itself is worth studying. It retains its original exterior outline. The rounded glass roof under which the trains arrived is still intact. There are four stories of art at one end of the edifice. When on the walkway between floors, one can gaze out over the central portion of the museum and realize the enormity of the building. It takes some time to get used to the unusual layout, but I am soon into the rhythm of the salons and start on the main floor. Many of the art works were originally housed in the Jeu de Paum Museum (former tennis court).

I am so excited to be here that I am filming each of the paintings with a short description. On the upper level I am behind one of the twin station clocks that face the street. How enormous it looks from here. I am close to the signature hoop roof. The glass sections are held in place by arches of iron that march from my end to the opposite end. I start with the earlier painters, some of whom I do not know, moving from Honoré Daumier, to Jean-Francois Millet, Jean-Baptiste-Camille Corot, and Gustave Courbet. I recognize many of their famous works I have known since I was a child. I hesitate before Henri Fantin-Latour whose paintings of flowers always engage my attention, then to Eugène Bourdin's scene of the beach at Trouville, Normandy, 1864. Bourdin was one of first painters to set up his easel to paint out-of-doors. What a trend he started.

I must take time to study "l'Atelier de Bazille, Rue de La Condamine" by Frédéric Bazille (1841-1870) 1870. He included himself in this iconic painting in his studio with early impressionist works of his close friends: Pierre-Auguste Renoir, Claude Monet, Édouard Manet and writer, Émile Zola. I have long admired Bazille as one of the painters who called Monet, Renoir, and Alfred Sisley his soul mates in creating the

Impressionist movement in the late 1800s. Bazille did not leave many works to posterity as he volunteered to fight in the Franco-Prussian War and was killed at the age of 28. I see Renoir's rendering of Bazille at his easel and also Bazille's glorious "Family Reunion" with his eleven family members seated and standing around a table with flowers and a walking stick on the ground. Bazille was born in Montpellier where some of his paintings can be viewed.

How can I **not** mention the infamous "Le Déjeuner sur l'herbe" ("Picnic on the grass"), by Édouard Manet, 1863, a treasure of contrast in hues and shocking state of dress and un-dress and his jaw-dropping, nude "Olympia", both right here in front of me! I am nearly breathless as I see one famous painting after another. "Femmes au jardin" ("Women in the garden") by Monet 1867; "Coquelicots" ("Poppies"), Monet 1873. I am stunned by Camille Pissarro and Paul Cézanne next. Winter scenes, water, fields of poppies and all at once, Berthe Morisot and Mary Cassatt cover the walls with their lovable, irresistible mothers with children. My daughter, Heather, and I have sent each other some lovely copies of mothers and daughters by Cassatt over the years. They really speak to us Moms. Then it is Renoir's turn to please my senses with his "Bal au Moulin de la Galette" ("Ball at the Galette Mill") 1876, Monet's "La Gare Saint-Lazare" ("Rail station Saint Lazare") 1877 with a train disgorging steamy smoke at the railway station much like the former Gare d'Orsay.

Time for lunch. Whew! I sit down and try to sort out all these masterpieces. I meet Judith on the roof deck on top of the museum. Another staggering sight; from up here we can see all over Paris, and we recognize many of the historic buildings including the new "Arche de la Défense". Looking down on us is a line of larger-than-life statues of women decorating the top front of the old 'gare' (station). We take a couple of photos with one of us standing next to a large Rubenesque statue and the city beyond, then go inside to eat and relax. We have both had an extraordinary morning with the paintings we have both seen. We make a plan to finish viewing those masterpieces that each has not yet seen and part for another hour or so. Can we make it? Our heads are spinning. We are in seventh heaven!

I make my way back to my stopping point, and so does Judith. It is a smooth transition to the world of Ballet dancers, like "L'Étoile" ("the Star') Edgar Degas 1917. In my childhood bedroom there were several of Degas's ballet dancers on the wall over my bed. Now I find two of Renoir: "Danse à la Ville" and "Danse à la Campagne" ("Dance in the city and country") 1883. Here come Monet's many interpretations of his famous garden at Giverney where in a later chapter my travel friend, Antoinette, and I, on a quest to follow the Impressionists to the towns where they painted, journey into Normandy. Next: Monet's familiar "Femme à l'Ombrelle" ('Woman with an Umbrella') 1886 and his large rendering of his famous water lilies 1917. I stand beside this one for a photo. Who is not fascinated by his shimmering water lilies? I shall see them in person chez Monet before long.

Later in this chapter we visit the region of Cézanne's Mont Saint Victoire in Aix-en-Provence. This is a preview with his "Les Joueurs de Cartes" ("Card Players") 1895 and his "Nature Norte: Pommes et Oranges" ("Still Life: Apples and Oranges") 1895. Another rapid change in style; I am staring into Post-Impressionist, Vincent Van Gogh's self-portrait, 1887. I have always liked his bedroom interpretation with elongated bed, chairs and window, 1889. I am inspired by his "L'Église à Auvers-sur-Oise' ("The Church at Auvers on the Oise River") 1890 that I am eager to see in person. Today it is the oil version on canvas. Later in another summer it will be the actual church in situ. This is a foreshadowing of the later chapter when I visit Van Gogh's final rented room before his death. Remember, we are getting close to the final breaking point for Van Gogh, as his paints thicker with purer colors.

Time for another change of style with Pointillism coming into view in artist Paul-Victor Signac's renderings of two women at the well on the beach 1892 and his "La Bouée Rouge" ("The Red Buoy") 1895. Both works in my estimation are good examples of painting by dots and George Seurat's "Le Cirque" ("The Circus") 1890. These two Pointillists created beautiful scenes that must have taken untold hours to complete. Their paintings can be examined from two perspectives, close up and far back. We transition to yet another expression in oil, that of Henri de Toulouse-Lautrec. I study his work carefully, mostly posters he did on commission, but aren't they special in yet another way? Albi, where he was born and worked in his youth, is on our itinerary, and we plan to tour the Toulouse-Lautrec Museum where most of his paintings reside. Evidently, upon his death, the town of his birth purchased most of his paintings. At the Orsay they have one of Toulouse-Lautrec's favorites: "Jane Avril à la Can Can" ("Jane Avril doing the Can Can") and his "La Toilette" ("Washing/Dressing"). Both are much to my liking. In a later visit to Albi I spend hours poring over Toulouse-Lautrec's works, painting by painting for a full day, getting to know his subjects.

Lastly, I examine Paul Gauguin, another favorite of mine, since I have visited his hometown of Pont Aven, Brittany. He painted there before going to Tahiti. I like the Pont Aven paintings as much as I do the Tahiti ones. He portrays the Breton women so well in their pure white, starched 'coiffes' (typical Breton headdress) in contrast to their surroundings that are applied in deep jewel hues.

There are a few lesser-known artists and sculptors, but I think I am all done for the day. I see Judith arriving at our departure point, both of us exhausted but happy. Well, hooray for us, another great day in Paris. The weather has been a little on the cool and rainy side but promises to be clear and warm tomorrow for our trip to the greatest château of all, The Palace of Versailles. For now, a tasty dinner near our hotel followed by a restful night's sleep, are in order.

A Fanciful Visit to Versailles

Versailles is only twelve miles from Paris, and we take a train that will let us off almost at the entrance to the large courtyard. It is a fine summer morning as we arrive in the town of Versailles. We spot an outdoor market near the gates and stop to examine the excellent produce, locally grown. I see perfect stacks of spotless, fully ripe red tomatoes, lemons, white asparagus, all the varieties of lettuce a cook could ever want. I am drawn to the tall pile of artichokes side-by-side with clouds of white cauliflowers in their couches of green. The plump eggplants glisten in the sun, while generous bouquets of a multitude of fresh herbs fill the bins. It is not lunchtime, so I must curb my food desires for now. As I look around at this sweet town, memories flood my mind for I have recently read a book in which the plot takes place both inside and outside the gates of Versailles. It is To Dance with Kings by Rosalind Laker. Although I have toured Versailles a couple of times, I now look at it with a different perspective.

Judith and I have already decided to take the tour of secret passageways. After purchasing our tickets, we walk down the long, cobbled courtyard and cross the threshold into the Palace. I am tempted to say, it is nice to be 'home' again. Just kidding! Being a student of French literature and history, I find much that is relative to my studies in these stately homes.

Right away we find that there are more rooms here than at the Château Chambord, 700 rooms, and 2,000 acres of gardens. The Palace of Versailles had humble beginnings with King Louis XIII's hunting lodge that grew to the huge proportions we see today thanks to Louis XIV's efforts. It was the seat of French power in Europe from 1682-1789. All this is held in the hand of one man, a king.

Our tour takes us from room to room, and I am amazed all over again at the sumptuous furnishings, the thick layers of gold upon gold covering the woodwork, the doors, and ceilings. As we walk through the Hall of Mirrors, we see it all around us in duplicate thanks to the mirrors from floor to ceiling. Oh yes, I see that the floor here in the Hall is made of black and white tiles – reminds me of the gallery at Chenonceau. Not sure which one came first. I vote for Catherine de Medici's gallery addition paved with black and white tiles, followed by Nicolas Fouquet's oval great room entrance at Château Vaux-le-Vicomte, then Versailles.

Fouquet's Grandiose Faux Pas

There are three artists, each one an expert in his field, who were hired by Louis XIV to create the splendor of Versailles: Le Vau – architect; Le Brun — painter and interior designer; and Le Notre – landscape architect. There is a shocking story behind the scenes of how Louis found these men of great talent and the unpleasant 'dénouement' (unraveling) of their original employer, Nicolas Fouquet.

This account is more than germane to the construction of Versailles, even down to the black and white tiles. Fouquet was Louis' Finance Minister. He wanted to build a château to showcase his high place in society. He searched for the best craftsmen he could find to bring this dream to fruition. He hired Le Vau, Le Brun and Le Notre. Under their creativity and Fouquet's finances, the Château of Vaux-le-Vicomte that I have visited, was built. In August 1661 Fouquet exhibited prideful hubris in by inviting his King and the entire Court to his version of 'Open House' for festivities to celebrate his great good fortune. The famous chef/ maître d'hôtel/party planner, François Vatel, created ambiance and menus of the finest quality for both Fouquet and Louis XIV (see the film 'Vatel').

For his grand opening, Fouquet, the financier, employed the popular playwright, Molière (whom we met at Chambord), who presented one of his plays. After sundown, there was a display of fireworks that illuminated the impeccable gardens, statues, water features and canals on the extensive grounds. For the sake of comparison, Fouquet's grand salon, a large oval room at the front entrance, is adorned with a Le Brun ceiling painting and the floor design is (guess what?) black and white tiles! Now we know which came first or at least prior to Versailles.

Well, all this magnanimity was absorbed by King Louis XIV in one sickening gulp that caught in his craw. The King and his court were courteous as they departed late that evening, BUT, a few weeks later when Fouquet was doing business in Brittany, Louis's men seized him and threw him in prison, from which he never left until the day he died. He never saw his wife nor his family again and left them in deep misery and poverty. It is a miracle that their beautiful Vaux-le-Vicomte still stands, judging by the extent of Louis' wrath at Fouquet's show of stupidity and pride.

Now I know you cannot wait to see the Château of Vaux-le-Vicomte after learning of the sad ending behind the glorious exterior. I left off at the three men who built Louis XIV's new Palace of Versailles where we now stand. We look around as we proceed through the rooms and get goose bumps at the stories that history carries down to us.

Secret Passageways
Rituals of King Louis XIV and Marie Antoinette

On our way to see the secret passageways, we start at King Louis XIV's public bedchamber. Standing inside this golden room, I wonder what it was like for visitors who crammed in by lottery to ask the king questions or favors at his 'lever' (waking up in the AM) or at his 'coucher' (going to bed in the PM), during which time he was either dressed for the day or undressed for the night by his servants. Meanwhile, his people observed from beyond the golden fence that separates them from their sovereign King. The fence of gold follows the horseshoe-shape of the bed, leaving just enough space inside for the King and his attendants to carry out their dressing duties.

I stand now in the Queen Marie Antoinette's public bedchamber where the same ritual takes place twice a day. I see the same fence of gold that separates royalty from subjects. From my own experience in dressing in 18th c. garments I have learned that it can take at least an hour just for lowly me to be dressed by a lady friend. That is not counting coiffing my hair in the true 18th c. style. This I do not attempt. I can but guess it might take hours to build up the Queen's hair to accommodate a ship or a bird's nest as she was wont to do in her glory days. I learn later that the 'lever' and 'coucher' were just for show and that the royal couple then retired to their private, but separate, bed chambers where they could be themselves out of the limelight.

We follow our guide through a hidden doorway to find the narrow stairway that connects the King's room with Queen's. There are many secret stairways going up and down from here. The entrances to these hidden passageways are not that easy to recognize, as they are doors flush with the wall and hard to see, skillfully cut in the fabric of the wallpaper. We enter one where the doorway is behind a series of similarly framed paintings on one wall. One simply has to know which painting hides the secret door. It must take ages to learn all these secrets in such a huge domicile.

I attended a Sound and Light program many years ago on my first visit to Versailles. With the crowd assembled on the grand outdoor terrace, it began at dusk with synchronized sound and light systems that the French have mastered over the years. Scenes of the history of Versailles were projected realistically on the side of the main edifice. While listening to the history over a giant sound system, the lights go on and off from window to window as the King and the Queen progress through secret passages while following the storyline. It is a powerful way to portray history.

Judith and I both love the private rooms of Marie Antoinette embellished with the works of Rococo painters, François Boucher and Jean-Honoré Fragonard. Their tender scenes of cherubs riding on clouds and young girls swinging over blooming gardens can be seen on walls as well as ceilings. The Queen's apartments are delicious in miniature with the expected Louis XV ladies' armchairs. Exquisite.

Lunch in Marie Antoinette's Backyard, Miniature Farm

While on the subject of Marie Antoinette, we decide to take a self-guided tour of her 'Hameau' (small hamlet) that her husband, King Louis XVI, installed on the grounds just for her pleasure and that of her 'ladies' and their children. We walk quite a distance, passing 'Le Petit Trianon' (The small château on the grounds of Versailles), looking for the Hameau. The Petit Trianon is a jewel of a hideaway, safely set apart from the prying eyes of court. Louis XVI said to his young wife, age 19:

"Vous aimez les fleurs. J'ai un bouquet à vous offrir." ("You love flowers. I have a bouquet to give to you.").

We find the Hameau and enjoy it very much. When Marie and her friends visited the Hameau, they dressed down as we say, in comfortable clothing and straw hats to feed the goats and milk the cows. Well, take a look at Judith and me, at our nearby perch on the edge of the round, columned garden 'folie' (A costly period building serving no purpose but fun!), swinging our legs, eating our ham and cheese on baguette and sipping 'un coca' (coca cola). From where we sit, we can see the Hameau and envision Marie enjoying the simple life down on the farm.

Galloping Through the Louvre, Loving Every Moment!

Our next destination for tomorrow is the Louvre Museum. By the way, it is not advertised as a château. Nonetheless, chronologically it was first a château, then a museum. It can be added to our list of stately homes visited outside the Loire Valley. It is gigantic. Why am I using these Gargantuan adjectives to describe these places? Because, every aspect of the Louvre is larger than the last.

The first thing we see as we approach the Louvre is the enormous and astonishing 69-foot t glass and steel structure called "La Pyramide", completed in 1989 for the bicentennial of the French Revolution. It is the design of world-famous Chinese American architect, I.M. Pei, whom you met in the Bicentennial Chapter. "La Pyramide" stands in the center of the courtyard of the Louvre with three small pyramids. The arms of the giant Louvre behind the pyramids wrap themselves around the ultra-modern structures like a mother protecting her brood. "La Pyramide" has become the new entrance to the grand museum. I find it to be stunning from all angles. Unlike many French and foreign tourists, I do not mind the mix of ancient and ultra-modern. When it opened there were many who detested the 'look' of it. 'Pas moi' (Not I). I adopted it from the onset.

Judith and I walk under the Arch of the Carousel toward the La Pyramide. Looking around, we see the Louvre Museum in perfect unity as a backdrop to the new Pyramide. Before we enter, I begin to read the history of the Louvre itself, taking us back centuries before it became a museum. The original fortification was begun in the Medieval period (late 12th c) when King of France, Philippe-Auguste, (a contemporary of English King Richard I) needed protection from invaders and built a 'château fort' on this site. His walls were massive, built to protect the 98-foot central keep. There were the usual deep moats, both wet and dry, walls within walls and towers at each of the four corners. The enclosure was completed in 1202. In the 14th century, King Charles V converted it into a royal residence. It was used off and on by French kings until, in 1793, the year that King Louis XVI and Queen Marie Antoinette were guillotined, after which it became the Louvre Museum that today houses 70,000 pieces of art and hires 2,000 people to run the museum smoothly.

After entering, we spiral down to the lower level and pick up a brochure. We learn that, in excavating for the Pyramid, the underpinnings of the early château were found and uncovered, preserved for visitors to see. This is our first goal. We walk into a low-lit area beneath the street level. Apparently, we are in or near one of the major moats. The sign reads that people who lived here through all manner of items into the moat. Hundreds were recovered through archeological digs. Some items were identified as belonging to kings. We walk past the foot of some of the original towers. They are in good shape. So, the pyramid project has added another layer of interest to Louvre visitors. Also, below grade level is a brand-new shopping mall with all the amenities. This gives visitors another option and maintains the clean, uncluttered appearance at ground level and attracts even more visitors for a full day visit. Smart planning.

My Quest at the Louvre:
Find the Wedding Gift from Queen Aliénor of Aquitaine to her first husband, King Louis VII, 1137

Now we are ready to take an elevator to our chosen floor of the Louvre itself. We finally enter the second-floor gallery that I have chosen. I am searching for two things: first, to show Judith the "Mon Lisa, La Joconde" (My Lisa, the jovial one) by Leonardo da Vinci and second is my personal quest, the wedding present, a rock crystal vase, gifted from my ancestor, Aliénor d'Aquitaine, to her first husband, King Louis VII of France. My research tells me it is here. The information desk says it is on the second floor against the wall behind the central case containing France's crown jewels including Napoléon's crown. Here we go. The parquet floors are well kept, but they creek as I walk over them. I follow directions straight to Napoléon's Crown, the one that he snatched out of the Pope's hands to place on his head. Artist Jacques-Louis David immortalized this moment in a magnificent oil painting. Perhaps I can find his painting here too. I have a print of it in my house. This gallery of the Louvre is heavy with importance and deep meaning.

It is with true excitement in my heart that I turn around to gaze upon the vase (pronounced "vaaze"), for this is truly an ancient relic worthy of the second pronunciation of the word. In my play, "Conversations with Queen Aliénor of Aquitaine", I give a complete description of the vase and its provenance. In the clip I am inserting here, the 'A' is Aliénor speaking, or the 'J' is Jini (myself) who speaks:

Excerpt from
"Conversations with Queen Aliénor of Aquitaine"

by Jini Jones Vail

"ALIÉNOR: There was one more thing that I never saw again; that was the beautiful rock crystal vase I gave Louis as a wedding present when we married in 1147. Light diffused through the crystal, turned into shimmering strands of rainbow hues. Not long after *I* gifted it to Louis, he gave it to his favored Counselor, Abbot Suger of Saint Denis, as I stood by in shock and horror.

JINI: Dearest, it is not lost to us, your downline family. Believe it or not, I am familiar with that magnificent vase. It sits in the

Louvre Museum in Paris opposite the crown of Napoléon. I was thrilled beyond compare when I discovered it there in the early 1990s. Hard as it must have been to see your husband give away your most special wedding gift to him, perhaps, in so doing, it has been preserved for posterity. The Abbot Suger, I believe, had it mounted on a gold-over-silver base encrusted with deep filigree and semi-precious gemstones. It is a priceless artifact to behold, especially knowing that it was once in your hands.

ALIÉNOR: (She cuts in to finish the description of her vase) The history of the piece goes even further back in our family as it belonged to my father and to his father before him. Did you remark that the neck of the vase is covered with a honeycomb pattern of twenty-three rows of tiny hollowed-out hexagons? It resembles ancient Samarian glassware, dating back centuries to Islamic and Byzantine designs.

My quest is achieved! I could not be happier. The Mon Lisa is the frosting on the cake after this. My first visit here ages ago, the "Mona Lisa" was totally unprotected. Today it is behind a transparent wall on three sides. The stories that accompany this painting are numerous. Mona has done quite some traveling over the centuries, from Italy to Amboise with Leonardo da Vinci, and back and forth from country to country, even to America. During the John F. Kennedy administration (1960s) she was sent to New York for her first trip away from home since her hiding places in World War II. Jackie Kennedy requested that it be sent to New York City for a special exhibit at the Metropolitan Museum of Art.

Sculptures and Paintings Galore

The rest of the day is spent here looking at some of the most well-known masterpieces of art in the world. Here are a few: "The Winged Victory of Samothrace" c. 190 BC – She announces our visit as she stands at the top of the main staircase leading to the upper level, surely a shining star in the collection; the sculpture, "Decent from the cross", Burgundian 12th c.; Jean Fouquet's "Charles VII", King of France 1420 (Tours); François Boucher's, "Diane Reading" 1742; Jean-Honoré Fragonard's, "The Music Lesson" c 1769; Jacques-Louis David, "Madame Recamier" 1800; Jacques-Louis David's, "The Coronation of Napoleon" (detail) 1807 – David is one of my personal favorites. I keep my copy of this painting in my French powder room; Eugène Delacroix's, "Liberty Leading the People" 1830; Claude Monet's "Rouen Cathedral in Full Sunlight" 1893; (I visit the actual Rouen Cathedral in a later chapter with in-depth description); Leonardo da Vinci's "Mona Lisa" 1452; Johannes Vermeer's "The Lace Maker" ca 1665; Rembrandt Van Rijn's "The Supper at Emmaus" 1648; "Self Portrait", by Albrecht Durer, 1493; Diego Velazquez de Silva's "The Infanta Margarita" 1660 and many more.

It is a full and wonderful day at the Louvre with Judith. Naturally, we paused before many more paintings and sculptures than we could ever mention. We decide on a scrumptious gourmet dinner under the portico of the left wing of the Louvre in open air so to speak. This is a great find for us, since how far could we walk after such a big day? We just wanted to be spoiled!

We are on a roll here in Paris. It is like a candy store for lovers of art and history as they are often lumped together. The next day we arrive at the "Orangerie" Museum, famous for huge, tennis court sized mural of Monet's "Water Lilies". We are fortunate that it is not crowded today, affording us an unobstructed view of the entire oval painting. This important work by Monet's hand is painted directly on the walls, not in frames, but is one continuous scene of his pond at Giverney. It is magnificent to behold. Stay tuned, as I will visit his home and famous water lily pond in a later chapter.

The Marais, Place des Vosges, Victor Hugo and Carnavalet

Afterwards we travel by Métro to the "Marais" (former swamp) section of Paris where we have a pleasant stroll around "Place des Vosges", looking in at the darling shops and tiny museums. The "Marais" in the 13th c. was swampland with a high road down the center, like a dike, above the water line, originally a Roman Road. The walls of Philippe-Auguste (1165 -1223) and those of Charles VII (1403-1561) extended to this area. A tower of Philippe-Auguste still stands. The Marais gradually was included in the Paris city bounds, and the swamp, drained. A few elegant homes were built. By the beginning of the 17th c. the center Place Royale became known as the Place des Vosges. Nobility and courtiers built splendid mansions here as well, designed by noted artists. Salons, free thinkers, philosophers and writers were drawn to the area.

Many of the famous residences remain intact and are recognized by the word, 'Hôtel' such and such, according to their most prestigious owner. For example, the Hôtel des Tournelles, Place des Vosges, is the place where the Duke of Orléans was assassinated. It was then acquired by the crown in 1407 and became the residence of King Charles VII; it was also the site where King Louis XII died, as did King Henri II. The latter's wife, Catherine de Medici, tore down the mansion as it held bad memories for her. By 1612 the residences in the newly transformed Royal Square were built in a similar architectural style of shared elegance. Now the Square is charming, symmetrical and harmonious of design.

Not by mistake, we find ourselves at the doorstep of Victor Hugo (1802-1885). We recall our favorite writings of Hugo: dramatist, poet and novelist. First: "The Hunchback of Notre Dame" and running a close second: "Les Misérables", both can still be read in French class or seen in film and on stage on Broadway, New York, City and beyond. The action of two works takes place in Paris. In 1903 Victor Hugo's house, the former Hôtel de Rohan-Guemee (early 17th c.) in Place des Vosges, where we stand, became a museum to the famous writer. He resided here between 1832 and1848. Judith and I climb the stairs to his apartment at the rear of the fashionable Place des Vosges. We do a self-guided tour of his home. The walls in the main living rooms are painted a shocking, deep red. They are tastefully decorated, however, with intricate wall shelves tailor- made to fit Hugo's collection of Chinese porcelain. Apparently, the Chinese items are from his home in Guernsey. Hugo was the designer and builder of most of the display. We also see some of his original drawings, family photos and mementos. I wish they had piped in some music from Les Mis (short for the Broadway play: Les Misérables).

The rooms are organized to follow the life of Hugo in the three stages: Pre-exile, exile to the Island of Guernsey and post-exile. The finale is his bedchamber featured in brilliant deep blue that appeals to me. The furnishings are of his period and in excellent repair and arrangement according to 19th c. Paris style.

My friend and I are off now to the "Musée Hôtel Carnavalet". The collection began in 1548 detailing the history of the city of Paris. No small feat. Carnavalet is made up of two Renaissance mansions, the first is Hôtel Carnavalet and the second, Hôtel le Peletier de Saint-Fargeau, recently opened to the public in 1989. The layout reminds me of the Frick Collection on Fifth Avenue in New York City. Both museums are known for their lovely inner courtyard gardens. The collections here at Carnavalet are housed in former mansions (thus the name Hôtel de…). This museum has more information than we can digest in the short time left of this afternoon. The collection begins with Paris in its early times, when it was called Lutetia, then on into the Medieval period covering historical events and special celebrations, to the present era.

I am familiar with the early name of Paris, Lutetia. I am curious to learn about the earliest known habitation of the "Ile de la Cité" (City Island), the island epicenter of Paris. The island was inhabited by the Parisii, Celtic Iron Age people, in the middle of the 3rd c BC until the age of the Gauls. Between 250BC and 200BC during the ancient civilization of Gaul, some 'Gallic' (inhabitants of Gaul – later named France) fishermen set up camp here on the largest island in the Seine River. In 52BC the Gallo-Romans took over the island and named it Lutetia. Even in the 12th c. under the reign of King Louis VII and Queen Aliénor, the Ile de la Cité was the seat of the entire country of France.

We only had time to finish these early years at the Carnavalet, but we gained new information on which to build in future visits.

The exhibit is comprehensive and well laid out. I make a note to return someday when I can spend a whole day or more here. And Judith agrees.

TGV to Provence/Chance Encounter with Vercingetorix

It is our last night in Paris, so we find our tickets to take the 'TGV" (the bullet train) to Aix-en-Provence in southern France for a very different atmosphere and slower pace of life in contrast to Paris. Our destination is the Luberon (can be written with an accent over the 'e' or not) in North Central Provence. The region is dominated by three mountain ranges. The highest mountain is about 4,100 feet in elevation. There are several attractive hill towns that spark our curiosity and broad tillable flat lands well-suited for agriculture. We expect fresh fruit in season and cannot wait. The area was once an important part of the Roman Empire, and thus, many ruins remain. You may know the Luberon from having read Peter Mayles's books. We will explore this charming part of Provence for ourselves.

It is a colorful region of open-air markets and good food in unpretentious restaurants. Once on the train, we sit back and enjoy resting our feet for a part of a day at least. The landscape goes by very fast but is interesting, nonetheless.

An amazing thing happens as we speed on. In 1990 I spent the summer of graduate study at the University of Bourgogne in Dijon. Our class went on day trips on Saturdays just as we do at Tours. One such trip included the statue of Vercingétorix, French hero of ancient Gallic Wars. I had heard his name before but knew nothing of his life or why we still remember him. The short of it is that in the time of Julius Cesar, there were accounts written detailing his Gallic Wars against what is now France. In fact I had to plough through them in my high school Latin class. What a chore! In 1990 I was brought up short when I heard that Vercingétorix is a French hero. I recall him being the subject of contemporary French adventure comic books, a part of pop culture. What he lived through was not simply an adventure, but a battle to the death worthy of remembering. He fought a protracted war to save his country, Gaul (early France), from the mightiest emperor of the Roman Empire, Julius Cesar. Vercingétorix soon became my hero too.

Why am I telling you all this just now? We have just passed his statue, clearly seen from the train. I just happened to look up at the right instant and recognized him high on his plinth, alone above the surrounding countryside. He was the last Gaul standing after a siege that left him and his small band defending the mountaintop we just passed. When water and supplies ran out, he was seized by Caesar and taken to Rome where it was their tradition to put him in a cage and parade him through the streets in total humility. He died in one of their prisons, a valiant solder who fought his best to save his people from extinction. His statue was erected on Mt. Auxois, Côte d'Or in 1865 by Napoléon III. Thanks to him for resurrecting my hero and thanks be to God that I saw him again today while flying by on the TGV!

By car to our Hotel in Lacoste with stop at Castle Ansouis

In no time we are in the South of France at Aix-en-Provence (Artist Paul Cézanne's country), where we pick up our car and resume our trip to our Luberon. The small village of Lacoste where we will spend the next nine days. We have lots of big plans. En route I am reading the Green Guide and see a possible stop for us. It is the small Château d'Ansouis, of which I know nothing, but the write up looks intriguing. The sign reads: Château of the Dukes of Sabran Pontèves. We go to the front gate and are met by a servant who bids us enter. He will give us a short tour for a few francs.

When the guide mentions a member of Aliénor's immediate family, I say that I am descended from Aliénor of Aquitaine and that I carry in my wallet the list of my ancestors back to her time in the mid-1100s. I ask if the owner of the château is home, and she says that he is. "Would it be possible to speak with him?" I ask. She goes to fetch him. He walks out to talk with us and is most hospitable, pointing out portraits of our family and his. Apparently, after showing him my genealogy sheet, the owner is convinced, and we have a nice conversation. His gardens are like miniature Versailles with an 'Orangerie' (A collection of tender potted citrus plants that must be protected inside in winter). Soon we are on our way wondering how on earth we happened upon the Château of Ansouis. I do not believe in coincidences. It was fun!

Oh, Happy Day! We find our hotel in the tiny little 'bourg' (small town) of Lacoste. The tone and tenor of our trip south is a change in our modus operandi from big city to remote village. Doing a little reading on Lacoste, I find it is in a large Nature Park and sits at just under 1,000 feet above sea level. There are at least four neighboring towns we will visit: Bonnieux, Rousillon, Gordes and Loumarin. Our lodging is in the former "Hôtel du Procureur" (Residence of the Public Prosecutor). The 17th century hotel offers period-furnished rooms with all amenities, including a private pool on the roof 'en plein air' (in the open). We take the elevator up to check it out, and it is serenely private and adorable. With the warm weather here in the south of France I am sure we will enjoy using the pool.

High above the hotel, dominating the bluff, above us, are the ruins of the Château du Marquis de Sade. Voilà! Another château for our list. There is a tall tower that remains, but most of the rest was demolished over the centuries. Today there is a group of university students on site doing an archeological dig. They sit or kneel quietly, notebooks in hand digging and examining the relics. Hmmm. They will be quiet neighbors. The history of the Marquis de Sade is somewhat on the steamy side. We ask a few questions about how their archeological dig is progressing and move on.

Starlit Night Over Bonnieux

From our room we can see Bonnieux on the opposite side of the peaceful valley. Following each night of excellent dinners in nearby restaurants, we sit on the terrace looking across that valley toward

Bonnieux and pondering the moon, the stars, and the peaceful quiet of this corner of the Luberon horizon. I am so inspired that I compose a French poem so I may better recall the good sensations I feel by being here. I name the poem "Nuit d'été Provençale" ("A Summer Night in Provence").

NUIT D'ÉTÉ PROVENÇALE (Jini Jones Vail)

Pleine lune nuit au-dessus de Bonnieux; ciel noir
Éclaire de Diane Chasseuse. Vapeurs de mercure
Cascadent le long de la taille Tannebaum,
Surveille de "Son" étoile comme la Sainte Nuit.

Pic ville surmonte le belfroi médiéval.
Ange-en-douche reflète la teinte jaune étincelante.
Lune sphérique grimpe jusqu'à onze heures
Et là, y pend, y monte la garde de la valée du Luberon.

La Nuit étoilée de Van Gogh, violente, bleuâtre noire,
Est bien moins irrésistible que cette couronne pavée
De diamants, que cette cape constellée
Cette belle nuit chaude de juillet.

English version:
Summer Night in Provence (Jini Jones Vail)

Full moon night over Bonnieux
Black moonlit sky, front-lighted.
Mercury vapors drip along Tannenbaum shape
Like 'His' star on that most holy night.

Pinnacle town, steepled medieval belfry.
Shower-shone angel in soft yellow hue.
Sphere moon climbs to 11 o'clock high
And hanging, keeps watch over the Luberon sky.

Van Gogh's Starry Night, violent blue black,
Far less compelling than yonder circle crown
With its cloak-full of stars this hot July night!

Open-air Markets, Van Gogh's Night Café and Arles Below Ground

The open-air markets in Provence are a real go-to for tourists, so we visit a few. They are tempting and colorful. We try the one at Îsle-sur-La Sourgue, and it does not disappoint. We decide, since it is near lunchtime, to buy a picnic of all our favorite delectables. We start with a roasted chicken just the right size for two; then choose a tapenade and a salade niçoise. We find a spot under a bridge on two rocks in order to get out of the hot sun. The tapenade is the best I have ever eaten and can never seem to duplicate it at home.

The next day we drive to Arles. It is a city of 52,000 near the mouth of the Rhone River, very near the Western Mediterranean between Montpelier and Marseille. It is in the department (similar to a 'county' in the US) called "Bouches- du Rhone" (Mouths of the Rhone). We plan to see the Roman ruins. It does not take long to locate their open marketplace where we are surrounded with herbs and spices as far as the eye can see, all colors of the rainbow. There are tables of fresh and dried lavender as well, a welcome treat to our senses. As we marvel at the variety of spices and fragrances, we hear music coming toward us. Everyone in the market looks up to see a group of musicians playing pan flutes and stringed instruments. They are from Peru and wear the bright colors of their country with flat top black hats. Their music is uplifting. We later learn that the Peruvian wandering bands are all over Europe in the summer, especially where there are lots of tourists to toss coins into their baskets. We love their native music.

After lunch we go to the museum that houses Vincent Van Gogh's letters, handwritten, numbered and framed. He wrote often to his brother, Theo, who helped him financially during his poverty-stricken years as a painter and acted as his agent in selling his work. I am reading from letter #338 (not sure if all are translated into English). After some confusion trying to describe his surroundings in this particular missive, from the town of Drenthe, The Netherlands 1883, Vincent wrote: Here it is "inexpressively beautiful". He signs off: "With a handshake. Yours sincerely, Vincent." We spend quite an enlightening, if sad, couple of hours reading Van Gogh's letters. This small museum is a find we did not anticipate. So glad, once again, that Judith and I share the same interest in French art.

Vincent came to Arles on 1 February 1888 and, while here, produced 187 paintings and 100 drawings. Van Gogh's paintings during his Arles period include his "l'Arlesiénne" (The Woman from Arles), "La Maison Jaune" (The Yellow House), "The Bridge of Langlois", several scenes of a weaver, harvest time, flowers, and the Hospital at Arles. It was a very fertile time for his creative brush. However, by December that year, he had more fits of depression; his friendship with Paul Gauguin was severed. Van Gogh cut off his own ear (See his self-portrait with bandaged ear), was sent into a downward spiral and by May of 1889 was relegated to an asylum in St. Rémy-de-Provence.

Finally, Judith and I find the location where Van Gogh painted 'The Night Café' in Arles. It is on a corner of a quiet boulevard and is now a business, closed for the night. I press my nose against the windowpane to peer inside but cannot make out the room in order to equate it to Van Gogh's rendering of it with a billiard table, shiny lights and men slouching over small tables. This famous 'chef d'oeuvre' (masterpiece) is of interest to me, as the original resides at the Yale University Art Gallery New Haven, CT. I take my students on a French art trip every year to admire original works. I spend time with my French students expanding their horizons, knowledge and vocabulary, with this type of valuable field trip.

Back in the open-air market, we stop to look longingly at the famous Provençale fabrics, the ones by Souleiado, so expensive in America. (There is a small town, Chester, Connecticut, where there is, in the 1990's a boutique called Souleiado where their fabric by the yard, tablecloths, skirts, even wallpapers, are sold. I can see that the price here in Provence is indeed a bargain.) Also, in Arles are the remains of ancient buildings, most in excellent condition. The Theatre (27-5BC), the Roman Amphitheater or Arena (end of 1c AD), and the Church of St. Tromphine (begun 3BC and finished 11c). All very impressive.

Next, we literally 'fall' into something else unplanned. Inside a shop Judith reads a small sign that indicates an entrance to underground caves that can be accessed here. We are very curious, so we descend the stairs with a guide. Before we know it, we are in the subterranean granary of the ancient Romans. We are amazed by what we see in the low light down here. Vaulted ceilings throughout, with entrances to what we are told were ancient caves built expressly to preserve wheat and other grains over the fall, winter and spring until it is consumed and replaced each year.

There is evidence of fancy, carved capitals of huge pillars, some upright and some lying in pieces on the ground. The walls are of perfect brick, all excavated and cleaned, still as strong as when they were built by those once-creative Romans about the time of Christ. There are some air vents. The guide says that this cool, dry storage space extends as "a web-like system of subterranean galleries carved out in the first century AD" under houses and town buildings. Who knew that all this existed and that it has been excavated? It is not featured in the guidebooks either. According to importance of sights to see in Arles, I finally find a reference to 'Cryptoportiques'. So that is the name by which they can be found. Tuck that new term away in our vocab list. Tomorrow we shall see another of the Roman masterpieces, the "Pont du Gard" (bridge over the Gard River).

We drive back to our hotel, freshen up and rest for a while then go to Bonnieux to their only restaurant on an outdoor terrace. I like the uncrowded countryside, so clean, so friendly, so charming in every way. This trip is almost too good to be believed.

Hilltowns:Rousillon and Gordes/Ancient ruins: **Bories and Oppidums**

After breakfast, we start out early for a full day of touring the Luberon and the Vaucluse regions. We start with the tiny town of Rousillon. The village sits atop one of the highest hills near the Vaucluse plateau. We get out and walk around, climb some steps for a better view. The earth is orange here. One might say that everything is yellow-orange as a result. This is one reason that it is famous. In fact, I read a book, "Lisette's List" by Susan Vreeland about life in the early 1930s in this nearly forgotten place.

The lives of the inhabitants revolved around the mining of ochre. Like most people who are not painters, I had no idea before reading this fictionalized account that ochre was mined. Rousillon's unique product was in demand around the world years ago because it was at the time the singular source of this pigment. It is used as raw material for the oil paint that artists <u>must</u> have to complete their palette of hues. When other countries found and sold it at a lower price, Rousillon's mines went dark. For all the above reasons, Rousillon is called the 'The Colorado of Provence'. There is so much to learn when we travel.

Our little car climbs these hills quite well, but on the way down near the center of the residential area we find ourselves 'coincées' (cornered) or blocked on a hairpin turn. I guess our car is not small enough! We cannot go forward or backward. We cannot turn around. As we get out to assess the situation, a group of young men out for a stroll come down the hill on foot. They see our predicament and offer to help. In a matter of a few minutes they have lifted the car around the turn, and we are freed! Are we lucky or what?

On we go through the countryside of ochre and lavender (both colors and both native here). We are already looking for a place for lunch. It is hot, hot, hot, again. We are sticky, but happy, sailing through fields of lavender. We are aching to get out and pluck a few stems as souvenirs. We refrain as long as we can, not wanting to tread on someone's private property. Then we see a huge field of blooming lavender with no sign of a house, a farm or a boutique. We stop the car. There is no traffic. We jump out with our manicure scissors to clip a few stems. We are stopped short by the buzz of a million bees who got there first. Crazily we manage to bring a few stems into the car without bees following us.

They are really the guardians of these fields. We know that now. I recall my first trip to Provence; my mother and I drove up from the Riviera to Grasse, perfume making center of France. Its location was perfect for the collection of flowers needed to produce scents that would be sold the world over. I am not far from Grasse as we speak today.

Gordes looks like a good place for our midday meal. Again, it is a hill town and the earth is still ochre in color. Per our trusty guidebook, Gordes faces the Luberon Mountain and is at the edge of the Vaucluse. We are mostly visiting single star towns on this trip. We chose that standard to avoid the crowds. It is working for us and the cuisine is dependable. With its Neolithic and Celtic influences, the name finally morphed into Gordes. Again, we two intrepid travelers walk for a while before choosing a restaurant. We pass under ancient vaulted walkways, climb tall walls and rampart ruins.

Many of the villages have a central fountain from which the women carried their daily supply of water. Now the fountains are kept for their beauty. There are a few more tourists here, but the atmosphere is agreeable. Our attention is taken by a Soulieado boutique. At the peak of the hill, there stands a Renaissance château built on 12th c. ruins. This is not a new concept for us. Finally, we are tempted by a restaurant with a view of the surrounding valley with, naturally, a terrace under an awning. I am in the mood for 'steak aux pommes frite' (steak with French fries). Judith orders the trout.

In our several days in the Luberon we often pass 'Bories' (prehistoric stone huts) and 'oppidums' (ancient Roman shelters) sites. There are mountains all around and hill towns on top of most. Everyone talks of hill towns in Italy, but truth be told, hill towns are everywhere. They are the easiest to defend. Makes sense that everyone would want to build their castle and/or town on one.

L'Abbaye de Sénanque is our next destination. On the road from Gordes it is visible from on high with its central tower and oblong gray building. Most notable, even from our mountain road, are the full rounded rows heavy with lavender in front of the Abbaye. This is for us! We can hardly wait until the twisting road reaches the level of the fields. It is high season for the lavender plant that is grown is such profusion in Provence. I take pictures of the Abbaye and well-tended rows of lavender-in-bloom first from the road and then next to the undulating rows. The 12th c. Abbaye is a fine example of Romanesque architecture with its rounded arches and well-preserved cloisters. The scent of lavender is in the air. How heavenly is that? Contrary to what I just postulated on the attraction of building on hilltops, the Abbaye is tucked deep in a canyon surrounded by steep hills. Oops!

Pont du Gard and Cavillon Melons

Our route toward the Pont du Gard takes us through Cavaillon, a town best known as the epicenter of melon growing in France. These are the sweet melons I have enjoyed for years at Mado's. They are smaller than our melons at home. Their size is just right for the way Mado serves hers. Each person receives a full half; whereas, ours would be too large to serve in that manner. The Cavaillon melons are just right for filling with 'Porto' (sweet, red dessert wine). The Port wine and sweetness of the Cavaillon melon make a tasty pairing. (I bring a huge poster from the Cavaillon Tourist Bureau home with me to post in my French classroom in September). As we drive through this town, the scent of sweet melons wafts over us, and lavender is left behind!

Last stop today is the Pont du Gard! We approach it and are awed by its age and size. This is a Roman ruin at its best. Yes, I have been here before. I want Judith to experience it first-hand. No amount of descriptives from memory can match its beauty. It spans the Gard River as a bridge and aqueduct of three stories, built ca 19 BC as a link in a system of aqueducts carrying water from the towns of Uzes to Nimes. It is composed of colossal dressed blocks without mortar, some weighing as much as six tons each. The stones were lifted via block and tackle and propelled by a human treadmill. Some call it one of the Wonders of the Ancient World.

When I stood here many years ago, I was in the middle of a four-month student exchange program, The Experiment in International Living, and lived with the Weber family in Belfort, Territoire de Belfort, just south of Alsace in northeastern France. We Americans and our French brothers and sisters traveled for several weeks by bus and bicycle to this very spot. Our leader gave us permission to swim here in the Gard River that long-ago day. We all walked across the top level of the Roman aqueduct to the other side. What a thrill! Today I believe no one is allowed to step foot on it. There is an attractive restaurant near the aqueduct, with a terrace enlivened by red umbrellas overlooking the river and the Pont. I go in to make a phone call, wishing we could stop here for supper, but we will turn around now and eat in Lacoste. It has been another memorable day in the Luberon.

Tickets for "Carmen"
at the Roman Amphitheatre in Orange

Our final day is fast upon us. Tomorrow marks a special event. We have tickets for Bizet's Opera, "Carmen" to be performed in the ancient Roman Amphitheatre in Orange. We know that the town of Orange is about 30,000 in population, is in the département of Vaucluse, and like Arles, is in Provence "Alpes Côtes d'Azur" (French Rivera) region. The literal name of Côte d'Azur reflects the beauty of the brilliant blue waters of the Mediterranean Sea.

Parking is easy as we get to Orange early. We walk under the elaborately carved Triumphal Arch to pose for photos. The "Théatre Antique" (ancient theatre) where we will attend the opera tonight, is touted as the "best preserved Roman theatre in the Roman Empire period!" That means that our seats on the top row, #37, are very high, but safe after some 2001 years. The semicircular seating section is built into a sloping hillside. We make the long climb up to our seats very carefully. I sense acrophobia when looking forward. The lowest, front tier seating was meant for the kings and magistrates. We are just peons. The climb is quite steep, and when we get to our top rung and attempt to slide past several people in our row, there is only a slim iron rod to grasp at knee height to prevent a tip and a fall forward. The seats are crude, ancient stone and offer no comfort or back rest.

I am gazing down at the stage. It is about three or four stories high and very wide. There is a royal doorway in the center of the stage And, in a niche, standing near the top of the wall, is an imposing, if incomplete, statue of Augustus, first Roman Emperor from 27BC to his death in 14AD. It is an impressive backdrop for any play or opera. "Carmen" is part of an internationally famous summer series that was inaugurated in 1869 called "Chorégies". This summer's operas feature the music of Bizet, Berlioz and Verdi. I had to make several phone calls back home to purchase our tickets. And it looks like we got the last two!

The role of Carmen will be sung by Kathryn Harries and Micae, by Barbara Hendricks, an American who concertizes principally in Europe and therefore is best known by European audiences. I have seen her in Stockholm as well. The National Orchestra of France will be conducted by Charles Dutoit, born in Switzerland and has conducted most of the major orchestras in America. (Judith and I have seen him at the Tanglewood summer festival in Massachusetts.). Tonight, the choirs from Marseilles; Nancy and Lorraine; Avignon and Vaucluse will be accompanying the orchestra and soloists.

The performance begins at 9:30 PM. It is a warm, clear night with stars overhead. The two of us are in our element. We have been attending concerts together for many years now all over Connecticut and Western Massachusetts and now in France. Georges Bizet was born in Paris in 1838 and died in 1878. He wrote "Carmen", his last composition, in 1874, (Premiere, March 3, 1875). When he completed it, he stated: "I have written a work that is all clarity and vivacity." It is the opera that many Americans recognize and sing the "Toréador" song by heart. Despite Bizet's optimism, at first, "Carmen" was rejected because it included prostitutes and smoking. The composer was depressed with the bad reviews of the first performance. After only 33 performances, Bizet suddenly died. In a matter of a few years, his "Carmen" went on to become a success all over Europe, America and Russia. The song, "Toreador", is so famous that most Americans can sing it or hum the tune.

Returning to Judith's and my night at the opera, the actors/ singers are a long way from our top seats, but we manage to follow the story line (sung in French) and are mesmerized from the opening to the finale. It is the highlight of our Luberon tour. How lucky we are to have heard the Vaucluse choir supporting the lead vocals, so meaningful for us now that we know our way around the Vaucluse and Luberon!

We pack the next day and set out in our car for Tours and Mado's house in the Loire Valley. En route to Tours we stop briefly in Limoges for lunch and check out some shops on the main street to view formal tables set with contemporary Limoges fine china. The new designs are bright and lively, but nothing compares with my grandmother's Limoges from the early 1900s.

Serendipity at the Medieval Town of Martel

Then, back on the road again, we are looking for a place to stop for a cooling glass of 'citron pressé' (freshly squeezed lemonade) and find a surprise waiting for us in the small town of Martel. Little do we realize, the road we are on is similar to, if not the actual one, a messenger from English King Henry II had taken with an important scroll of forgiveness from father to eldest son (son's formal name: Henry Courtmantel). His parents, Henry and Aliénor called him Harry.

The back story is depressing, but suffice it to say, that at a very young age, Harry had been crowned King of the English at the bequest of his father. He claimed he did it to assure unquestioned inheritance of the crown. Highly unusual. King Henry lived to regret this hasty crowning of his young namesake. After years of family infighting, especially between Harry and his father, things were going very poorly by 1183. Young Harry wanted more power, more land and more funds to call his own; yet while Henry still lived, he was not willing to cede these to his son. The father King finally cut off his son's financial support altogether.

In desperation, willful pride and revenge, Harry ransacked churches and monasteries in Aquitaine to garner funds. In so doing he became crazed with greed beyond reason. When he reached the holy place of pilgrimage, the monastery of Rocamadour, it is said Harr broke into the treasury and stole Roland's famous sword, "Durandel", and sold it.

As Harry was leaving Rocamadour with his loot, he heard the tower bell begin to toll all of its own accord. Stunned, Harry believed it was a sign from God announcing his sinfulness. In dread and terror, he fled across the mountains toward Martel. Harry eventually entered the small, usually quiet town, feeling very ill and weak with a fever. He was taken in by a local man who tried in vain to aid him. Harry quickly deteriorated and died in the upstairs room where we are standing.

Meanwhile, in Limoges, not far from Martel, King Henry heard of his sons' thievery but refused to come to Martel, thinking his son was crying wolf as he often did. At length, Henry received the messenger bringing more news. This time Henry realized that Harry's illness was dire. Immediately he dispatched another messenger with a letter of forgiveness from father to errant son. Henry arrived too late to speak to his son before his miserable demise.

After leaving Limoges, Judith and I had driven down into the valley of the Dordogne River, heading toward Martel, as did King Henry's messenger some 800 years prior, rushing a message of forgiveness to his dying son. My friend and I have no notion of this important page of history re-enacted by us today en route to a cool drink. Later, I ask Judith why we happened to turn off the road at Martel, not having it on our itinerary. She said that we found the town in our Green "Guide Michelin" and read something about Queen Aliénor's son in Martel. So that was enough to choose Martel. It turned out to be a propitious choice as we soon discovered. This is what unfolded for us in Martel.

We drove into the small village and parked near the center. We did not see a café, so we stopped to ask a local man. We begin a casual conversation that led to why we are in Aquitaine all the way from Connecticut. I piped up to say that I am following in the footsteps of my progenitors, the

Plantagenets. I have learned over the years that I might not get a positive response as often people from Aquitaine still carry resentment against Aliénor and her family because she wed an Englishman.

The man asked if we knew that King Harry, eldest son of Queen Aliénor and, King Henry II, died right here in the center of town? I was caught off guard and said my research had not gotten that far, but that I was very curious to find out the circumstances. The man went on to say that he lives in the house where young King was taken for help. The house was nearby, and the man beckoned us to follow him. We decided it was okay as he was most eager to show us. We waited on the sidewalk while the kind monsieur entered to tell his wife they have visitors. Soon the whole family came out and invited us in to see the second-floor room where Harry died. This was indeed extraordinary! How could I be so fortunate as to learn history in this way, in faraway Aquitaine? For me this was a pot of gold at the base of the rainbow. I forget now if we ever found our lemonade that day in Martel, but I shall always carry the vision of the small, upper room where a king of England spent his last hours in 1183.

Returning to the Loire Valley and Mado in Tours
Warm Welcome and a Yuri Bashmet Concert

Turning once again toward Tours, I am eager to introduce Judith to my endearing friend, Mado, and her family. So far on this trip I have strayed far from the Loire Valley but can stay away no longer! We shall spend our last few days in Tours with Mado. How happy I am to be returning to my home away from home in Touraine. Mado gives me my usual room overlooking the courtyard; Judith's is across the hall. I have told Judith about Mado's hospitality and her gourmet cuisine.

Our welcome home dinner is, as usual, in Mado's garden. Following our meal Judith and I are treating Mado's daughter, Maryse, to a concert in the "Semaines Musicales" series. It is not by coincidence that we have already purchased our tickets. The concert will be held at the Cathedral in Tours, and the featured musicians, the "Les 'Soloistes de Mosocou",

Yuri Bashmet's group of which I have so often spoken. They will play Rossini's "Petite Messe Solennelle" (Solemn little Mass). The selection of music is in honor of 200th anniversary of Rossini's birth, an auspicious occasion. Yuri will conduct the supporting orchestra and choir. I know the awesome Cathedral of St. Gatiens well, having attended mass there many times.

When I met Mado and Maryse in 1988, and we attended our first concert with Yuri Bashmet, world's foremost violist, I learned a wonderful new French word that describes all three of us tonight. The French have used one word to describe what we, in English, need at least two words to express. It is 'mélomane', (music lover). You, dear reader, know by now that I am certainly one of those. Music makes my heart tick and when it happens in France, I am ecstatic. I am in good company.

On that high note, a 'double entendre', Judith and I fly back to New York and are met once again by her son, Charles, who drives us home in his limousine. A perfect ending for a perfect trip.

Chapter Five

The Little-Known Little Loir

IT IS MY SEVENTH SUMMER in France, and I am planning something completely different from the preceding summers. I am going to do the first part of this trip alone, renting a car at Charles De Gaulle airport in Paris, and going directly to my friends', Anne and Carlson's, house. Their country home-away-from-home is called 'L'Abri aux Chouettes' (Safe place for Owls) and is in the area of the little Loir River (spelled Loir). This is about 40- minutes west of Tours and the big Loire (spelled Loire). There I hope to spend three peaceful weeks just letting the lovely French summer air, sights and smells, waft over me, providing inspiration to write. Of course, I will visit my great, old friends in Tours, the Renaud family, and take in some concerts. This will be a test to see how I fare on my own.

At the end of three weeks, my son, Rusty, will fly over to meet me at about the same time Anne and Carlson will be arriving. We will spend some time together, then Rusty and I will head out on a long-awaited two-week trip following in the footsteps of the pilgrims to Santiago de Compostela in Spain and then to the Southwest of France, into Cathar country.

I have completed my required number of graduate course hours at the University to satisfy two Master's Degrees. So, though my formal education is over, my life experience education goes on 'ad infinitum'. I have an insatiable hunger, even after all these years, for all things French. I daresay this appetite doubles when I am on French soil. I am forever, observing, taking notes, asking questions and reading everything in sight. Although I have my first computer at home, I do not have a laptop to plug in at 'L'Abri aux Chouettes', where I will be staying, but alas, I will have to be content with the old pencil and legal pad routine.

Winter research – next summer in France

I continue my self-required reading over the winter: "Le Journal Français d'Amérique" a French language newspaper which I receive monthly; my seasonal "France", the magazine; a similar "France Today"; my British publication of FRANCE; the weekly newspaper, "France-Amérique"; the "France Discovery Guide" published yearly by the French Government Tourist Office in NYC; the most helpful monthly session of "Champs Elysées en Français" which keeps me up on all things old and new, cultural and historical in France including all around news coverage on cassette with written script; my favorite, a radio program airing every Sunday evening emanating from Five College Radio in Northampton, Massachusetts capsulizing politics, music theatre, literature and business and called "Tout en Français"; the wonderfully informative magazine, "European Life" and last, but not least, my "Paris Notes" newsletter. I am an ever-renewing blotter for a variety of French news. Ask any of my friends over the years and they will testify to my French mania. Trust me, I do not exaggerate.

Systematically, I organize all my materials, making them easily accessible, to be used, first in the classroom, and then on my yearly trips. As you may imagine, my files are bulging, my bookcases crammed full, and my cupboards filled to bursting with all this indispensable French information. Ask me if there is a summer chamber music festival in the tiny bourg of Thoronet in the southwest of France; ask me to tell you if there is a nuclear power plant in Touraine and where it is; ask me who did academy award work on the invention of special movie-making lenses in the late 50s in France; ask me when the open air market in Île-Sur-Sorgue sells antiques as opposed to food; ask me where can I find the best fresh fruit and cheeses in Versailles for a picnic? Ask me how to get tickets for the opera in the Roman amphitheater in Orange from my desk at home; ask me how and where to purchase the best price on tickets for the Russian music festival called "Semaines Musicales" in Tours. All this in 1993 and for me, pre-internet!

With all this knowledge crammed into my head and condensed into this summer's notes, I take my leave of home and hasten to the skies on Air France. I arrive in Paris, not too tired to check out my car and start on the four to five-hour drive to the small town of Beaumont near Vendôme on the 'Little Loir'. This will be my first trip to their French country home, "L'Abri aux Chouettes". I am more than thrilled to be going to my friends' home even if I will be arriving ahead of them. They have owned it for about two years. It feels like a dream to me as I drive closer and closer.

Anne and I first met when we were working at the French Embassy on Fifth Avenue, New York in 1960. began our meeting of the minds on our favorite subject, France. It has continued ever since. Some years ago, Anne and her husband decided they loved the valley of the little-known little Loir as I call it and purchased "l'Abri aux Chouettes" (safe place for owls). I shall call the house, "L'Abri".

Settling in at "L'Abri"

So, here I am, in late June, excitedly driving past fields of poppies on my way to their front door. My expectations are very high, and I am not disappointed! I pull up to the bottom of their driveway by their mailbox. I cannot see the house, only a very steep drive. Once at the top I am rewarded with the sight of a lovely country home with a 'grange' (barn/garage) on the right across the terrace and grassy courtyard. The house is tall and fashioned of local 'tuffaut' (limestone) like the châteaux of the Valley of the Kings. The façade of the barn is alive with thick 'hedera helix' (ivy). The graceful ivy surrounds three charming Dutch doors streaked with nail stains from years of rainy days. The sturdy double garage door belies the existence of a vintage utility car resting in the shade of the interior. I will look inside tomorrow. Behind the barn is a tiny 'étang' (small pond), overhung with low tree boughs.

Turning back toward the house, I see that it is surrounded on three sides by fields of 'tourne-sols' (sunflowers) ready to explode into sun-color momentarily. The fourth side is an open, dipping-down pasture populated with three Holstein cows munching their cuds, interested but quite unflapped by my arrival. As I stand there drinking in the luscious, peaceable kingdom that surrounds me, I hear the ubiquitous French cuckoo calling behind the barn as he hunts for his supper.

The exhaustion of the trip is beginning to catch up to me as I walk up to the front door with key in hand. The sun is shining; a sunbathing chameleon noiselessly flits out from under my footfall on the doorstep. I later learn that he is a regular inhabitant who is always given deference by humans in the know. The door is a bit hard to open, but it does at last give way to my pushing and pulling.

I enter to see a sparely furnished, definitely old-world home. The living room is on the left with a tall ceiling, aged beams revealed, stone fireplace, large French windows at either end of the room, an old 'escritoire' (writing desk), some chairs and a couch, all with a distinctive European look.

The kitchen is on the right. Spanning the center of the kitchen is a long, sturdy trestle table covered with a cheery, new, Mondrian-like red and white oilcloth and a fresh bouquet of flowers. Opposite the table is a small wood stove sitting in the kitchen fireplace, while on my left I see a lovely Monet- like blue and white ceramic counter with similar patterned skirt to the floor. The tiled floor the color of New Mexican Adobe bricks, reflects the light from two large windows giving out to the cow field on one side and to 'la Terrasse', (the terrace), on the other. There are, also, of course, the requisite small frig, adequate stove with oven, flanked on one wall by an antique, mirrored hutch. Who could ask for more?

I realize that the flowers must have been cut from the garden by Ghislaine, a neighbor who, with her husband, Michel, are caretakers of Anne's house. I am eager to meet them. Before I can haul my luggage into the house, there is a tap on the door. Ghislaine and her daughter, Marie-Laure, arrive to bid me welcome. They undoubtedly saw me pass their house on my way into town. It is so small a 'bourg' (village) that when a strange car, especially a rented one, passes by, they take notice.

We have a spirited conversation as Ghislaline answers my many questions about 'la maison', (the house), the village, and what I expect to do in the next few weeks. She wastes no time in telling me that her son is to be 'marié' (married) on Saturday, this coming Saturday and that I am invited to all the festivities! A friend of hers, 'une jeune fille Américaine' (a young American girl) who works as an attorney at the American Embassy in Paris, will be joining us early Saturday AM, and would I mind if she stays with me at the house for one night? I am happy to have a visitor. And so, the summer of '93 by the little Loir River begins on a very busy note.

Café Surprise - Luisette

The next morning, I make an early trip to the one and only café in the village, just opened, to try their 'café au lait avec tartine', (strong coffee with warm milk served with horizontally cut French 'baguette' (bread), slathered with fresh Normandy butter and this season's raspberry jam) my favorite French breakfast. It being the end of June, the raspberries are just coming into season. I briefly contemplate walking down to the café, only 3/4 of a mile, a nice quiet road with just a few houses on one side but feel lazy and drive 'à l'Américaine' (American style). As I enter the brand-new café, I discover it serves as a pickup spot for the newspaper, the fresh-baked daily bread, and last-minute groceries, including fresh veggies. On the side near the corner are a few tables with chairs. I think these are mainly for coffee imbibers, but soon find out I am wrong. For, on occasion, when I am there inevitably, a car or 'moto' (motorcycle) roars up to that entrance, a man strides into the counter and asks for some red wine, always before lunch. I am not too shocked since I know 'les Français' (the French), don't let the time of day interfere with imbibing their share of wine.

I introduce myself to the owners, M. et Mme. Chatelaine. They will kindly reserve my baguette for me each day. I will be asking their advice on many things while in town this month. Having ordered my continental breakfast, I sit alone at a small table by the window to read the paper.

Soon I am joined by a sweet-looking, diminutive, well-dressed, elderly lady at the next table. One of us, I cannot recall which now, breaks the ice by speaking to the other solo woman. From thence begins a friendship which continues for nearly a decade, until her death. Her name is Luisette Anquetil. She is 80 years young and lives just up the street one block. She was born here, lived in Paris during her married life, bringing up her children in the capital city. After her husband died, she retreated to the countryside of her youth to live out her years in peace amongst old friends. She is delighted, as am I, that the café has opened. This broadens her daily routine. And mine too! I find she is an educated, fine lady with whom I can discuss many aspects of French life, politics and art. We agree from that day forward to meet every day at the small café. One day I will buy; the next, she buys and so on.

I scoop up a few groceries in the nearest town and return to the house to make a few phone calls and to begin writing. But first I call Mado to say I have arrived. She immediately invites me for supper in two days' time. I will see the whole family and meet her current students from around the world.

Even Queen Aliénor is here too!

Next, on Anne's recommendation, I call her new acquaintances in the village. Louis is a 'marionnettiste', (puppeteer), and his wife, Dominique, his assistant. She fashions the costumes and helps write the script for their presentations. I have already seen a flier announcing their show at Chinon in the couple of weeks. It will be a presentation of the story of

Eleanor of Aquitaine and Henri II and their life at Château Chinon. How perfect! I know Chinon and would love to attend their performance.

In the meantime, they invite me for cocktails the next night. Well, at least initially, I will have my days free to write and my evenings occupied with seeing friends. Really, quite a perfect life, I would say, for a foreigner in a totally new town. in what one might call 'La France Profonde', (deepest, most remote, France). Remember, this town has no post office, no grocery store, except for the newly opened quick-pick café, no gas station even. There is, however, a church. But, pursuant to the post-World War II trend in France, this town, like so many others between cities of Tours and Le Mans is no longer a flourishing farming community. Instead, it is peopled in large part by the retired and elderly. France has become centralized around Paris, the big draw for young people.

To get a feel for some of the other residents, Ghislaine and her husband, Michel, are mushroom workers. They work about 15 minutes from home, together, at a mushroom farm. They work all day 5 days a week in the dark, all hunched over, planting, weeding, and harvesting the mushroom crop. They are from a large a fun-loving large, family who has lived here for generations.

It is Michel who does the handiwork at Anne's. In fact, my second day at the house, I make a call for help to Michel. The upstairs tub faucets are not functioning properly, and the back door leading into the furnace room had flown open in a strong wind, making it impossible for me to fasten the next morning. Michel bails me out quite nicely.

Marie-Laure, my guide to the area

Their young daughter, Marie-Laure, age 11, becomes my companion on excursions since she is relatively free during the summer and knows her way around locally. During the first week Marie-Laure shows me how to find the local goat cheese farm just over the hill en route to the grocery store. It is a fascinating excursion. We drive off the main road to a very old farm owned and run by an elderly couple whose children have long since grown up and moved to the city. Marie-Laure leads me, following the lady cheese maker into one of the sheds where the goat cheese is curing.

At first, I am not sure if I want to buy the cheese, since there are flies and cobwebs galore in the storeroom, no light, except the filtered light of day coming through the loose boards. Plus, it is about 85 degrees Fahrenheit, and no refrigeration. Nonetheless, I forge ahead and point to two cheeses. The farmer's wife wraps them up, and I take them. I reason to myself; everyone else eats this cheese. After all this was the tried and true method until recent improvements in refrigeration. Why should I complain? Outcome: I eat the goat cheese, relish them and live to tell the story. The cheese is marvelous in fact. No preservatives either.

On our way out, Marie-Laure asks for some 'oeufs verts' (green eggs) that apparently are cholesterol-free! So much for the old-world methods. I have no idea what these might be or from what feathered bird!!

By way of comparison, two weeks later I take on a little sojourn with Mado's daughter, Maryse, to visit some friends of hers who raise goats and make cheese. The contrast is marked! Their herd of goats, though sizable, is impeccably clean, The entire operation is today's state-of-the-art, and is handled much like a cow-milking operation. Stainless steel vats and milking machines, everyone wearing uniforms, white hats and rubber gloves. Not a fly in sight. No cobwebs anywhere. I enjoy very much seeing both the old and the new methods. Both cheeses are excellent.

Whenever Marie-Laure and I take a short trip, whether to the grocer, the florist or on a more distant excursion, we develop a little game that we play in the car. I ask her the words in French for parts of the car or other words I rarely have occasion to use. She writes them down in French using the proper article, feminine or masculine. Then I give her some words in English. We keep the notebook in the car and quiz each other on the previous trip's vocab. In this way we both enrich our vocabularies while I drive. She is a charming, lively, young companion.

Meeting Guy, the Ebeniste (cabinetmaker)

Another of Anne and Carlson's friends is their closest neighbor, Guy (pronounced, ghee). As I drive up the road toward the L'Abri, I pass only three houses before coming to theirs. The last one on the right is Guy's workshop. He is an 'ébeniste' (cabinetmaker). He makes furniture to order. And, like Ghislaine, when a car passes that he does not recognize, he is alerted. Every time I drive past his workshop, I am aware that he is aware I am there. It is much like my Vermont experience. I have owned a parcel of land in Stratton, VT for 40 years. It is on a road where very few people live. Whenever I drive in, Mr. Brazer, the original owner of the land, always sees me and comes over to say hello, whether I pass his house or not, be it day or night. It is much the same with Guy.

Anne forewarned me that Guy would stop in to say hello and expect a glass of wine with conversation in the first couple of days. Sure enough, in two days, just after lunch, before he resumes his work, there is a knock on the door. There is Guy to introduce himself. He is a man about my age who actually resides a few miles away with his family but has made this his workplace for some 30 years. Of course, after his visit, he returns the favor by issuing me an open-ended invitation to his 'atelier' (workshop), to see his work and to partake in his after-lunch wine ritual.

The next couple of days pass very quickly. At the end of the second week, I take some time after my lunch to stop by to see Guy. I am rather curious to see the kind of work he does. I was told he fashioned the trestle table in Anne's kitchen, so I know his work is first rate. When I arrive, he shows me the cabinets and tables he is working on. They are beautiful in design. After we talk awhile, he welcomes three friends, two women and a man, apparently, old friends. He introduces us all around. I decide this is a good opening to take my leave. Guy, however, insists they have come for a 'coupe', (a cup of wine), and would I please join them. He leads us all out of the workshop, around to the right, under the thick, hanging fronds of a weeping willow, parting them and disappearing into the darkness.

I am somewhat bewildered, but I follow the others, stooping down under the willow. Once inside the 'cave' (wine cellar) we continue our animated chatting. It is the height of a steamy July day, but here, in the shade of willow at the entrance to Guy's wine stash, it seems rather cool in more ways than one. Presently Guy returns, emerging from his hidden 'cave', (wine cellar), having quickly chosen a bottle for us. Uncorking it, he tells us the origin of this wine and its vintage. He produces some plain, sturdy, glasses and fills one for each of us.

The talk turns from the broiling temperatures to local politics, most interesting for me, as an outsider. I cannot stay long, nor can I drink much, as I am in the midst of writing and need to stay awake for the rest of the afternoon. Apparently, this is a long-held tradition for Guy and his friends. I find it quaint, if not way too much for my unaccustomed head on a hot midday. Before long I express my thanks and bid them all good day as I struggle to part the willow branches and walk unaffected under the hot sun toward my car.

A French Country Wedding

I am very pleased to be invited to the wedding, being a rank newcomer and all. This dispels all pre-conceived notions about the snobbish attitude of the French toward Americans. Although I had witnessed weddings before in France, in cathedrals, or in the streets, I have never been invited to attend one. So, this is going to be special.

Saturday morning the lady from Paris arrives and becomes my companion for the day. We first assemble at the town hall in a nearby village, with all family members sitting around a large table. The bride and groom sit in the middle side by side. Across from them sits the Mayor who pronounces the vows and officially marries them in the eyes of the French government. Then we all file out behind the bride and groom. She clutches her bouquet while her flower-bedecked hair becomes wind-blown. We all trip through the tiny town, across the square, and into the large church. There are no bridesmaids to carry her bridal train. Only a small boy and his young sister seem to be a part of the bridal party, now leading the cortege up the aisle.

Once in the church, the bride and groom prepare to be married again, this time by the local priest. They sit alongside each other in upholstered high-backed chairs, facing the altar as they repeat their vows for the second time. The bride and groom then exit the church, passing under a gala archway of hand-held fire nozzles created by the groom's fellow 'pompiers', (firefighters). How very quaint!

Afterward, with photos having been taken in front of the church, the entire retinue of principles and guests walks, again, through the streets, out of the center of town and finally up a long dirt road past a line of flowering trees to the summit of a hill where a 'vin d'honneur' (toasting) reception party is waiting at a small inn. We move inside and mill out on the terrace, choosing from large trays of red and white wines as well as champagne, very little in the way of food. I duck out early, having talked with most of the people and thoroughly enjoyed myself. They party will carry on well into the night.

The fun surprise comes the next morning after my houseguest leaves to return to Paris on the early train. I am driving down to the café for my morning coffee. As I 'round the corner at the bottom of the hill past Guy's workshop, I see several people in the road and much commotion. A few cars are parked by the side of the road, and I first wonder if there has been an accident. Why else would so many people be out on a Sunday morning when you usually see not a soul. I pull to a stop and recognize Ghislaine, Michel, Marie Laure and the rest of the family. The crowd is, in fact, in front of their house. I get out as they beckon me to join in whatever they are about to do.

They and about ten other friends and family members were waiting, I am told, for the best man to go inside their house to the nuptial bedroom. The tradition is that they arrive early on the 'lendemain', (the morning after), rouse the newly-weds, physically pick up the bride and carry her outside in her nightie. The groom is in his shorts, chasing after them. They carry with them a bedpan crock filled with blobs of chocolate mousse and whipped cream. As we stand there the best man appears carrying the bride with her hair in disarray, her eyes not fully open, scantily clad. The groom hustles along behind trying to catch up, clutching some clothing around himself.

Everyone is laughing and making much ado. They take the bride across the road and into her father's vegetable garden before letting her down. They then give her and the groom spoons and bid them eat from the chamber pot.

Mado told me about this tradition some years ago, but I never thought anyone actually does it still! We are all in stitches before it calms down and I can gracefully bid 'adieu' (farewell), and travel on down the road for my own albeit mundane breakfast. Such is life in France in a small country town, and I thought It would be so quiet! Wrong!

Finding Aliénor, Henry II,
and Berengaria in Le Mans with Maryse

The following Sunday I drive off to meet Mado's daughter, Maryse, at the train station in Le Mans. It is the week of the annual Medieval Festival there, and I am in seventh heaven. We park the car near the open-air market. We stroll past mounds of neatly stacked colorful fresh vegetables and fruits and eventually find the parade of costumed revelers wending its way through the medieval streets of the 'la vieille ville' (the old town). I swiftly learn that Le Mans is not only famous for a car racing.

We take our time perusing the vendors' booths, eyeing specialty foods and local artisans' wares before going into the Saint Julien Cathedral for a tour. I am quite taken by the in-depth history of the Plantagenets we see displayed in dioramas inside the ancient (mostly) Romanesque edifice. For example, King Henry II's parents were married here, and Henry was baptized here. It is known that Queen Aliénor accompanied her husband here many times.

The west façade, the oldest entryway at St. Julien's, with its surrounding tympanum is still beautiful. The 11th century nave is said to be one of the oldest in the Romanesque style. There is at least one stained glass window that survives from the time of the 11c Plantagenets. It depicts the Ascension of Christ in vivid color. I learn that over the millennia there were fires that destroyed large portions of the great cathedral, but enough remains as blend of architectural motifs (from Romanesque to Gothic) to be a treasure trove for historians and genealogists likes me.

Of particular interest, "Aliénor d'Aquitaine", (Eleanor of Aquitaine), and her second husband, Henry II, attended a re-dedication of this cathedral in the aftermath of one of those devastating fires, circa 1160. Furthermore, Henry made one of his last stops here before he died in 1189. Wherever possible I follow in Aliénor's footstep. Over course of my 10 summers in France, I continue to be grateful that Maryse has planned meaningful side trips like this one, relating to Aliénor and Henry.

Maryse, much like myself, "travels on her stomach". Not literally of course. When we meet in the summer, we do indulge our gourmet tendencies whenever possible. Naturally, she knows of a fine restaurant in nearby Coulaines called, "Les Rosiers", ("The Rose Bushes"), where we dine in splendor for a good two hours on their terrace. I order a trout that looks and tastes much like salmon, because of its pink flesh. Maryse tells me it is a 'truite saumonisée' (salmon-like trout) a specialty of the Loire River. It is succulently adorned with a 'tapenade Provençale' (spicy olive paste), an intense mixture of olives, anchovies and garlic, with a side of eggplant. We conclude the elegant outdoor repast with a Grand Marnier soufflé, while lingering in the shade at our table. Eventually we must venture out into the still- hot afternoon sun, she, being much more used to the extreme heat than I.

After lunch we visit the 'Abbaye de l'Épau' founded in 1229 by Queen Berengaria, the wife of King Richard I, the Lion-Heart, and daughter-in-law of Queen Aliénor We discover that Berengaria is buried here. TheJ H 'gisant', (her effigy), on her sepulcher is stunningly well preserved even after these many centuries. Preceding our visit to the abbaye, as we are looking for a parking spot, a troubling scenario presented itself. I desperately wanted to park in the shade to facilitate our return to the car on this sweltering day. However, we met with a deterrent. As a result, I was so miffed by the ladies who thwarted us that I penned this short poem to crystallize the frustration of the moment.

I wrote this poem on a hot day in France, and my daughter obliged by creating this beautiful painting.

Painting by Amy Dyer, inspired by Alina Maksimenko.

THREE FINE FRENCH LADIES

Three fine French ladies sitting on a bench.
Three fine French Ladies on a hot LeMans day before lunch Three fine French ladies at L'Abbaye de L'Épau.
Three fine French ladies in no hurry to go.

Along came us, une Française, an American from New York.
Seeking a place under a shade tree to park.
Fancying a return to a cooled down car
After burying the wife of old Lionheart.

Spying the one shady spot
In front of a bench in the parking lot,
We drove in and commenced to alight
When came an assault which gave us a fright.

Three fine French ladies sitting on a bench.
Three fine French ladies watching from hence
Three fine French ladies intolerant of our choice!
Three fine French ladies calling in unison voice,

"You daren't park here,
Not in front of us!
Your car smells queer!
Your engine stinks of gas!

We faced them in shock,
Turned to each other, unable to talk.
Do we unseat the three,
Retort or retreat?

Alas, what choice did we have,
Two threatened tourists, the finer of five,
With clenched teeth lipped in, we smiled, and we waved,
Then drove 'round and 'round still craving the shade.

Three "fine" French ladies glared us down.
Three "fine" French ladies sat their ground.
Three "fine: French ladies smug with their win
Three "fine" French ladies out with the sun.

Semaines Musicales in Tours

The next few days are spent in securing tickets for the series of concerts I usually attend in Tours. This year marks the 19th year for "Les Semaines Musicales de Tours", (Musical Weeks). The featured musicians as usual, are the "Soloists de Moscow" (Moscow Soloists), conducted by its founder and soloist himself, Yuri Bashmet, plus a full Russian orchestra, the National Symphonic Orchestra of Russia, The Branko Ksmanovis Chorus, an opera troop, chamber players, even dancers. I have been enjoying their varied concerts every summer since 1987. By now I know the musicians I want to hear again. My favorite is fast becoming a Russian violist named Yuri Bashmet. I have since found that he is touted as 'numero uno', violist in the world! This year I hope to attend most of his concerts. Even at home in Connecticut I hear him more and more often on Public Radio. I know he plays regularly at Tanglewood, Lincoln Center and Carnegie Hall.

Yuri Bashmet comes with his family to Tours each summer, for the month of July, to give master classes and to perform in the evenings at the different churches in town, as well as other inviting venues where the acoustics are supreme. The concerts are indeed one of the most special highlights of my summer. Usually I go into Tours early to join Mado, Lucien and Maryse and her family for supper in their garden. On occasion, Maryse will accompany me to the evening concert. Best of all are the nights when Maryse's employer, the well-known chef of a four-star restaurant in Tours, Jean Bardet, gives us complimentary tickets.

After several days of intensive writing, I feel I have toiled sufficiently hard enough to merit the first of the Yuri Bashmet concerts. I leave the L'Abri aux Chouettes for the 40-minute ride through rambling countryside, passing through the outskirts of Tours where the Walmart-type stores are growing like mushrooms after a rain. There is Mammouth, one of the largest. They learned it all from us, the Americans.

Aren't we Americans proud? In place of lovely rolling hills dotted with cows and neatly arranged haystacks, we boast of a network of huge stores, 'round points' (round-abouts), traffic lights, billboards galore and tons of smoking cars. They are just getting the idea of lead-free gas in the summer of 1993. Few people see the advantage in shelling out the extra francs for higher priced gasoline to clean up the air they breathe.

Oh, yes, let me digress to tell you about the French billboards I pass en route to Mado's. I have seen them in France for years now. The large rectangular sign is made up of many blocks that are moveable. Each block of the entire picture rotates every few seconds, thus producing an entirely new ad. The process reminds me of the cubes we had as children with pictures on all six sides. To change the picture from that of the three little pigs, to a scene depicting Jack and Jill tumbling down hill, each cube must be rotated in the same direction at the same time, and so on until you return to the original nursery rhyme. This is a very clever use of space. Some rotate vertically; some horizontally. I find them quite innovative. I wonder why we have not picked up on this method of advertising in the US.

Evening with Mado; Supper in the Garden

Soon I arrive in center Tours. I alight from my parked, air-conditioned Citroën on Rue Victor Hugo and begin the walk down the alleyway to the Renaud stronghold. The air is oppressive, but my spirits are high. It has been many months of letters back and forth from my house to Mado's all winter, waiting for just this moment. I ring the bell and knock on the gate. The large English sheep dog barks my arrival. Soon I hear Mado calling, 'J'arrive' (I'm coming)! Oh, it's you, Jini!! Oh, là là!! It's been so long since we said good-bye last August! It makes my heart warm to welcome you again, Jini!"

We start our conversation through the gate as she makes her way to open it for me. At last, 'nous voici' (Here we are)! We made it another year! There is always activity in the combined households and gardens of Mado and her daughter, Maryse's. Maryse has not yet returned from work, but her daughter, Paloma, is sitting at their table at the far end of the garden talking with a close friend. I greet everyone with a usual 3-5 'bises' (kisses) on both cheeks. Paloma's brother, Martin, comes out of the house with a great smile and an added 2-3 inches in height since last year.

When it quiets down, I follow Mado into her kitchen. So much to talk about. Lucien is taking his afternoon nap upstairs. I imagine he has awoken by now, with all the high-pitched voices in the courtyard. Mado has just returned from doing her errands. Dinner is cooking. She is always so beautifully organized when it comes to meal preparation. I guess that large numbers at the table are second nature for her after all these years. The students from Japan are studying upstairs. I will meet them at dinner. So, there is some quiet time before we eat. I offer to help Mado set the table. There will be only five tonight at her table under the banana tree. Maryse's family will eat later when she returns.

Our supper tonight is light fare due to the extreme heat. Lucien comes downstairs and we greet each other with affection. He goes to the 'cave' per usual to pour from the cask, his favorite wine, a good local red wine. Mado piles the plates three high at each person's place. The first one will be for a cooling course of 'crudités' (cold veggies) made up of 'crevette salade' (tiny Brittany shrimp salad), punctuated with fresh celeriac, 'carrottes rappés' (grated carrots) and cold white asparagus served with a wonderful homemade herb mayonnaise. I already feel relief from the heat.

For the second course Mado clears the top plate and brings in a simple trout amandine in a lovely tarragon sauce. I mop up every morsel of the sauce with more than my share of French bread. I think I could live by bread alone if I were French or at least on French soil!

The third plate is for her signature 'salade verte' (green salad) - again, I need a few more pieces of baguette to clean my plate. Mado returns from the kitchen bearing my favorite, every-July-dessert, fresh raspberries in 'fromage blanc' (a tasty, runny white cheese). For the rest of my life, even though I grow raspberries in my own yard, I shall never forget the taste of her succulent raspberries, smothered in fromage blanc. It is not too sweet, not too sour, jussssssst right!! Mado may not have enough to serve the others at the table, but, if she has her way, I will have mine, come hell or hot July night. Accordingly, I am in heaven, hoping this moment will never end!!!

Finally, the Bashmet Concert and Not by Chance Meetings

Tonight, I am going to the concert alone as Maryse cannot make it. I drive to the university auditorium and park just outside, since I am early. Most concerts start at 9PM in the summer in France. I have ordered my tickets-with-discount through my Club France membership. I go to La FNAC (large book and CD store) with a list of CDs that I want to buy. For example: CDs to use in my French language classes at home. It is the best place to find the old standbys, like Brassens, Piaf, Josephine

Baker as well as the contemporary songs my prof at the Institut plays for my class each summer, Marie Antoinette's dance favorites, and some medieval Spanish music I heard in a concert last summer. I will special order Yuri Bashmet's most recent recordings.

I find my seat easily. It is on the left side of the auditorium, about 8th row. My seat is the second from the aisle. Soon I have a neighbor sitting to my left on the aisle side. It is well before the beginning of the concert, so we strike up a conversation. It is a young girl of about 14, blond and effervescent. I soon discover that she is one of Yuri's pupils this summer. She is from the Bordeaux area and will be spending the month of July here under Yuri's tutelage. This will be her third summer as his student.

Only this summer is to be different. She has just won the 'young violist of the year' competition in Bordeaux. She is not here alone. In fact, her parents have rented a house in Tours, as they have in past summers, to be with their daughter in her pursuit of her viola education at the highest level. We have fun talking about what it is like to study with the foremost violist in the world. Annette offers to introduce me to Yuri after the program is over. At intermission I meet her parents. They speak neither English, nor Russian, and therefore cannot communicate with Yuri. They ask me to speak with him on their behalf: They want me to convey to him the fact that their daughter has just won the prestigious prize in Bordeaux. They know that their daughter will not say a word about it. They hope Yuri will take more interest in her as a result of her recent success.

The concert begins about 30 minutes late! According to Annette, her viola master is consistent in this respect; he is always late for her lesson, thinking nothing wrong with arriving 40 minutes to an hour late. Like Annette, we forgive Yuri as he starts the concert with Schubert, followed by Grieg with his 'Soloistes'. The depth of emotion in the music draws us completely under his spell. I cannot help but notice, through the strains of Grieg, how the spotlight reflects the droplets of Yuri's perspiration fanning out from his forehead on this steamy night.

The program draws to an end. Annette and I move out ahead of the crowd, still clapping for a fourth encore. We work our way backstage where friends and the press are waiting to speak with Yuri. Patiently we stand on one foot and then the other while Yuri gives a lengthy taped interview in his native Russian to a Russian radio reporter. We wish we could translate, what must be, his descriptions of the evening's performance from Yuri's point of view.

Finally, with the radio interview completed, we step up in front of Yuri. His wife is not far away, tall, slender, ebony straight cropped hair. She looks bored. Probably is.

Annette congratulates her mentor in English. He is all smiles now, relaxed, still sweaty and hot. Then she introduces me to him. I shake his valuable hand and mutter a few words in praise of his incredible talent. I remember to give him the message from Annette's mother. He replies that he already knows of his student's impressive achievement in June.

Yuri's hair is a shiny chestnut, cut in a long bob like so many artists. He is smiling, and has mischievous eyes that draw the listener in. I am just another one of those listeners, attracted to his expertise and yet in total awe, standing weak-kneed before him. Next thing I know it is over, and we move out into the street where Annette's parents are waiting.

This is but one of many such concerts I attend with Yuri Bashmet playing his heart out on the stage and then greeting me more and more as a friend as the years melt one into another. I easily find my car and head back to Beaumont. It is close to 2 AM when I cross the threshold and climb the steep stairs to find my bed.

Luisette and I Stroll Around Her Hometown

Tomorrow comes early with the song of the mourning dove sounding just like the ones that awoke me at Mado's in previous summers. I am up at a decent hour, and I join Luisette as usual for 'un petit café et conversation' (a little coffee and talk).

This day she says she wants to take a little walk around Beaumont to show me a few places special to her. We walk about ten minutes or so to a country road not far from Anne's to view the house where Luisette was born. She tells me some Americans have bought the house, some antique dealers who are away most of the time. There are tall walls around the house obscuring the view. I can see that part of the wall along the long driveway is made of tall stacks of firewood, evidently more to form a barrier between, their house and the neighbor's, rather than to burn. In front of her house, as we stand on the narrow country road Luisette points out the 'lavoire' (washing place) where, in the early 20th century, her mother used to do the laundry "en plein air", (in the open air). The small stream which runs by the front of the houses on this road provides the source of water, not only for her laundry, but further up the road, for her neighbor's as well. There are a couple of large, flat, stones strategically placed at the water's edge, so her mother could kneel beside the water and scrub the clothes. Primitive by our standards, yet our early settlers did much the same thing.

Next, we pass by the old dark, stone church, now virtually closed for lack of parishioners. Then we climb up the small hill going away from the center, past Luisette's small abode and up to an impressive gate with a long curving drive disappearing under the tall trees. She tells me an American couple bought this large estate a few years ago and that they are in the process of restoring the house. Some townspeople are part of the work crew, providing bits and pieces of info regarding the ongoing work. Luisette tells me their name is Oldenburg, He is a sculptor and she is a writer. Their name rings a bell with me. I think she wrote a short account of the life of Aliénor d'Aquitaine. In fact, I have the book. They are an elderly couple of Scandinavian origin. This must be a great source of excitement for the locals since this château is the only large property in the village. We have had a lovely walk and talk together. I leave her at her tiny house near the church and return home to finish my projected writing for the day.

Mary-Lure and I Visit the Abbaye de Solesmes

The weekend after the 14th of July I'm walking into the Abbaye de Solesmes overlooking the Sarthe River in Solesmes, still in the land of the Little Loir. I am accompanied by Marie-Laure. We utter not a word, for the compline (evening prayer), has already begun. The Benedictine monks are entering from behind the altar single file. They are wearing brown monkshoods tied up with ropes around their middles. Their hands are clasped before them. Their heads are slightly bowed. Marie Laure and I find an empty seat. Their Gregorian Chant fills the 11th century Abbaye de St. Pierre. They are singing the office of compline service that will include several psalms. The service began with the ringing of the abbey bell and will end the same. My little friend and I are mesmerized by the quiet spectacle, new for us both. In a few minutes, we are joined by a lady who silently slides in beside Marie-Laure. The lady is dressed all in black with a black scarf covering her head, tied in the back. She bows her head and sits back to listen with the rest of us.

My gaze wanders left and right with the undulations of the Latin chant. In the half-light I see the church is decorated with sculptures and sepulchers. As I am about to whisper to Marie-Laure to notice the elegant recumbent figure to our left, I see she is already listening intently as our neighbor lady is explaining something to her. I realize the lady, in fact, has taken a shine to her and is filling her in much better than I could. I wait to hear the descriptions after the service.

Forty minutes later the monks return from whence they came and disappear along with the music. The bell takes up the peel as we begin to leave. I lean over to introduce myself to the kind person who has sat with us. She gives me her hand for a French greeting with a beatific smile. On the way out we three talk a bit. I learn that her name is Jehanne (archaic spelling of Jeanne). She comes here every day to all the services, matins, complines, vespers, etc... I daresay in a year she misses not a day. I am stunned to be in the company of someone so saintly.

We offer her a ride home as it begins to sprinkle. She tells us she lives just across the bridge on the north bank of the Sarthe. In turn she asks us if we would like her to come with us in order to have a guide in her small town. We would indeed love that. The three of us climb into the car and we two are shown the sights of Solesmes.

After a couple of hours, we find ourselves walking along a path opposite the Abbaye, marveling at the beauty of its architecture when Jehanne says in a very quiet, hospitable voice, "We are now in front of my house. Shall we stop in for tea and sweets?" This we did happily, sitting on her tiny front porch facing the impressive abbey, now bathed in the rays of the setting sun. We talked of many things. One thing I recall vividly was her telling us she had just returned from the royal necropolis at St. Denis Church, North of Paris, where she met many friends for their yearly gathering to recall the glory of the last real King of France, Louis XVI and his wife, Marie Antoinette.

Arrival of Anne and Carlson

The next week passes all too quickly in observing my surroundings, writing, and preparing for the arrival of Anne and Carlson and my son, Rusty. Anne tells me later, how they love having me arrive at L'Abri ahead of them. I take care of all the details, opening the house, working out any glitches with Michel, gathering the local gossip, buying the groceries, even preparing their first evening meal on the eve of their arrival. Anne adds: "Quelle luxe!" (such luxury!) I love doing it for such good friends.

With Anne and Carlson finally in residence, we spend two delightful days just enjoying the local delicacies, especially the fresh fruits and veggies of the season at every home-cooked meal. Anne and I love to cook together. We prepare a very special dinner for some of their new French friends, artists from Chinon, after spending the day in the country visiting antique shops 'til we drop.

Later on, at night, after the usual leisurely meal in the French style on Anne and Carlson's terrace we practice a new occupation: waiting until the summer sunglow disappears, allowing for the moon and all the celestial bodies to find center stage, as we sit back in our chairs to gaze at the sky. Just a reminder, it can be fairly light until nearly 11PM in July and early August in France. So, in order to fully appreciate the brilliance of the stars, one has to be a bona fide night owl. We three lean our heads back and watch for shooting stars. It is the first time since I saw Sputnik in the mid 1950s that I actually identify satellites moving across the night sky. At first, we get excited and think it is a shooter, but upon further examination, find that it moves slowly, much more slowly than a shooter, maintains a continuous path, and can be tracked for a comparatively long period. It must be a satellite. Thus, we spend our late evenings before retiring that summer of 1993 getting sore necks but happy all the same in the Valley of the Little Loir.

Chapter Six

Meeting Rochambeau: Comte and Maréchal

YES, THERE ARE THREE MORE excursions to come at the end of my
packed summer of 1993 in the Loire Valley and beyond. The first one is
close by in the Little Loir region. The second adventure takes me into
unknown territory south of the border in Spain. And the third brings me
back into France, just north of the Spanish border into Cathar country
of the 13th century. All three are life-changing for me. Happily, these
new landscapes are shared with my son, Rusty (Richard Hemenway
Dyer III), who has recently launched a film production business in
Washington DC. Near the end of July, he flies over to join me at the
country house where I have been writing for the last three weeks.

Rochambeau had written me earlier, as he promised, to say he was
not feeling well. He said he would call when he felt better. Then, we
would arrange a visit. I do not recall if I told him the date Rusty and
I would be leaving for Spain. I could only hope his timing would be
fortuitous and catch us before our departure. Time was running out.

The Fête Rochambeau and other Background Events

Rusty and I are about to meet the Rochambeau family at their
ancestral home. In order to discover what it is like to be at home with
the Rochambeau's 225 years ago as well as today (1993), I will tell you
how I met the present day 'Comte' (Count) Michel de Rochambeau
and how I came to visit this real life castle, once owned by his ancestor,

Général Jean-Baptiste-Donatien de Vimeur de Rochambeau, America's long-overlooked hero of America's War for Independence.

At the close of last summer, I picked up a brochure advertising a Sound and Light extravaganza named 'Fête Rochambeau' that took place at the Château de Rochambeau. That was the extent of my information on the subject. At that point I knew nothing of any Rochambeau, either living now or in the past.

During the intervening winter at home I finally took a moment to re-read the Rochambeau brochure. I checked the map and discovered that the Château Rochambeau had a post office address in Vendôme only about 40 minutes from my friends' house where I planned to write for three weeks.

Then I checked online to see what the Fête Rochambeau was all about last summer. According to the write-up, the château facade was used as a backdrop for the projected historic scenes of General Rochambeau and his military campaigns, primarily in America, beginning in 1780. The fête involved 1300 French and American re-enactors in period dress along with 3000 extras, 150 horses and riders, artillery units, boats, lighted fountains. All this created with 700 computer-regulated projectors with quadraphonic surround sound and fireworks topped it off. The French really know how to put on a show! I can hardly wait to see it in person. I add the Fête Rochambeau to my list for this coming summer.

Maybe some of you have witnessed a Sound and Light presentation in France. They have been producing them since the 1950s. I saw my first one at Versailles the summer of 1958, and while working for Air France, Public Relations, Fifth Avenue, wrote an article on the origin of Sound and Light performances three years later for the "New York Herald Tribune" and the "New York World Telegram and Sun" newspapers. My, does that ever date me! At any rate, now you can see why I am so eager to see the spectacle at the Rochambeau Château.

Ancient Origin of the Château de Rochambeau and the Derivation of the Plantagenet Royal House

What is needed was further research on Rochambeau, for I know nothing of the history surrounding this famous name and house. I found that the present-day Château de Rochambeau was built on the ruins of a 'château fort' (fortified castle) built and owned in the early 11th century by the great and powerful feudal lord, Fulk Nerra III (970-1040), Comte of Anjou, of the Angevin Royal family. It was he who built some 100 châteaux in the Loire Valley and reinforced several others, many of which I visited in the chapter on Château Hopping: Angers and Langeais (Not included here, but visited early on with Mado and Lucien), Amboise, Chinon and Loches. Fulk's son, Geoffrey II, Martel, Comte of Anjou, was followed in 12th century by his grandnephew, Geoffrey V Martel, Duke of Anjou, the first Plantagenet. My upline progenitors, all. So, I have a remote connection with the Rochambeau house.

I know this sounds complicated with details about feudal lords and their many castles from 1000 years ago, but stick with me, and I will bring you up to the present in a flash. That same Geoffrey V, Duke of Anjou, eventually became known as Plantagenet. The reason he was called Plantagenet came right out of thin air, you might say. Geoffrey had a habit of wearing a sprig of the 'gênet' flower in his cap. In old French that plant was called. 'planta-gênet' (gênet bush). We know it today as the shrub, Scotch Broom, or cytisus, genus name: 'genista' for you gardeners.

At any rate, the reason I am taking you off into the plant world is because it is truly relevant to my interest in Rochambeau's château. 'Planta-gênet' soon became Geoffrey's surname. Therefore, Geoffrey V Plantagenet as we know him today, is the founder of an entire royal lineage. And it came from a flower!

My Verified Connection to the Plantagenets

Well, now to find the connection between this flower, Rochambeau and myself we must go to a 30-year genealogical study compiled and published in 1974 by my mother's first cousin, Leslie Aulls Bryan, Ph.D. In a bound, hardcover volume, he traced our family back to the Plantagenets, the Fulks, Charlemagne and more. Voilà the connection I have stumbled upon with the Château Rochambeau. My ancestors built the earliest-known castle on the site where the Château de Rochambeau now stands!

So, in the winter of 1993, I wrote to the address on the Fête Rochambeau "Sound and Light Festival" brochure, inquiring if the event would be held the next summer as so many sound and light shows are in France. I waited.

In the interim, the name of Rochambeau was one I began to hear more and more in the Southbury, CT area, only ½ hour from my home, as area historians were planning a Rochambeau celebration of their own come spring.

When I had almost forgotten about my letter of inquiry to France, I received a very cordial hand-written response saying: "Chère Madame, I am very sorry, but the event of which you speak was a one-time thing". It was signed Michel de Rochambeau! Naturally, I was surprised to hear from the Comte himself, not even knowing there was a living descendant at that point. Even more astonishing, I discovered that he inhabited the same château where his famous ancestor, General Rochambeau had lived well over 200 years ago. I was ecstatic! What girl doesn't dream of meeting a Comte? Never mind, it is only on paper.

Correspondence with Michel, Comte de Rochambeau

I was thrilled to hear from the Comte, but at the same time I was sorry beyond words that I was a year too late to attend the Fête Rochambeau. If the truth be told, I was 'extrêmement désolée'! (extremely disappointed) with the news, especially since I had been in Tours within an hour of the Château Rochambeau at the time of the celebration last summer but had no idea that such a special event was being held there. All was not lost, however, as you shall see.

In the meantime, I attended the Rochambeau commemoration in Southbury, CT gathering souvenirs, brochures, and lots of historical information relating to Rochambeau's 'March to Victory' through our area. En route from Newport, R.I. to Yorktown, VA I even buy a Rochambeau tee shirt for the Comte!

As I stash away my Rochambeau memorabilia, I begin to hatch a plan. Since I would be writing for a three-week period near Vendôme in July that very summer, I wondered if the Comte would want me to 'drop by' and give him all the Rochambeau mementos I had collected. With this in mind, I pen the Comte a note suggesting just that. Again. I wait.

He writes back saying indeed he and his wife, (la Comtesse), would be pleased to receive me at the château in late July. The Comte promises to call me in July at my home-away- from-home in the valley of the Little Loir. He says that he will let me know when it will be convenient for him to visit, as he had not been feeling well.

Now, fast-forward to the end of July, and my son, Rusty Dyer, joins me for an extended religious pilgrimage over the Pyrenees into what they call 'Green Spain' (northern Spain) to Santiago de Compostela. That will be the far away part to this chapter.

Long-awaited Phone Call

Rusty is with us at L'Abri now. It is two days before our departure from the Little Loir region. It is nearing the close of my so-called 'uninterrupted, quiet period of writing', and I am literally crossing my fingers that Michel, Comte de Rochambeau, will call with the much-awaited invitation. Still, no word from him, but I remain expectant.

Then tonight, during dinner, the phone rings. It is Michel de Rochambeau asking for me. He hasn't forgotten! He is feeling much better after a hospital stay in Paris. He invites Rusty and me for cool drinks at the château tomorrow! I accept without hesitation.

I recount here my first visit with Comte Michel and his wife, Comtesse Madeleine. To make this visit more meaningful and one that will have a lasting effect, Rusty, a budding film producer, hopes to film the entire visit with the permission of the Comte.

Warm Reception Chez Rochambeau

We approach their driveway after a short ride. We see the small unimposing sign that reads, Rochambeau 'privée' (private). It is here at the foot of their drive that Rusty stops the car, jumps out and puts on his tie using the side view mirror. I fix my hair and straighten my casual designer dress, hoping I am properly attired to meet le Comte and la Comtesse de Rochambeau. We are both very excited and giddy as you may imagine, not knowing just what to expect, but knowing it will be wonderful!

Now, back in the car, Rusty begins driving down their long, unpaved roadway with no dwelling in sight. Oh, I should mention here that Rusty has a favorite filming technique that he uses when we are driving, and we don't want to miss an inch of scenery. He films nonstop while driving. He does this while holding the video camera outside the car window with his left hand while he drives with his right. He used this technique in Paris as we were driving from our hotel by the Louvre Museum one time a couple of years ago, all the way up to Montmartre. The results were fabulous! So, once again Rusty is filming as we glide along this long road that we know has to lead to the château, but we see nothing but countryside for ages. We are so full of suspense that we barely speak.

Along the Banks of the Little Loir

We pass through a tranquil, almost medieval, forest. Then, on our right, we observe some men fishing with simple bamboo poles along the bank of the Loir River, which we were following along the right side the roadway. It seems to me that we have already stepped back in time, seeing the fishermen emerge from the serene, bucolic landscape, as if from a Watteau painting. Apparently, the little Loir River flows through the Rochambeau property paralleling the road toward the château.

In France, unlike in America, they revere their rivers; they keep them pristine. This famous small river, Le Loir, has lovely green banks, often covered with wildflowers in season. There are often bike paths and picturesque centuries-old stone bridges, providing a place for picnics and quiet walks. They are not strewn with ugly factories, garbage heaps and castaway cars, as in America.

In contrast, today we observe this stretch of the Loir as idyllic in many ways, as it leads us back in history to a time of revolution on two continents. General Rochambeau played a part in both the American and French Revolutions. Please note that henceforth, I shall be referring to General Rochambeau as the 'Maréchal' as they do today within their family and to his present-day descendant, as the 'Comte'.

Now, returning in suspense to the long drive toward the Château de Rochambeau, we note the double line of tall shade trees that flank the road. I learn many of the details later but will sew them into our narrative as we go. These trees were originally planted here by the Maréchal. If one dies, it is to be replaced. The present-day Comte has done just that, thus perpetuating Maréchal's wishes. After the American and French Revolutions many 'trees of liberty' were planted in America and in France, gifted by various patriotic organizations between the two newly liberated countries.

Can you picture the Maréchal arriving home after a long, distant war campaign by carriage or on horseback, hurrying to greet his wife, Jeanne-Thérèse, after a long separation? There would have been a cloud of dust announcing his arrival as he galloped down the long 'allée' (alleyway of trees). I learn that at least once he brought a part of a regiment (some 150 soldiers) to be billeted in the cave across from the château, raising as even greater cloud of dust!

It was also along this unchanged road that Rochambeau returned home a free man, after being held for months in the infamous Conciergerie prison in Paris. Unlike thousands of other nobles and clergy, he escaped an appointment with the guillotine blade by one day! All the same, his spirit must have been heavy with the loss of many officers not as lucky as he, who also served in the American campaign but died under that same blade. Some of these were the Duc de Lauzun, the Prince de Broglie, Colonel Dillon, and Admiral D'Estaing. As the dirt road turns into crushed stone, the château comes into view at last.

The Maréchal and Comte Chez Rochambeau

Stepping out of their doorway to welcome us warmly are Comte Michel, handsome in his casual attire, and his diminutive wife, Madeleine, accompanied by their nine-year-old granddaughter, Virginie. The Comte offers to give us a tour before being invited into their private salon. We are very fortunate because their château is not open to the public except on rare occasion.

Conte Michel begins the tour in French noting the changes in architecture that the Maréchal made when he came to live here as a married man after 1749. Until then only the central structure was in existence. The Maréchal had two new "pavilions" (structures) built on either side, tripling the size of the façade; he raised the existing roof to match the additions, enlarged the windows adding mullions as well, achieving a harmony of style. The clock above is 18th century, and the bell, 15th century. The more formal front entrance that we cannot see, faces the Loir River with sloping grass down to the water's edge where a family of swans glides by. After this introductory word, we do an about face, leaving the main house behind us.

We step into the 18th century chapel where family services are held. It is freestanding within the chiseled–out limestone, with stained glass windows on the side facing the courtyard. Like most grand châteaux in the greater Loire Valley, this historic family home was constructed from limestone found on the property. Thus, the huge hollowed-out cave across from the house that shelters the chapel and other dependencies.

Crossing the courtyard, we enter the main house via the foyer, where our guide draws our attention to a small statue saying that, in February 1796, Thomas Jefferson said to James Madison, "The Count of Rochambeau has deserved more attention than he has received; why not set up his bust in your new capitol?" In reality, no bust was made, but there are four life size statues of Rochambeau in existence today. They are in Vendôme, Paris, Washington DC (in Lafayette Park opposite the White House), and Newport, Rhode Island. The model for these is here in the foyer where we stand.

Next, we move into the Blue Room, once the Grand Portrait Gallery, where the Comte mentions the sixteenth century ceiling. Then we see the full-length portrait of the Maréchal de Rochambeau wearing the 'cordon bleu' (the blue sash) of the order of "La Sainte Esprit" (The Holy Spirit), followed by the oval portrait of his mother, the Marquise, and the rectangular one of his father, the Marquis. We are stunned by the beauty of the next portrait. It is the Maréchal's wife, Jeanne-Thérèse Telles D'Acosta de Rochambeau. This lovely pastel is attributed to the French painter Maurice Quentin de la Tour. The Comte is quick to add that her beauty is well-known and that the painter did not need to enhance her aristocratic likeness to render it pleasing.

Nearby is the oval portrait of their son, Donatien, Vicomte de Rochambeau who accompanied his father to the United States on campaign. (1789-1783). Donatien was given the happy task of returning to France to tell King Louis XVI of Rochambeau's success at Yorktown. Later during a posting in the Caribbean (Haiti) he was captured in San Dominique and held in an English prison. His incarceration prevented him from being at his father's deathbed in 1807. Donatien eventually died in 1813 on the battlefield at the Battle of Nations in Leipzig, Saxony, Germany. It was a decisive battle during the Napoleonic Wars. Rochambeau and his son, Donatien, were but a link in the family continuum of military men of noble birth who served their king with distinction.

Moving along to the next salon, the Comte turns to the twin gouaches (since sold) painted by the artist Van Blarenberghe. The first represents 'The Siege of Yorktown' and depicts the taking of British Lord Cornwallis' last redoubts #9 and #10. This final assault on the part of American and French allies pushed Cornwallis' back to the sea, while the French fleet under Admiral de Grasse prevented the British from escaping by ship. The Comte points to Rochambeau in the painting and tells us that each of the hundreds of faces in the two paintings is unique.

The second gouache, on the left, is 'The Surrender of Yorktown'. Thousands of American and French soldiers form two long columns in preparation for the laying down of arms by the British. These two paintings (later sold by the Comte) were a gift from King Louis XVI to the Maréchal. The original pair, also commissioned by the King, hangs in the Palace of Versailles.

We turn to follow Madame la Comtesse Madeleine to see the 'fauteuil' (armchair) near her. She tells us that it once belonged to the Maréchal. It is a delicate Louis XV style chair upholstered in fine needlepoint. The needlepoint was re-created and hand stitched by the Comtesse herself, who recounts how much she loved doing it. She adds that she re-did all the furniture in this room in the original design. What a feat! When I ask if she still enjoys needlework, she replies she only has time now for her grandchildren's layettes.

Upstairs we pause to look at an aerial view of the château. Sitting in the front are two souvenir cannon (in singular military speak at the time) that the United States Government sent to the Maréchal after his triumphal return to France. Their stay here was short-lived, however. During the French Revolution Jeanne-Thérèse, in an effort to appease the revolutionaries, sent them to Vendôme. They were never seen again.

We enter the Maréchal's private bedchamber. Here again are beautiful examples of 18th century handwork. The story goes, once again revealed by the Comtesse, that when the Maréchal was in America supporting our battle for independence between 1780 and 1783, Madame Jeanne-Thérèse de Rochambeau created this fine work as a surprise for her husband. He was gone just long enough to see it completed on his return. The Maréchal and his wife were married for 59 years until his death in 1807. She was a capable, supportive 18th century wife who weathered his extended absences with dignity. By all accounts, they were very devoted to one another.

On the desk in this room is a photo of the present Comte with President George H. W. Bush the elder in the oval office in Washington. D.C. Bush is quoted as saying: "France was America's first friend in the world". Also, in the bedchamber is a near life size painting of George Washington commissioned by the Maréchal of the American artist Charles Wilson Peale. (Soon after our visit, it was sold at auction in c 1995). It had hung in that spot where we see it, for 220 years. While on campaign in America, Rochambeau learned some English so he could better communicate with his allies. Afterward he and Washington carried on their friendship by letter for years. Their ties were strong, each one eager to hear news of the other on opposite sides of the Atlantic. Following Rochambeau's death, eight years after his friend Washington, 'The Ladies of Mount Vernon' planted seedlings from trees planted at Washington's tomb, around the Maréchal's gravestone in France. Gifted were: two elms, two maples, two red bushes, and six ivy plants.

Military Orders and Honors

Now we are asked to look at a case of royal orders, state military honors, and medals that tell the story of the Maréchal's leadership qualities as appreciated by his king and later by his emperor. These memorabilia, now moved to a place of safety include: the military decoration known as the Cross of St. Louis, created by Louis XVI in 1693; the blue and white ribbon of the Society of the Cincinnati founded in 1783. (This medal is awarded to officers and their descendants even today, both American and French, who fought side by side in the American Revolution); the baton of Maréchal of France awarded to Rochambeau in 1791 by Louis XVI in recognition of service to his country. It is the highest military order in France (Thus, Rochambeau wears seven stars – much more than our American Generals' five stars; the gold ribbons of the Grand Officer of the Legion of Honor conferring knighthood, granted to him by Napoléon Bonaparte in 1803); and lastly the Maltese Cross, recognized by the sign of the dove worn with the 'cordon bleu' (blue sash) as in the portrait we saw earlier. It is known as the Royal Order of the 'Saint Esprit' (The Holy Spirit). It was created by Henri III in 1578 under the old regime and was limited to 100 recipients. It is the most prestigious order of knighthood in France. The medal is worn with the gold mantle at the back of the case.

Regarding the Society of the Cincinnati, curiously, it was named after the Roman farmer/senator/soldier, Cincinnatus, who was called to leave his fields and lead the Romans into battle. When he had successfully completed his mission, he wanted only to return to the peace and quiet of his farm. Does this story remind you of two founding members, American and French, who fit this model perfectly?

In the library, the Comte pauses to tell us the story of how his ancestor fared during the French Revolution. It is one thing to survive and actually be on the winning side in one revolution and then to return home across the Atlantic to be caught up in another revolt of epic proportions in which nobles were persecuted. Six years after his homecoming the Maréchal (then still a General) was imprisoned in the Conciergerie in Paris, thinking that each day would be his last. Many of his friends, military comrades and relatives lost their heads to the Guillotine blade. Some even fled France if they were able to do so early on. Rochambeau wrote letters seeking his release but to no avail. Finally, one day he was called with a small group of men and women to climb into the crude wagon that bore the unlucky ones to the "Place de la Révolution". The Comte was fairly whispering this into my ear as he told me that, as Rochambeau was to climb into the wagon himself, there was a lady near him, and he offered her his hand as she mounted the steps saying: "Ápres vous Madame'" ("After you my lady'). At that precise moment the guard called a halt to the dispatching of the unfortunates to their untimely deaths and said: "C'est finis pour aujourd'hui. À demain". ("That is enough for today. Come back tomorrow"). And with those words Rochambeau was rescued from a horrible demise. The killing was stopped that day, and the revolutionaries themselves were eventually guillotined. "La Terreur" (the terror) of the French Revolution was finished! Rochambeau was saved from the devilish blade by one person and one day of grace! Not a coincidence, by my reckoning!

There is one more memorable anecdote from the tour that day. The Comte showed us his ancestor's Memoirs, his fine library, and some memorabilia – one that tickles my funny bone. It is a medal with a story. Engraved on the medal is Mother England giving birth to her baby, America, which she in turn is trying to kill. France is shown saving the baby! I love the symbolism.

We exit the house and cross the courtyard again to enter the 'RochamBar' a clever play on words! There we see young Virginie, the granddaughter of the Comte, and Comtesse, perched on a bar stool with a phone at her ear. With a sparkle in her eye she is saying: Allô! Allô!

With this moment of comedy, our tour is complete. We follow Comte Michel, Comtesse Madeleine and Virginie, into their private salon for a cool drink and conversation. Rusty puts down his camera to thank the Comte and Comtesse for their indulgence in letting him film this once in a lifetime experience. After a while Virginie beckons Rusty to go out to feed the swans that are silently swimming in the Loir, cooling themselves this hot July afternoon.

Comte Michel points out to me a two-volume boxed set of books:

"Rochambeau's Military Campaign in America". As a Commissioner on the Connecticut Governor's Advisory Commission on American and Francophone Cultural Affairs, I was aware of this fine set of books detailing his ancestor's troop movements in America. I passed up an opportunity to purchase them at a much-discounted price several months ago, thinking I had no real need to own it. It was not until later, following a decade of enjoyable and fruitful correspondence with the Comte, that I realized I would indeed need these treasured books as essential reference material for the biography I would soon write.

I began to write a biography of the life of Rochambeau along with his military campaign in America. Title: "Rochambeau, Washington's Ideal Lieutenant; a French General's Role in the American Revolution". But I do digress. This is simply a peek into the future, for as of my first visit chez Rochambeau, I had not a single thought of such a project.

Virginie and Rusty: Swans and Song

Virginie and Rusty re-enter the salon with smiles on their faces. Rusty shares with us that that Virginie has taught him a French children's folk song about her ancestor, Maréchal Rochambeau. She sings the ditty for me too. It went something like this: "Rochambeau, Rochambeau,

Ton bateau, ton bateau (Your boat, your boat)
Rochambeau, si tu savais, (If you only knew)
Rochambeau, si tu savais (If you only knew)
Rochambeau, Rochambeau,
Ton bateau n'était pas beau!" (Your boat was not beautiful!!)

It is charming to hear Virginie sing this children's song, even if it berates her ancestor. Our wonderful, informative visit is at an end. And we have it all on Rusty's tape. The Rochambeau's accompany us to our car. And Virginie waves a goodbye to us saying: "I hope the video turns out well."

Little did I know that afternoon spent in the company of the Rochambeau family, that in ten years hence I would be deep in research on my first book, a biography/military history: *Rochambeau, Washington's Ideal Lieutenant, A French General's Role in the American Revolution.*

As we slowly turn our car away from the imposing silhouette of the château, we are so very grateful to the Comte Michel and Comtesse

Madeleine for generously giving of their time and their privacy to show us the wonders of the Château de Rochambeau. Rusty and I agree this is a day to be savored for a lifetime.

Michel, Comte de Rochambeau, and I, together at our first meeting at the Château de Rochambeau in the summer of 1993. Following this pivotal day, we corresponded until I received his last hand- written letter in April of 2007.

Chapter Seven

Pilgrimage to Santiago de Compostela: Basque Coast, Biarritz and Pied de Port

FOLLOWING OUR BEAUTIFUL AFTERNOON WITH the Rochambeau's at their family château, Rusty and I make the transition to our next adventure on foreign shores. It begins the day after our visit with the Rochambeau's. We shall be crossing over the Pyrénées into Spain. We know by now, that when we travel in Europe, we can no longer be cavalier about the unexpected wonders that we find along our way. Therefore, as I learned in my logics class at Sweet Briar College, I am prepared to expect the unexpected! And I welcome the serendipity of it all! So, hang on to your hats. Here we go full tilt toward the southwest corner of France and in Northern Spain.

We drive through much of southern Aquitaine and into Basque country for old time's sake. My son and I have ventured into this area of southwestern France at least once during another trip shortly after I began my studies in Tours. Soon we are driving along France's picturesque Basque Coast.

When I think of Basque country, I recall with fondness La Côte Basque restaurant in New York City. In my day, it was an elegant restaurant I used to favor for a special occasion, as it was on East 55th close to my Air France Public Relations office at 666 Fifth Ave. Lunching there, comfortably seated on the red leather banquette, my Francophile friends and I were fully aware we were worshipping at as the Temple of French cuisine.

Today, however, we are exploring the real thing. Rusty and I spend an evening in Biarrritz, where we ingest a sumptuous dinner of 'fruits de mer' (seafood) under the stars high on a rocky cliff overlooking the Bay of Biscay. We choose the Bouillabaisse with the requisite Rouille sauce, croutons and grated cheese. The various shellfish are piled on a tall, tiered serving dish set for us in the center of the table. During the meal, strolling Spanish singers serenade us at our table with guitars to our hearts' content. We take our time savoring succulent dinner until 11:30PM. It is a breathtaking setting as the moon rises, shedding its reflected light over the sea.

We spend this first night on the Basque Coast in Anglet at the Hotel/ Spa Atlanta in the Pyrénées-Atlantique department of France where our rooms overlook the sea. In the morning Rusty swims in the Bay, and I 'take the spa waters' as they say. Refreshed, we drive on through St. Jean de Luz and pick up an easterly direction to St-Jean-Pied-de-Port where we have reservations for the night at the Hôtel des Pyrénées. From there will follow the Pilgrim 'Camino' (route) in general, and specifically for us, the trail taken by Queen Aliénor's father, William X, Duke of Aquitaine to Santiago (St. James) de Compostela (the starry field), Spain. It is in part, for this reason, that we are here, to retrace the 1137 route of our ancestor.

St.-Jean-Pied-de-Port, foot of the Pyrénées

Pilgrims have been tripping through St-Jean-Pied-de-Port for over a thousand years. Even in the 21st century, if one chooses to go on foot as many do, it is a difficult trip. The pilgrims relied on the hospitality of strangers such as in St-Jean-Pied-de-Port to feed, house, and even clothe them on their journey. The ultimate destination for pilgrims passing through France entails the crossing of the Pyrénées mountain range. The faithful walkers are undaunted by the heights and stormy weather while tramping narrow, precipitous, often icy paths.

The pilgrim trails in Europe begin in the north, east and west, funneling into France and merge into one or two paths at the foot of the Pyrénées where we now at St. Jean-Pied-de-Port. From here, all trails lead to Santiago. Their ultimate goal, like ours, lies some 500 miles distant at the northwestern corner of Spain hard by the Atlantic coast. This means crossing the breadth of what is euphemistically called, 'Green Spain, into Galicia'.

In the Footsteps of Charlemagne and St. Jacques

As we prepare to cross the Pyrénées, I am reminded of much earlier ancestor, "Charlemagne" (Charles the Great), King of the Franks, who, in 813, the year prior his death, heard a voice in a vision say: "This is the path of Saint James, and I am that apostle, servant of Christ, son of Zebedee, brother of John the Evangelist whom Herod slew, appointed by God's grace to preach His law: Look you, my body is in Galicia, but no man knoweth where, and the Saracens oppress the land. The starry way signifies that you shall go at the head of a host and free that land, and after you, peoples in pilgrimage will follow until the end of time." And so, the story goes, in his effort to unite Europe, Charlemagne did vanquish the Saracens from (Galicia) Northern Spain. He literally chased them off the 'Finis Terre' in Galicia.

It is also said that Charlemagne walked out into the water, and a boat appeared, the same mystical boat that centuries earlier had carried the body of Saint James from Palestine. His body was not found until long after, as the result of yet another vision. This vision was the gift to Pelagius (360-420), a hermit/theologian in the mountains of Galicia. Suddenly he saw a new star in the sky accompanied by strange celestial music.

Pelagius related his vision to his bishop, Theodomir (413-474), King of the Osthrogoths, and to the local people. They all turned out to dig directly under the star until they discovered a stone tomb. In it lay a body, with head intact, sweetly perfumed, and beside it lay a letter that read:

"Here lies Santiago, son of
Zebedee and Salome, brother of

Saint John the Apostle whom Herod
beheaded in Jerusalem. He came by
sea, borne by his disciples....".

Upon this spot the original church was built, and a town grew up beside the church. The town was named Santiago de Compostela.

Not everyone puts credence in this story. It is an explanation of a questionable happening. Why else build a church in such a lonely and desolate spot where no one lived? Usually churches are built because there are people living in an area who want a place to worship. In this case the church came first. Because of the church's proximity to the ocean, the scallop shell became the symbol for St. James and for his faithful pilgrims.

Another name for St. James is St. Jacques, so I feel compelled to mention that growing up, my mother, who was an excellent cook, prepared a fancy dish named 'Coquilles St. Jacques' (St. Jacques shells) for special luncheons. She used real scallop shells in which to bake and serve the savory scallops. I guess I was keyed into the name all those many years ago.

It is not a secret that my son and I are not roughing it as many pilgrims do. We do not wear sackcloth, shirt of hair, nor do we walk barefoot. Instead we find our lovely 4-star hotel, the Hotel des Pyrénées with a 5-star chef. The address is Place du Général- de- Gaulle. This 'auberge' (hotel) is run by a father and son Arrambide and has been the resting place for pilgrims beginning their trek over the Roncesvalles Pass.

For Rusty, the stay is most memorable. Tonight, he relishes his first ultra-gourmet meal prepared by a world-renowned chef. Rusty orders the 'fillet de boeuf' (steak filet) with all the trimmings, and finishes with a specialty of the house, a lovely pudding of fresh raspberries smothered in a Sabayon sauce. After this gastronomical apogee, he raves that he is already in heaven, and the journey is just barely underway.

Following a good night's sleep with the windows open to let in the cool, mountain breeze, we set out the next morning to explore new territory. Just eight kilometers from the Spanish border, we start by walking around St-Jean-Pied-de-Port, capital of Lower Navarre, on the northern side of the Pyrénées. We know that Navarre has a checkered history of being fought over by Spain and France since the early Middle Ages. Strolling around the town, we take in the sense of the long history that surrounds us here. Along the Route St. Jacques (Saint James) we look to our left to see the 'Ville Haute' (upper town) perched on the hill with the ancient citadel and church high above. We come to the river Nive that bisects the town and cross over via the 'Vieux Pont' (the old bridge).

From the bridge, we see the picturesque street of very old homes and notice that many of the windowless front doors display the sign of the scallop shell. The tired pilgrims know they will receive a safe, warm bed for the night with food for sustenance graciously supplied. The scallop shell signifies that the residents of these ancient homes through past centuries, as well as today, are ready and willing to aid the many Christian pilgrims who pass through St-Jean-Pied-de-Port. The old Navarre homes have wooden balconies that lean out over the Nive River. The ancient bell tower can be seen far above the river with the mountains fading into the mist of morning. Rusty photographs the interesting doorways, each one slightly different from the preceding one. Some are quite colorful and all as welcoming as promised.

This summer (2018) as I edit this chapter once again, our Cousin, Trip Stevens, is walking the Route St. Jacques on foot as we speak. Nothing happens by chance. I feel that I am with him as he walks. Surely Cousin Trip has marveled at the charming town of St. Jean-Pied-de-Port we are seeing this morning.

In my research I discover, much to my chagrin, that St-Jean-Pied-de-Port was flattened by Aliénor's son, Richard Lionheart, in 1177, prior to his crusade to Jerusalem. I can only hope that he took up the cross to assuage sins he committed here. Not always happily, I continue to meet my grandmother of 29 generations ago and her family at the unexpected turn.

Let us briefly consider Christian pilgrimage throughout France and wider Europe over the last 1200 years. In my short term of study, I reckon back to my first summer in Tours while on a comprehensive visit of the old section of the city, our first stop was the Basilica of St. Martin. There were religious relics stowed safely in the bowels of the church. Because of the rich history of St. Martin and the relics, this church became a destination on the pilgrims' progress through Europe. The idea of pilgrimage piqued my interest, so I purchased a book on pilgrimage routes in France and was off on another tangent to learn as much as I could about what continues to lure travelers to pay homage to certain saints whose memory is held dear today. The obvious reason is because of the hardships they faced making these difficult trips so long ago. Of course, we know many were martyred along the way. Even more reason to follow reverently in their footsteps.

William X, Duke of Aquitaine's Pilgrimage to Santiago

Three hundred years after the Charlemagne episode mentioned above, there was an event that took place in 1137, concerning the father of Aliénor of Aquitaine, William X, Duke of Aquitaine. When Aliénor was but a teenager, her father set off for Santiago to assuage his sins. It is because of our connection to Aliénor's lineage that Rusty and I are traveling this ancient route today. For centuries the preferred mode of travel, especially on pilgrimage, has been by foot. One really learns the meaning of penance through suffering in this way, not so much on horseback. I often pictured Aliénor of Aquitaine traveling alongside her father, William the X, Duke of Aquitaine, as together they crossed the Pyrénées on horseback with their small entourage. I have longed to do this trip on horseback, but for obvious reasons had to give up the idea. I find out later that Aliénor, although she accompanied her father in their lands, did not travel with him to Santiago on this fateful journey.

In the early 1100s the Dukes of Aquitaine were the wealthiest of men, having dominion over more than half of present-day France. Aliénor's father was likened unto a king, but under the ancient regime of the feudal system, he was, nonetheless, subservient to the King of France, Louis, VI. As a Christian, William was also subservient to the Pope, with whom he often had a contentious relationship. In 1137, when Aliénor, was 15, the Duke was forced to set aside his ungodly ways and to accept Jesus under the unrelenting guidance of Bishop Bernard de Clairvaux.

Duke William was a changed man after that experience and decided to make amends by taking up the scallop shell and walking stick to go on pilgrimage to Santiago. He and his small band of protectors trudged over the Pyrénées Mountains braving all kinds of weather. By Easter week they were within a few miles of the cathedral at Santiago de Compostela. They were eager to discard their boots and rest their sore feet at long last.

They made one last stop near running water and were hoping to have a drink and catch some fish. They had been warned the water was not safe. But William insisted on eating a fish and became very ill. He carried on the next day saying that he would walk on no matter how sick he felt. His body deteriorated at an alarming rate, ending in a horrible death for the poor Duke. His men carried his body into the cathedral and laid him to rest beside the tomb of Saint James, where they say, it lies today. (No one I know so far, including Cousin Trip, Rusty and myself, can locate his burial spot.) Duke William's trip certainly had an unexpected outcome. William had summoned just enough strength to prepare a will stating that his daughter, Aliénor, should wed King Louis VI's son, Louis, as speedily as possible in order to safeguard life and limb and most of all, his dukedom.

So, true to my quest of following in the footsteps of Aliénor, (and her father), Rusty and I, too, take up the scallop shell and hit the road to Santiago. We are both aware of the enormous reputation and purpose of such as trip, and we prepare heart and head to undertake the challenge.

Shortly we cross into Spain and follow the route over the mountains. In each of my trips to the Loire Valley, as well as today in Spain, I consider myself a modern-day pilgrim as I trace the steps of my ancestors from France into Northern Spain. Rusty and I make a pact that we will make it to the altar of St. James.

Our first stop on the Camino (road) is the pass at Roncesvalles, high in the Pyrénées. We barely leave France behind, and we are in Navarre Province, Spain, at an altitude of 5,000 feet at the highest. It was here that King Charlemagne and his army were ambushed by Christian Basques on their way back to France after a fierce fight against the Saracens in Spain. The King's nephew, Roland, who was leading the rear guard, was killed in the fighting. The epic poem, more a heroic myth, the "Song of Roland", is still read by students of French. The spot where this routing occurred in 877 is remembered today bypassing pilgrims like us. We pause to recall what happened here so long ago, to another of our French forebear, Holy Roman Emperor, Charlemagne.

We descend from the heights of the Pyrénées enjoying the delicious vista on left and right. The mountains are varied in height, are not snow capped at this season, but are tall peaks of majestic beauty. We rave about these mountains that are so little known by travelers to France, and yet so accessible. On the southern side we descend to the city of Pamplona, well known for the annual running of the bulls. We try to picture the craziness of those who come to take part in the death-defying challenge of running side by side, hopefully not under the hooves of the rampaging bulls as they race wildly through the narrow streets of this town. We do not linger.

Westward on the Camino

The pilgrim trail, the Camino, takes us westward now toward Santiago. We follow the sunburst signs that will lead us to our destination. This is called Green Spain, but in mid-summer we do not see any sign of green growth. We see desert-like stretches on both sides of the road. We are going to make up time here, as the way becomes flat, interspersed with rolling hills. After a while, I point out to Rusty, my superb driver, that I see something strange on top of the next rolling hill. It is black and very large. As we near it we make out the image of a huge bull cutout, probably made of steel. It is perched high on the hill with no explanation. No words of an advertisement even. We wonder and drive on.

We pass some walkers here and there, either alone or in small groups, as the Camino to Santiago crosses our road. That is to say that the walkers follow the ancient Camino, unpaved whereas we travel on fine black asphalt. The walkers look shaggy for the most part, with backpacks or small rucksacks, many men with long beards, most with a walking stick and a scallop shell around their neck.

We drive through the large city of Burgos next, a town of much charm. We know there is a Parador here. A Parador is a government-owned luxury hotel, formerly a palace, a monastery or other prominent building, long out of use, but of beauty and history worth preserving. We pass what looks like a Parador, a long, tall gray building with an elegant, sculptured façade. We also see the strikingly beautiful and decorative Gothic Cathedral of Burgos. It is hard to miss with its tall twin towers with pointed spires, accompanied by many shorter spires behind. Construction of this cathedral was begun in 1221 and was not fully completed until 200 years later. Sadly, we cannot take the time to visit it, in order to make or next stop on time. Rusty and I do not discover until much later, that our ancestor, Queen Eleanor of Castille (aka Eleanor of England), wife of King Alphonso VIII of Castille, is buried here, next to her husband in Burgos in the Cistercian Monasterio de Santa Maria Real de Las Huelgas. Queen Eleanor of Castille was the daughter of Queen Aliénor of Aquitaine and her second husband, King Henry of England. I write more on Queen Eleanor of Castille in the final chapter. For now, we choose to go on to Leon where we will find our Parador and reserved rooms for the night.

It is a long and desolate drive with very little in the way of remarkable landmarks. Once, we drive off the road to pass through a tiny, ancient village. Everything is gray here. The sand, the hills, the old and crumbling buildings of which there are very few. The town appears to be clinging to a rock outcropping. It is a bland landscape of gray. There is no one in the street. We pass what appears to be an old church. There is no sign of life at all. We leave quickly to return to our dull route.

Imagine what this path is like for the walker in this kind of landscape under the burning summer sun. He or she has plenty of time to contemplate life and the sins they are hoping to assuage while suffering through this 500-mile trail of trial. There are hostels along the way, with simple accommodations for the hikers. I am so glad, once again, that we are driving after all. Even on horseback it must be grueling in the heat by day followed by cold nights. The distractions are few whether walking or driving.

Our Parador at Leon

At last we come to Leon and find our Parador San Marcos. It is indeed a sparkling diamond in the sand for us and is the epitome of beauty and fine taste. 'Quelle surprise!' (what a surprise) It is a former monastery from the Middle Ages. I describe it as very 'old world', with marble floors, huge paintings on the walls, heavy carved wooden doors, an impressive cloister on a huge scale lined with ancient sarcophagi. Lots of history with atmosphere. Our rooms at San Marcos overlook a large labyrinth, formal gardens and the huge square.

The next day we are off again. The landscape changes into fields of grain. We see a somewhat shocking sight along the road – a man cutting his wheat by hand and his wife tedding it by hand. The resulting rows are twisted and irregular. I have not seen this since my first trip to France in 1958 when the famers could be seen pitching the hay by pitchforks onto haystacks of the Monet type.

When we finally see some sunflower fields, the flowers are stunted, compared to those in the Valley of the Loire. We learn that unemployment in this area of Spain is 20%, yet we are heading into what is called 'the breadbasket' of Spain. Clearly there is little regular work here outside the cities, and we are headed for one and getting closer. Santiago, here we come! We begin to see church steeples surrounded by small towns; tile red tile roofs all the same. These wheat fields waving! We pass a lady with folded table and folded chairs on her head! She must be going to a party. It is getting exciting. People are all headed toward Santiago.

Sunday, July 25, High Feast Day at the Cathedral

This Sunday is the high, holy day in Santiago. When the feast day of Saint James, July 25, falls on a Sunday, it is the highest feast day of the summer. My friend, Mado, back in Tours, has been telling me about this day for years. Our suspense is growing as we approach the famous city. Rusty and I will see it at its apogee.

We arrive on Saturday evening, July 24. The crowds are everywhere as we inch our way to our hotel near the center. We are happy to have a room at the Hotel Europa on Montero Rios. It is a second-floor walk-up. 'No problema'. We look out our window onto the busy street. People are here from all around the world. Lots of young guys and girls wearying backpacks and the requisite scallop shells – mostly college kids, I think. We do not take much time to settle in, just want to see the Cathedral and wander the streets a little to see the sights.

We see all manner of things we have never seen before. There are people eating in the streets, either at restaurants with outdoor terraces, or travelers munching on trail mix or dried fruit. We round a corner and see a person covered in white from head to toe, perhaps chalk dust, not sure, posing like a statue on a pedestal and plinth. We see revelers dressed in Middle Ages style, spitting fire from their mouths high into the air, acrobats on swings and high wires as darkness falls. Every corner brings new spectacles.

Very late, in the dark, we walk the few blocks to gaze at the Cathedral in the central square: Plaza de la Azabache. It is bathed in soft light from tiptop crosses to front steps where we stand. The first church here was ordered by Alphonso II in 897; by 997 Moorish Hordes razed it and the town that had grown up around it. They saved the tomb of St. James, as they feared harming it. The bronze bells were moved to Cordoba and were eventually returned to find their present home in the Cloisters of the Cathedral.

Ground was not broken for the building we see today until 1075 when construction began under the reign of King Alfonso VI of Castille, with the patronage of Bishop Diego Pelaez. It was built mostly of granite, according to the same plan as the monastic brick church of Saint Sernin, one of the greatest Romanesque edifices in France. The last stone was laid in 1122.

Some years later the bishopric was upgraded to the archbishopric of Santiago. The first bishop was the dynamic Diego Gelminez who remained in place for 40 years until his death in 1140. His reign as bishop is said to be the Golden Age of Santiago. Gelminez oversaw the Romanesque period, to include the towers, the Cathedral cloisters and the palace.

According to my reading, "In 1188 Master Mateo took over the construction of the cathedral and added one of its most spectacular features – the Gloria Portico, which is its main entrance. It is decorated with 200 figures representing the Apocalypse, and the figure of Saint James, welcoming the pilgrims at the end of their journey. The Basilica was finally consecrated in 1211 before King Alfonso IX" of Leon. Architecturally, the Cathedral at Santiago reflects several periods: Romanesque, Gothic, Plateresque and Neo-classical.

We take some time to reflect on our trip thus far and what it means to each of us to be here. For me, it is a quiet time of prayer, being thankful for a safe trip and being here together, mother and son. It is a privilege to stand here on holy ground where kings and paupers have stood over the ages. Over 1100 years have passed since this great cathedral was built. We are humbled to follow in the footsteps of countless saints and sinners who came before us. We are exhausted, so we make our way to the hotel and crash.

It is Sunday morning, July 25, 1993, the high holy day of the passion of St. James. We rise in great expectation of the day's events. After a continental breakfast, we head out early. Having walked to the cathedral last night, we know it is not far. There is a large, open, cobblestone square in front of the church. Pilgrims are gathering here, slowly at first. We know we must wait until the church doors will be opened to let us in. I do not know if it will be traditional church inside, even if there will be a mass said. We shall just have to wait.

Soon the numbers in the square increase exponentially and fast. We are beginning to feel squashed on all sides. I am not used to being in a large crowd like this and begin to feel a little claustrophobic. Even wonder what if there were to be an accident or the like, we would be trampled. Rusty is fine; I am uncomfortable. We know that today being the High Holy Day of the Catholic Church, Juan Carlos I, King of Spain since 1975, and his wife, plus Mario Soares, President of Portugal and his wife will be in attendance. But where will they be? We do not know. Our Spanish is not that great, so we do not know whom to ask.

We are moving ever so slowly toward the front steps of the grand three-spire cathedral. We are walking up the steps. Now I see what I did not find last night. To the left of the main entrance is the place where pilgrims fit their hand into a well-worn deep brass/stone handprint. It is to give solace to the walkers or riders like us and to prove we made it. It is a long, long tradition that we follow along with all the others.

Before we know it, we are being pushed into the church itself. There are crowds ahead of us. Everyone is standing. Somehow, I thought there would be seats, but that would limit the numbers, so we stand toe to heel craning our necks and stretching our heads to glimpse the altar I have read so much about. It is heavy with burnished, shining gold everywhere.

The 'piece de resistance' (main attraction), moving slowly from left to right and back again at the front of the altar, is the giant and I mean GIANT, censer. It must be taller than I am and much wider. I have read it is used only on this day. It is called 'Botafumeiro'. It emits incense amid the congregation. It weighs 117 lbs. and measures 4'9". It is not larger than I am after all. It swings back and forth 65 feet above us propelled at 52 mph by ropes and pulleys. I am not Catholic, but I have heard this custom began in order disperse or deaden the odor of the pilgrims who have been walking for days without bathing.

Sitting behind the censer are the King of Spain and his wife and the President and his wife of Portugal, just as we hoped. There they are in full view. This is our first time being in close proximity to royalty and world leaders. Rusty and I are in complete and utter awe in this place. The respectful silence is appreciated. We spot young men in white, dressed as acolytes or host bearers. They are going through the crowd methodically bearing the Host to us all. This is a touching surprise. Rusty and I receive the Host together. This is the ultimate gift that we can receive at the end of our journey. Think how much this means to those who really struggled to reach this spot. Surely, the love of our Lord fills this place.

We leave the main chancel of the church and walk around wherever we can, looking at the bounty of beauty that surrounds us here. We leave the church and explore the exterior as well. There is a gift shop where I purchase a small plate and a spoon to commemorate our visit. Once again in the square, we look for a place to stand to get a better look at the balcony where the dignitaries we just saw will be received quite soon. Again, the crowd swells as worshipers leave the church to wait in the square to hear their address. At my request, Rusty and I leave and walk back to our hotel well before they appear. We turn on the TV for a much closer look. The two ruling couples are still in the church. The camera's eye view brings them into focus larger on the screen than in real life. We watch them as they come to the balcony, waving to the crowds. The King and the President give short speeches, and it is all over. Later we go out to eat with the street revelers.

To be sure, we are amazed at the activity we see in the streets of Santiago. This High Holy Day in Spain is all and more than we expected. Of upmost importance, are our hearts changed by this symbolic march to the Cathedral where pilgrims have come since the 800s. Would we have been more humbled and more comprehending of the trip had we walked or bicycled as did our friends?

For me, it was the moment when I placed my palm in the well-worn spot at the Cathedral entrance, the same as thousands of pilgrims before me. And it was during the crush of believers inside the church that an acolyte, robed in white, suddenly appeared before me offering me to partake of the 'Host' with a multitude of other worshipers. These two events, to me, symbolize the unbroken chain of believers over the millennia. Yes, I stood near the rear of the church, not able to move any closer to the altar, after covering hundreds, even thousands, of miles from my home in Connecticut, to pay homage at the foot of the Cross.

Northern Coast of Spain

The next day we drive toward 'Finisterre' (land's end), as it was known in early Roman times, and end up in a small seaside village between Finisterre and La Coruna. For the Pilgrim, we have reached the end point of our adventure. Near here is the point of disembarkation where St. James's body was brought ashore so long ago. It is the westernmost point of Galicia, just north of the border with Portugal, of that we are sure.

We explore the area near the water and find a small restaurant with outdoor seating. All the tables are filled. We will stand and wait for a free one. As we wait, we spot a couple at a nearby table trying to catch our eye. They hail us to join them. How sweet is that? We go over and introduce ourselves all around. They are from Denmark. We converse in halting English and enjoy ourselves while deciding what to choose from the menu. They have just received their main course and encourage us to try it. It is fresh octopus with a dipping sauce. We always like a challenge, so we order it too. We try 'fruits de mer' (seafood) of a new variety, one we rarely see at home. It is different indeed. It is a bit tough to chew, but tasty. Eating an octopus' suction cups is not the norm for us, and I am here to remark on this new experience and to remember the kindness of the Danish couple.

The small harbor here is quiet with a long wharf where tourists like us walk to the end and listen to the breaking waves. Time to catch our breath and reconnoiter before traveling north and east into France via the Basque country. Rusty stands at my side as we have reached our farthest goal on this trip, having driven the breadth of Northern Spain from the Pyrénées to the Atlantic. It is a lovely spot from which to gaze westward and imagine our faraway home in America on the other side of the Atlantic Ocean.

We drive back to France, retracing our route, for the most part, stopping in Burgos for a night, then on to Pamplona, and the Pyrénées mountains once again. My son and I are eager to pursue our next quest, Cathar Country of SW France.

Chapter Eight

Cathar Catharsis

IT IS STILL THE SUMMER of 1993. As promised, there are more adventures to fit in before Rusty and I fly home. I am pursuing a tangent, suggested to me this spring from four different angles. The first came from Maryse. She wrote me of her recent trip to the Languedoc region of France, thinking it might be of interest to me. The Languedoc region lies south and east of Toulouse to the border of Spain and the Mediterranean. The reason for her visit was to focus on the history of the Cathars in the Albigensian Crusade, which took place in the early 1200s.

The second tangent came by way of an article on the same subject in "Smithsonian Magazine". It was given to me by a Macedonian acquaintance who spent the better part of last year in the Languedoc. Third, I was given another clipping, this time from the "New York Times", on the reinstating of ancient languages in France. Not coincidentally, one such dialect was Occitan, native tongue of the Cathars. The fourth angle came via my librarian friend, Jacques. Normally, I file away these bits of French travel info for future use, never knowing for sure when, how, or if, I will have the opportunity to follow up on them. I just know they will fit into my life puzzle somehow. Well, there will be no putting off this Cathar subject. Four nudges are enough to pique my interest this summer.

Rusty and I cross the Pyrénées back into France, and I am harkening back to the days when our ancestors were obliged to make the journey on mule back. Horses were not fit for the trip in inclement weather as the trails are very narrow and precipitous. In those days it took at least four days to make it to the other side. By contrast Rusty and I are buzzing along the modern roads, through tunnels and enjoying the view as we spiral down the last of the mountain roads into France. I am reading the guidebook as fast as I can, trying to decide where to commence our Cathar quest.

Our hub in Cathar Country is Mirepoix

I choose Mirepoix, southwest of Carcassonne, not far from Albi, for our center of operations. After a four-hour drive from St. Jean Pied-de-Port, my son and I arrive there and settle in comfortably at the Hotel Commerce in the middle of the small medieval town. Mirepoix is an intact 'bastide', or medieval village, fortified by its surrounding walls. The central square is edged with half-timbered houses supported by wooden arcades. The beams of the House of the Consuls are decorated with the original hand-carved heads of men and animals.

The region of Languedoc and the Cathars is squeezed in between Aliénor's Aquitaine on the west, its neighbor to the south – Arragon, Andorra, Catalonia (Spain) alongside the Pyrénées with the Mediterranean on the east. To the north is Carcassonne. It is an intense land of sadness, secrets and mystery. Referring to the article from Smithsonian Magazine, I find the story of the Cathars concerns an "ordeal by fire" and a "monster" weapon called the "bad neighbor". The "ordeal by fire" refers to the method by which many of the Cathars met their death, and the bad neighbor, "la malvoisine", is one of many medieval weapons used against them.

Who were the Cathars?
What was the Albigensian Crusade?

The terms, Cathar Crusade or Albigensian Crusade are relatively new to me but, suffice it to say that the Cathar story under any name encompasses the most savage of medieval wars. From my ensuing study, I determine that the appellation, Cathar, which has its derivation from the Greek word meaning "the purified", was rarely used in the Middle Ages, but has come into more frequent usage as a result of the book published in 1953, "Die Kathayer", by Amo Borst. It refers to a heretical, though still Christian, sect. Some say it is the forerunner of the Protestant Reformation gone awry.

Who were the Cathars, when did they live, what were their beliefs and what could possibly have happened to them that would spark our interest today? Let me quote the article I am studying in order to set down the Cathar beliefs. "The Cathars were dualists holding that all things on Earth were evil, and therefore, the creation of the devil who, in the strict version of the faith, was as eternal and powerful as God. The Cathars rejected the Old Testament, whose wrathful Jehovah was actually Satan in disguise. They denied the Catholic sacraments, including baptism at birth, marriage, confession and the Eucharist. Since all matter was evil, Cathars refused to believe that Christ had ever assumed a human body: his apparent incarnation was an illusion used by God to instruct the faithful. The only prayer Cathars said was the Lord's Prayer, which they recited as often as 40 times a day."

After reading several more accounts of the Cathar debacle, I find the British author, John Sumption's account: "The Albigensian Crusade", to be the most comprehensive. According to Sumption "The Cathars believed that all men and women were composed of a corrupt body; a spirit, which alone could find heaven, and, a soul, suspended between two abysses, which sought to unite with the spirit while being sorely tempted by the flesh." The Cathars were divided into two groups, an elite called 'parfaits' (perfects), and the larger population of believers.

To become a 'perfect' required a novitiate living in austerity lasting as long as four years, capped with a formal ceremony called the 'consolamentum', a kind of baptism by book and word rather than by water. Perfects refused to eat meat or any byproduct of animal procreation. They could never touch women. There were also 'parfaites' (the female equivalent of the 'perfects'). They resolved never to lie and to face death without fear. For a Cathar believer there was no better form of death than death by fire.

By the late 1100s Catharism took hold and prospered in the Southwest of France in the area known as Languedoc. Here they found a land, which fostered tolerance, in which the civil power was weak, and the powerful nobility had little reason to cooperate with the Catholic Church and the Pope.

All this in total opposition to the conditions in the north of France as we know it today. At that time (late 1100s) France was but a small country surrounding Paris. The Atlantic portion of present-day France extending to the Pyrénées was ruled by Queen Aliénor of *Aquitaine* (remember, she is my ancestor and 29th direct grandmother) and her second husband, King Henry II of England, while the Cathar region, further to the east, was controlled by Aliénor's uncle, Raymond VI, the Count of Toulouse. Even his fiefdom was larger than that of King Louis VII of France (her first husband).

This entire section of France, Aquitaine, Toulouse, and Languedoc were referred to throughout Europe as the most civilized, the most cultivated in Western Europe. Toulouse, too, was said to be more opulent and intellectually advanced than Paris. Like its neighbor, Aquitaine, it was the land of the troubadours, music and love poems with a strong cultural tradition.

Their language was Occitan, which was regarded by many intellectuals, like Dante, for instance, as more prestigious than French or Italian. Dante originally planned to write his "Divine Comedy" in Occitan. In fact, Sumption also states that the Midi, the south of France, rightly thought of itself as an independent nation, with Occitan as its language. He quoted the 7th century Bishop Isidore of Seville, stating that a nation was defined by a common origin and a common tongue.

Pope Innocent III's Involvement

Meanwhile, the peaceful, but sure, spread of Catharism was alarming to Pope Innocent III. He decided to stop the spread of the 'heretical' sect, and indeed to stomp them out altogether. Thus, "Cathar Catharsis", my title, takes on meaning here. The 'Catharsis' to which I refer is the purging of the 'purified' by King and Pope. And this is how and where it happened. First, the Pope sent orators, such as St. Bernard and St. Dominic, to preach the benefits of strict Catholic doctrine and to deny the Cathar beliefs.

This tactic had the reverse effect, however. On one occasion, when St. Dominic was debating in his hometown church at Fanjeaux, each side gave his gospel to an envoy of the opposing side, who threw them into the fire. As the story is told, the Cathar book burned to ashes, but Dominic's book leaped out of the flames and struck a rafter. The rafter still bears the mark today. In summation, the Cathars were excellent debaters and held their own in the face of the Pope's opposition.

The preaching of the crusade being ineffective, the Pope resorted to sending in troops to annihilate the heretics. By the late 1100s Pope Innocent III began relentlessly to wipe out what was now being called the Albigensian heresy, since the city of Albi was a center, rife with dualists. Innocent called upon the nobility to swear allegiance to him and to take up arms to rout them out locally. He sent papal legates into all suspected areas.

In January of 1208, the Pope's envoy was sent to bargain with Raymond VI, Count of Toulouse, who stubbornly refused to give in to the legate's demands. The next morning, as the legate was leaving, he was murdered. No one took responsibility, but Raymond was strongly suspected. This single act of violence served to galvanize the Pope against the Cathars.

As a result, in 1208 the church proclaimed a crusade against the "infidels" By July 1209, an army of some 15,000 marched into Beziers in northeast Languedoc to rid the city of heretics. The commander of the army, Arnald-Amaury, was asked, "How can you tell the heretics from the Catholics?" He replied: "Kill them all, God will recognize his own."

Embittered massacres followed at Carcassonne, Minerve, Lavaur and beyond. Whole towns were executed. The attackers built huge rock-throwing machines called 'trébuchets' (medieval engine of war with a sling for hurling missiles) and 'mangonels' (a military device for throwing stones) The largest of the trebuchets was named the "Malevoisine" (the bad neighbor). Remember the reference to this medieval war machine in the article given to me last spring? The "Malevoisine" used at the town of Minerve was remembered, as the defenders almost succeeded in burning it to the ground during the night. However, a soldier from the Pope's army got up to relieve himself and discovered the Cathars setting the fire.

The invaders also employed 'tours roulants' (rolling towers), that were built to extend to a height of 150 feet allowing soldiers to scale otherwise impregnable walls. The defenders used deadly, giant crossbows. It should be noted at this point that the mercenaries demanded by the Pope and recruited by the King of France, Philip-Auguste (son of Louis VII), were only hired on for a period of forty days. No matter where they were or what they were doing, these men left for home after their forty days were up. It made a successful outcome for the Pope and the King much more difficult.

Simon de Monfort

After the death of Arnald-Amaury, there was a need for a strong leader to replace him in this assault on Languedoc. Simon de Monfort was elected by his peers as head of the crusading army. He was a man of singular purpose and great military skill. He was the leader most successful in causing the downfall of the Cathars. He burned them alive by the hundreds. As Sumption stated, "He was a man filled with self-righteous cruelty of fanaticism." Those whom he did not kill he mutilated and sent home as ghastly exemplars. I will spare you the well-documented, ugly details.

By the end of 1212, Simon had conquered virtually all of Languedoc. As time went on the crusade became not only a papal war against the

Cathars in France, but a war between the North and the South, a war of acquisition for the King of France, allowing him to expand his influence, as well as his boundaries, to the Mediterranean. By 1223 Louis VIII succeeded Philip Augustus. He and the Pope would do their best to squash the Counts of Toulouse and force them into ceding their lands and allegiance to the King and the Pope.

Increasingly the brave Cathars were forced to live in secret, in high, inaccessible strongholds, veritable eagles' nests. These 'Citadelles du vertige', (vertiginous fortresses) were to be their last refuge, about 50 of them in all. These are the object of our interest as Rusty and I plan our travel through Cathar Country. After all there is very little else which remains as witness to the terrible century of religious and political purge and persecution.

During the 13ᵗʰ century, Mirepoix (our hub this week) gave shelter to the Cathar heretics. Pierre Roger de Mirepoix, Lord of the town, was a believing Cather himself. He protected his brethren in this town as long as possible. In 1289 the town apparently was washed away in a flood when the lake at Puivert suddenly emptied. Mireloix was rebuilt.

A Coll Respite – A Cool Citron Pressé

We head to the town square for a cool drink. Rusty and I take turns using his high-tech filming apparatus as we sit in the square and order our libations. Rusty has only been in France for a few days and wants to practice his French.

'Comme d'habitude' (as usual) I order my preferred 'citron pressé (freshly-squeezed lemonade) and he, a local beer. My 'citron pressé' arrives in an old "Ricard" bottle with a pitcher off water, a glass that has only the juice of one lemon in it, and packets of sugar. It is a 'do it yourself' thirst-quenching drink. With the camera running and pointed straight at me, I start to tear open several packets of sugar into my glass while speaking in French with Rusty who awaits his beer. We are discussing our drinks in rudimentary French, Rusty being the French student and moi, the 'prof'. So, what is new?

I request 'glaçons' (ice cubes). After a bit, Rusty asks me: "How is your drink?" I answer, "It is way too sour!" I proceed to tear open several more sugar packets and stir them into my tart lemonade. My son looks at me in total shock. How could I possibly want any <u>more</u> sugar after all those packets I just added? With our repartee in imperfect French we begin to laugh uncontrollably. The waitress returns to see if we need anything, but we are in such silly laughter we can barely answer. We catch it all on tape.

Puivert Stronghold

While I linger at the table to write in my journal, Rusty takes his still camera and his video cam to get close-ups of the many carved heads which support the arcade roof around the square. We rest awhile and change for supper at the hotel.

So far, we give Mirepoix three stars, as it is quiet and off the beaten path of most American tourists but harbors a staggering portion of French medieval history. We are about as far from Paris as you can get and still be in France. Rusty and I decide to start at Puivert castle, formerly the rendezvous of the troubadours playing their instruments and singing songs of courtly love. This castle, on the western side of Cathar territory, reckons back to a more festive, rather than fortification. Puivert, literally translated, means 'green well'. The tall walls and grand doorway, vaulted ceiling and chapel remain in part. The access road brings us most of the way up to the castle ruins. It is n to ride the rest of the way in a horse-drawn wagon, but we choose to walk, then to roam freely within the tumbling walls of its ruined perimeter. I make a note of the temperature. It is 100 degrees!

I open my black umbrella to shield me from the blazing sun. We climb up and down spiral staircases where it is briefly cool. Puivert's towers and impressive 'keep' still stand majestically over the town below. In reading of its history, we find that Puivert was taken by Simon de Monfort and his army of crusading knights early on, in 1210. The castle was seized after a three-day siege; all the Cathars escaped with their lives. Today it is silent and peaceful.

We hasten on our way to the next mountain stronghold, Montsegur. The castle is perched atop what is called a 'pog' or pinnacle of rock 3,960 feet above sea level. We are dressed to make the precipitous assent. Making our way to the base of the trail, we see a small monument, or 'stele', as they call it, erected in the 'Prat dels Cramats' (field of the cremated ones), to commemorate those who died by fire here. On this spot more than 200 Cathar Perfects, both men and women, were burned alive.

Monsegur, a Steep, Rocky Climb

The story goes that Montsegur (safe mountain) had been a long-time thorn of resistance in the side of the crusaders. The Cathars knew they needed to find a safe place, and Montsegur, was just that for many years. The crusaders could not get a foothold here. It, therefore, remained the spiritual hub of the Cathar Church, as well as asylum for persecuted brethren, especially after 1232.

Some 500 adherents of their faith lived here on a regular basis, either on the summit, on terraces, or at the foot of the mountain. In 1241, Raymond VII, the last Count of Toulouse, often the protector of the Cathars, was forced to promise the King and church that he would destroy the rebel castle.

Raymond's attack, however, was repelled. By then the crusade had turned into a full-blown inquisition. The next year, 1242, the Cathars of Montsegur sent a small band of men to assassinate two grand inquisitors at Avignonet. This infuriated King Louis IX who prepared, in retribution, yet another siege of Montsegur for the spring of 1243. The king vowed to "cut off the head of the dragon" once and for all. The final siege of Montsegur lasted 10 long months with the castle and the Cathar defenders finally succumbing. In the last days a few Basque soldiers scaled the sheer face of the pog and set up a rock-throwing catapult that threw the advantage to their side. With a two-week truce in place, the Cathars had to choose between renouncing their faith or being burned alive. I have told you the outcome. They chose the latter.

Knowing the sad story behind this tranquil-appearing place, Rusty and I, with mixed emotions, prepare to make the climb. We look around the flat place by the monument and try to imagine the horror of what happened here 750 years ago. How could the church be so intolerant, so repressive of a group who also believed in God, who were also their own countrymen, fellow human beings? As difficult as it is to comprehend, it still goes on today and is called ethnic cleansing. Often now, as then, many are killed who are not even a part of the oppressed group in question.

We climb for about 3/4 hour, passing a few people coming down from the summit, all exclaiming how beautiful it is. The pathway becomes steeper, and rockier. The trail soon melts away into bare rock.

Before long I call ahead to Rusty to say there is no way I can continue with no handholds to climb up over slippery moist gravel between pointed rocks. I hate to miss the summit, only about 80 feet higher and all there is to behold, but I know my strength is waning just now. I go back down a few yards to the last bush I passed. I sit down beside it in the small spot of shade it makes and tell Rusty to go on ahead. I will wait for him here, trying not to be too embarrassed as people pass me going up and down. I scrunch into the shady spot waiting to hear how magnificent it is up above.

While waiting for my son, I move around the bush to stay in the shade. I must be a silly sight! Never one to waste time, I inspect the flowers near me and enjoy the view from my vantage point, thinking how it must have been for those persecuted people years ago, carrying up and down this treacherous slope, everything they needed to live. Rusty will be my eyes. When he returns, somewhat out of breath, but energized by what he has witnessed, he is full of stories: mounting ancient, crumbling staircases to get good shots from the heights of Puivert; trying to converse in his broken French with a couple of tourists he met; simply being awestruck in this place. Soon we turn to make our way down slowly. It is a memorable visit for us both. We are getting a better sense of how difficult it was for the Cathar to survive, always being hunted, having to move from safe place to safe place year after year.

On our way back to the hotel, we drive through the town of Foix. As we draw near the town, Rusty, with his eyes on the twisty road, and I, with my nose in the map, look up at the same time to see the Castle of Foix perched high on a knoll in the center of town. With its crenelated walls and towers, it is the quintessential medieval 'château fort' (fortified castle). We are stunned by its beauty and size. The Count of Foix was a key player in the Cathar Crusade, helping to protect the victimized whatever way he could. In fact, the Count was implacable for years, dodging accusations and standing up to the cruelty of the king's armies. Simon de Montfort boasted that he could take the château easily, proclaiming that he would "fair fondre comme graisse le rocher de Foix et y griller son maitre!" (He would melt the rock of Foix into a puddle of grease and then barb-que its master!). Now I see by the size and location of his property, how influential Foix must have been and how he could have enervated Simon of Montfort. Sadly, all the influence, money and men couldn't protect the Cathars in their doomed struggle to remain free and to practice their religion peacefully.

We drag our tired feet back to the Hotel Commerce. After our afternoon of exertion, we make our way back to the calm of the hotel. While I linger at the table in the courtyard to write in my journal, Rusty takes his still camera and the video cam to get close-ups of the many carved heads that support the arcade roof around the square. We rest awhile and change for supper at the hotel. We decide to dine on the terrace to relish whatever fresh air we can as the sun goes down.

Puillaurens, a Serendipitous Hike

The next day we plan to visit Puilaurens. Rusty and I pull into the parking lot below Puilaurens at about 8:30AM. It is deserted. The area is forested, and it is therefore hard to catch a glimpse of the castle. The head of the trail is well marked. After my experience of the day before on the steep trail at Montsegur, I am a little reticent to start out, not knowing the difficulty of the hike. Rusty offers to go on ahead and check out the conditions; I will wait in the car with my reading material. After about twenty minutes I am thinking I will start out on my own when a car pulls in and parks beside ours. A friendly-looking petite blonde alights from her vehicle and heads for the trail. I quickly say that I am just starting out and ask if she is familiar with the walk. She answers very politely that, no she is not, but would I like to join her. Just what I would have hoped. We start out together introducing ourselves. She is Lily Ressouches from Albi, the center of the Albigensian Crusade.

I hope she can answer some of my questions as we walk. Happily, the trail is broad and not too difficult. Lily tells me she dropped her husband at work at 6AM and drove 2 1/2 hours to get here! We have much fun finding out about each other. I am afraid that meeting Lily is another of my "not by coincidence" happenings. I discover right away that she is a teacher of small children, about the 5,6,7 year old age group and that, most amazingly, she teaches the ancient language of Occitan, the language about which I read in the "New York Times" before coming to France this summer.

Lily and the Occitan Language

Lily tells me that her family always spoke Occitan as well as French, as did many of the people in her small village just outside Albi. In fact, there are still today people in her town of Le Travet, who speak Occitan. Am I lucky or what? Naturally they are pleased that their language is enjoying a revival. Lily tells me that teachers of Occitan are few and far between, and she feels fortunate to be able to contribute in this way to keep her regional tongue alive.

We are so lost in conversation that I lose track of the passage of time and of how far we have walked. I look up and see the crenellations of the ancient walls and three towers looming up ahead perched on stone outcroppings on the brow of the hill. Thankfully Puilaurens is not as high as Montsegur. I will actually get to see Puilaurens myself today. I call (out loud that is, no cell phones in those days except hard-wired in my Saab at home) to see if Rusty can hear me as we pass through the remains of fortifications and gates on our way. No answer. Finally, we pass over still more rubble stonework and enter a large inner courtyard near the summit. I call for Rusty again. He appears on a higher level with Video cam in hand, very excited at the vistas he has found.

The truth be told, Rusty has been so absorbed in the history and beauty of this place that he too, forgot how long he had been gone from the car. Lily and I do not skip a beat, but continue our intense discussion about teaching theories, French history, and the Cathars in particular as my son turns his camera on us.

Once inside daunting Puilaurens, it is hard to understand how this double-walled stronghold could ever be penetrated by an invading army. How fortunate we are to have our new-found friend, Lily, to explain much of what we are seeing. She tells us about the slanting narrow windows from which razor-sharp arrows are fired directly onto the path where we were just walking. We see the deadfall or chute built over the only entrance gate. This is effective for raining down boulders and hot oil on unwelcome intruders. On the opposite walls, in case anyone is clever enough to scale them are 'machicolis', another kind of chute from which are dropped all kinds of heavy rocks or boiling liquids. Lily points out there are windows with sentry benches on every side. A rare feature that we nearly miss is a speaking tube running through the wall, enabling people on different levels to communicate.

My new Albigeois friend is well-versed on the Cathar history and tells us that at one time The Count of Toulouse, Raymond VI, secreted himself here at Puilaurens, but was finally forced to flee with his army without engaging Simon de Montfort's superior forces. For several years the fortress successfully resisted the onslaught of the Albigensian crusaders and did not surrender until 1256.

After spending at least an hour exploring the deserted castle ruins under the near-roasting morning sun, we walk down together to the cars. Judging from our experience this week in Languedoc, I must conclude that one is not necessarily cooler in higher altitudes!

Puilaurens is neither an indifferent pile of rocks, nor a dead place to visit with guidebook in hand. Our visit here is unexpectedly enlivened by meeting Lily today. In parting, she offers us her apartment in Albi if we come back next summer. We promise to keep in touch and exchange addresses and emails.

Peyrepertuse

Next, we drive by Peyrepertuse, a fortress carved out of and seemingly growing upward from the craggy mountaintop on which it sits. We stop the car below to try and sort out which is rock and which is man-made castle. Obviously, it is a well-defended site, nearly unattainable to an attacking army. In 1240, after lengthy negotiations, Lord William of Peyrepertuse surrendered the castle intact to King Louis IX without a fight.

Hilarious Supper: A Faux Pas in Mirepoix

After a long day on the road driving and climbing the Cathar citadels we return to our hotel for a relaxing dinner 'en plein air' on the terrace. There is a slight breeze coming from the mountains as the sky darkens. We find our seats under the trees that shade the dinner space. We are ready for a late supper, and we know the cuisine here is excellent. Rusty brings his camera to the table for fun tonight. Subtly, with his camera turned on, he pans the tables and guests without disturbing anyone. The waitress arrives to ask for our drink choices. Rusty is better and better at 'restaurant French', and, as I hold the camera, he asks for a local beer and I for bottled water. Meanwhile, we look at the menu. I order a regional Languedoc dish, cassoulet. Rusty orders fresh trout to start and then a half of chicken, roasted with 'herbes de Provence' (an aromatic herbal mix).

I place the camera on the table, still running. When the waitress returns, we only get as far as the first course and decide to share a pot of 'potage' (thick peasant soup). Rusty misses some of the food vocab but is pleased we will start with a soup course. His college French is tuning up, so we continue our repartee while waiting for our first course, the thick soup. We are not in a hurry.

The soup tureen is brought to the table with a ladle. Rusty, being the gentleman that he is, picks up the ladle to serve us. The server has left a pile of dishes along with the tureen, apparently to use for the soup self-service. Rusty will do the honors and proceeds, while continuing our conversation, with the top dish in the pile. He begins to ladle out the fragrant hot soup into the first dish.

The film in the video camcorder is still running. It is focused on Rusty as he serves. Then I realize that there has been 'un grand faux pas!' (a terrible mistake). He is on his second ladle full, when I realize that he has picked up a plate, rather than a soup bowl, and is fast pouring the hot soup onto a flat plate. "Oh, my goodness", I intone: "Rusty, that is the plate that goes *under* the soup bowl! You are pouring the soup onto a plate!" Rust, who, no doubt, has been contemplating his next French phrase, examines the dish and guffaws, ending with a sheepish smile. I am now in fits of laughter as he sets down the overflowing plate. The camera has caught the whole procedure, and we are doubled over with mirth!

The waitress comes over when she sees what is going on. She has seen the camera from the start and clearly does not want to be caught on camera for posterity. She darts away with the soiled plates and points out the proper rimmed soups. So, this dinner starts out with a slip-up, quickly remedied. We are still speaking mostly "frenglish" (a combo of French and English) at the table. I am carrying on in French and Rusty in halting French. It is too funny for words.

My ever-hungry son orders his fresh caught trout while I am finishing my potage. Then come our main dishes: His is the roasted chicken and mine the cassoulet.

Cassoulet in Sarlat: Tasty Dish of SW France

To prepare the proper cassoulet: it begins with a 'confit' (pieces of meat cooked in their own fat and preserved in that fat in a screw top jar) of goose or duck. The confit is combined with sausage links. Next, add onions and tomatoes dredged in flour while the beans are cooking in another pot until soft. The procedure takes several hours, during which the two pots (meat and beans) are combined and put in the oven until a crust forms on the top. The crust is then broken about 2-3 times and incorporated into the stew. The result is flavorful and rich, fit for royalty.

I remember the first time I ordered a cassoulet in the town of Sarlat, in the Dordogne River valley where friends and I were seated out-of-doors in the central square of town. The cassoulet and the ambience were splendid, just as they are here in Mirepoix with Rusty. We finish our meal with a large tray of local cheeses, named by our server. A perfect end to a day in the Languedoc.

Following our unforgettable dinner, Rusty and I walk around town while he finds more pillar capitals with a myriad of carved men's heads and faces to photograph. We shall sleep well tonight!

Queribus

Last, but not least, in our Cathar quest is the fortress of Queribus. It is located at some distance to the east, closer to the Mediterranean Sea than the other Cathar castles we have seen. This one is not to be missed. On our way, we pass through a small town named Cucugnan. We stop for a cold drink, a sandwich and a little shade, though I must say the car has been delightfully cool. I am glad I asked for the air conditioning in the car. Without it I think we would have perished from the heat. Speaking of Cucugnan, I recall a short story by Alphonse Daudet, called "Le Cure (priest) de Cucugnan" and wonder if this is the same place. Cucugnan is a dry, desolate place not far from Queribus. None of that was mentioned in Daudet's account of a priest and his several "hot stops" (in the lower world) on his way to heaven. We quench our thirst and continue on.

At last we find ourselves nearing the foot of Queribus. From our vantage point rounding a wide curve in the road, we catch our first sight of the citadel known as Queribus. It appears to be perched like a gemstone in a Tiffany setting high atop a mounting of bare rock. From the summit one can glimpse the blue Mediterranean far to the east. To reach its pinnacle, one must pass a series of three interlocking massive walls and surmount hundreds of steps hewn from the stone mountain itself. Queribus was the last bastion to hold out against the marauding crusaders, finally surrendering in 1255. The siege was not as bloody as that of Montsegur. But nonetheless, its fall was a turning point in the Albigensian crusade. After Queribus, the few remaining Cathars were forced underground for next few decades under the growing Inquisition, gradually to disappear entirely.

Queribus is not quite as high as Montsegur, but fully as impressive. The route to the top is rocky and difficult. That is evident. Once again, deferring to my better judgment, I encourage my agile son to carry on without me. He takes the cameras and easily makes it to the top. Again, he explores every nook and cranny to his heart's content, filming as he goes. I know it is a thrill for him to discover it by himself, and since he is starting out on his own as an independent film producer, I am sure he will get footage he can draw on for years to come. I wait contentedly at the foot of our last craggy mountain, writing in my journal.

Quillan, Roussillon (Languedoc)

Not yet ready to leave Cathar country, we find a small hotel in Quillan in the Roussillon region of Languedoc, closer to the Mediterranean, not to be confused with the village of the same name in the Luberon Region of Provence. After supper, we wander the narrow streets of the old town, thinking how little things have changed in southwestern France in the last hundred years, maybe longer. The houses, wooden doors and window shutters are washed in earthy Mediterranean colors of ochre, rust and blue-green. The ochre hues we see here are reminiscent of those of the Luberon. The evening is hot and quiet. We hardly see or hear a soul, except for the wail of a hungry cat or the splashing of a fountain in a small square. We turn in early, after a cup of strong coffee in the hotel bar. It does not mar our sleep. We start out very early in the morning to drive back to the valley of the Loire, our starting and end point.

As we leave Cathar country, the one redeeming feature of this horrible siege that lasted for most of the 13th century is the resultant unification of France under one King, one flag. But that is a Machiavellian theme, that the end justifies the means. Were all those deaths worth such an end? Was such an end worth the destruction of an advanced civilization and language? Was such an end worth the elimination of a peaceful religion? For the most part it was indeed a Catharsis.

Regarding the language, Occitan, like the six other former French regional tongues, was banned in the schools and in the streets for over 400 years. It almost became extinct. How prescient was it that I was handed that "New York Times" clipping, dateline, Nîmes, France, May 3, 1993, just preceding my trip? The timing was impeccable, especially in the light of our meeting with Lily, the Occitan teacher, on the trail to the mountain fortress of Puilaurens. She is now teaching the all-but-dead Occitan language! Happily, the French government has reversed its policy in favor of enriching its language by tracing its heritage and retaining its roots. In point of fact, a living legacy of the Cathars remains today in Lily's classroom as she teaches young children to speak the language of their ancestors.

An uplifting postscript to this story is that, now, twenty-four years later, my husband, John, and I are still corresponding with Lily and her husband, Claude. In 1997, John, and I accepted her gracious invitation to visit her and her husband, Claude, in Le Travet, just 1/2 hour south of Albi. While there, we were fortunate to be able to attend a local street fair in their tiny village. There, Lily and Claude introduced us to several elderly townspeople who still speak Occitan. It was a pure delight to hear Lily conversing with her friends in their ancient idiom. Also, of interest, Claude is a metallurgist working for a large company. He travels throughout the world looking for mineral deposits to supplement those that are depleted or never existed in France. Lily has been most helpful in sending me information on Occitan and the history of the Cathars as well as the Albigensian Crusade (centered around her hometown, Albi).

Through our long years of correspondence, Lily and Claude have kept us abreast of the re-construction of the Marquis de Lafayette's second ship to America, the "Hermione". They sent me photos and videos of the building of this magnificent replica ship as it was being built over a period of 20 years! It finally arrived in Newport, Rhode Island in the summer of 2015 with much fanfare, and John and I spent four days there for the welcoming ceremonies of the "Hermione" with all the French and American dignitaries in attendance. We cherish our transatlantic friendship with Lily and Claude beyond words.

I leave you to contemplate the words of **Victor Hugo in his poem:**

"Revberies Albigeoises
0 murs! 0 creneaux! 0 tourelles!
Ramparts! fosses aux ponts mouvants!
Lourds faisceaux de colonnes frêles
Fiers châteaux! modestes couvents!
Cloitres poudreux, salles antiques,
Où gemissaient les saints cantiques,
Où riaient les banquets joyeux!
Lieux ou le coeur met ses chimeres!
Églises ou priaient nos mères,
Tours ou combattaient nos aleux!"

English translation:
Reminiscences of old Albi
"Oh walls! Oh crenellations! Oh turrets!
Ramparts! moats with drawbridges!
Heavy stacks of frail columns!
Proud castles! Modest convents!
Dusty cloisters, dirty antiquities

Where saintly hymns were moaned;
Where they laughed at joyful banquets!
Places where the heart hung its dreams!
Churches where our mothers prayed,
Towers where our grandparents fought!"

To Hugo's lament, I add my own: Remember the Languedoc, 'la langue d'oc' (the language of the south), the land of my forebears. Oh walls, crenellations and turrets, and ancient, crumbling castles where our ancestors roamed…moldering convents where our grandmothers died. Please remember where Rusty and I have climbed; the steep, rocky trails to fortresses long lost! In concluding this episode of retracing the footsteps our ancestors once trod, we do not forget: Charlemagne, King of the Franks (also known as Holy Roman Emperor); William X, Duke of Aquitaine; his daughter, Queen Aliénor, Duchess of Aquitaine and her husband, English King Henry II, Plantagenet; and their son, King Richard I, Lionheart. We stand here in Languedoc, nearly 1,000 years later, inhaling and exhaling the same Occitan air as they did. Listen for the hoofbeats of their horses returning from battle, victorious or beaten. Where we stand this day, they stood. Harken back, as even the French king, Phillippe-Auguste and Pope Innocent III in the early 1200s successfully murdered the peaceful Cathars to a single one but were unsuccessful in purging the Cathars from history.

Cathar Catharsis

Rusty and I have completed our three part quest this summer: Meeting the Rochambeau family, completing our pilgrimage to Santiago de Compostela, Spain and lastly, our exploration of the Cathar Country. It has been a fulfilling and fruitful time of travel together, making long term friends in Albi (Le Travet), Lily and Claude, spiced liberally with laughter along the way.

Chapter Nine

Tours to Quimper; Vouvray to Sancerre and on to Reims, Saint-Denis, Notre Dame Cathedrals

ONE OF MY GOALS THIS summer is to tie up loose ends, to visit the Cathedral of Reims, to learn more about Jeanne d' Arc whom I have already followed extensively in the Loire Valley, and to visit the Cathedral of Saint- Denis where I will find the tombs of famous kings and queens. Both destinations are in the extended Paris region. My trip this time includes more travel with my son, Rusty, who joins me for a foray into Brittany on a quest to buy a wedding gift in Quimper for his sister, Heather. I conclude with Lore Valley wine tasting.

Jeanne d'Arc and the Dauphin Charles VII

Once again, I find my hub, Mado's summer garden, in time to relish an appetizing dinner prepared by my French hostess. She presents me with my annual all-natural, gourmet treat of her homegrown raspberries smothered in 'fromage blanc'. After breakfast the next day, I head out in my rented car to my first destination: the city of Reims, unofficial capital of the Province of Champagne, 80 miles northeast of Paris. My second destination will be the Basilique of Saint-Denis, roughly six miles west of Paris, where the Kings and Queens of France are buried. My first leg, to Reims, will be a bit of a trudge today in the heat, but I am up for it. Reims Cathedral is where the Kings of France were crowned. If I am to understand Jeanne d'Arc and her quest to have the Dauphin, the uncrowned King Charles VII, anointed and crowned, I *must* go to Reims. The cathedral is an exquisite sacred place with a history of much importance to France. As I approach, I notice that Reims façade is covered with heavy, white canvas and is ready for a Sound and Light performance that will portray the story of Joan and Charles VII, and how she accomplished her God-given mission by bringing him here for the ceremony of sacred investiture.

I do a self-guided tour of Notre Dame of Reims and read that behind the canvas is the constant re-furbishing and replacing of eroding building stones, arches, capitals and carvings of all kinds. There is no end to the travail of repairs. This is true wherever I go, be it church or château. The French government, the Catholic Church, and even private citizens (often American), shoulder this enormous never-ending undertaking. For France, it is well worth it, since tourism is 'numero uno'.

The cathedral I explore today, is built on the site of an early Gallo-Roman Bath. There was a church here as early as 401. It was dedicated to the Virgin Mary in the mid-5th century. On Christmas Day 508, Clovis I, King of the Franks, accompanied by his wife, Clothilde, received a Christian baptism by Saint-Remi here. I descend into the bowels of the cathedral to see the spot where Clovis stood at the ancient altar on that day so long ago. Further along the timeline of the edifice, King Louis VII was crowned King of France here at Reims by Pope Innocent II. Apparently, his coronation at Reims was his second crowning, the official one, with much pomp and ceremony. Louis' first coronation happened only a short time after Louis and Aliénor's wedding on July 25, 1137. Louis' father, King Louis VI, had died unexpectedly as the young marrieds were 'on progress' from Bordeaux to their new home in Paris on the Ile de la Cité. As a result, Aliénor's first husband was hastily crowned King Louis VII at Bourges Cathedral (I have visited there also) to safeguard his rule over France.

In ca.1210 the Carolingian-early Gothic design Notre Dame of Reims was destroyed by fire. The re-building of Reims started in 1211 and was completed in 1345. There are outstanding architectural features of the high Gothic period on the façade of Reims Cathedral, for instance: the twin towers that stand 267 feet above the street. The south tower carries two enormous bells, one of which weighs about 11 tons and is named Charlotte (not sure why). Adorning the West entrance is a large Rose window with three smaller, less decorated windows below. Rose windows are large, circular windows made up of many intricate stained-glass designs, depicting scenes from the Bible. They are also found in other French Gothic Cathedrals such as Saint-Denis (visited later in this chapter), Notre Dame of Paris, and Notre Dame of Chartres (both visited earlier). After World War I shelling by the Germans, there was heavy destruction of the rear section of Reims, once again, rebuilt. This is a cathedral that has suffered the pangs of almost insurmountable war and fire damage, yet she now stands erect, the proud example of man's undaunted persistence to rebuild God's house in the face of doom.

Notre Dame of Reims and Notre Dame of Paris

There is similarity to be found between the façade of Notre Dame of Reims and that of Notre Dame of Paris. Both façades have two square towers. They both have three pointed-arch doorways on the front-facing façade; Notre Dame of Paris has only one large Rose window on the front façade, whereas Reims has one large and three smaller round windows on the front (there are other Rose windows on the sides). Reims is remarkable for the graceful 'piercing' of the stonework, easily visible from the front, making it look lacier than the Paris Cathedral. The Reims Cathedral looks taller than the Parris Cathedral. Looks can be deceiving however, as Paris has 387 steps up the tower, and therefore must be taller than the Reims tower of 267 feet. Both structures were among the first to use the amazing 'flying buttresses' (exterior supports used where there are windows cut in the outside walls). The addition of windows weakens the structure.

To continue with the west façade of Notre Dame of Reims where I am today, one of the outstanding full-size sculptures beside the north portal is "the smiling angel" nearest the entrance. She has a beatific curl on her lips, and well she should, as she too, suffered damage during the German bombardment and, unlike her neighboring angels, was restored to her original beauty with wings intact. I believe there are about 120 sculptures on the west front alone.

The building of Notre Dame of Paris was conceived under Bishop Maurice of Sully with construction having begun in 1163. Like Reims, it is built on the site of a Gallo-Roman temple and a later Romanesque church. After many additions and innovations, the Paris Cathedral was completed ca.1345. Notre Dame of Reims was begun around the same period; both churches were built under the reign of King Louis VII and Queen Aliénor.

Remembering here my many visits to Paris and to Notre Dame. I always hold it dear to my heart because my favorite hotel is just opposite the cathedral on Rue Saint-Julien. The cozy balcony off my room looks directly only Notre Dame. Many a late night or early morning I sat there to stare at the façade lit by the sun in the morning and the floodlights at midnight. I have mingled with school groups from far away countries following their tour leaders speaking numerous languages I did not recognize. There were choral groups assembling for a conference. I recall admiring groups of students, dressed in matching uniforms and brightly-colored bandanas. Others were musicians preparing for a concert in this extraordinary space.

Already mentioned here is a third cathedral in the Paris region, the Basilique of Saint-Denis (patron saint of France). I shall be standing before it very soon. The Abbott Suger, advisor and sometimes antagonist of his King, Louis VII, and especially a thorn in the side of his Queen, is remembered as the innovator of what we know as the Gothic style of architecture. It was a daring innovation in those days, but a natural one in the progression of creating larger, taller, standing structures. Built earlier than the Reims and Paris Cathedrals, Saint-Denis was Suger's 'chef d'oeuvre' (masterpiece). Suger was the first to use Gothic, pointed windows and arches in his newly renovated and greatly expanded royal necropolis of Saint-Denis. Under the direction of Suger, building commenced in 1136, 24 years before Notre Dame of Paris. It was built with two front-facing square towers on the west façade and includes a central Rose window. The taller north tower was crowned with a breathtaking spire. However, the north tower was dismantled in 1845, leaving the façade with an unfinished appearance. The west front was completed in 1140, and the choeur (choir) was finished in 1144. Much to Suger's credit, for posterity he introduced the following architectural features now signatures of his new Gothic creation: the ambulatory, the radiating chapels, the ribbed vaulting, the clustered columns for better support of the ceiling, the embellished rose window, and the flying buttress, all of which have been incorporated in churches from Suger's time to this day. This is only a cursory taste, examining the exteriors of these massive, early Christian churches.

As I sit here today on April 16, 2019, doing a last edit of this chapter, I have to report the horrifying, sad news received last night via television: It was the live, on- screen burning of Notre Dame of Paris Cathedral! It is said that a wealthy Frenchman donated $300 million of his own funds, and two days post fire, there is more than one billion, to begin the re-building of this beautiful and iconic cathedral to the glory of God. My fond memories of this most holy space, now desecrated by flames, are replaced with chills running up and down my spine. I feel the shared sadness, now followed by the sense of hope. Like the Cathedral of Reims following the destruction of World War I, the 850-year old Notre Dame of Paris will rise again.

Sound and Light Performance Tells History of Reims

At the appointed hour in semi-darkness, having enjoyed a fine supper near my hotel, I am back at the Cathedral of Reims for the Sound and Light performance. No sense in belaboring the fact that the façade is covered with canvas; artists have faithfully recreated the delicate outlines of the front-facing elevation to give the same impression as the real stone and glass. The show begins in the street and concludes in the interior of the church. The theme of the exterior re-enactment is the building itself, wartime destruction and succeeding years of re-building accompanied by loud narration over a multitude of hidden speakers, lots of explosions, flashes of light and military music. The theme for the interior portion of the program is coronation, highlighting that of Charles VII and how Jeanne d' Arc achieved her goal to have him crowned inside this magnificent double-towered edifice. I can barely believe that I am here where this supreme moment in history took place on this sacred altar over 500 years ago. It was the apogee of Jeanne's struggle against heavy odds to do God's will. There are many renderings in needlework and on canvas of the event with the notables of the church and the nation assembled around the kneeling king. Jeanne is depicted as standing nearby in her full suit of armor near the high altar. When the music and the light of the performance dim at the close of the presentation, I remain in my seat near the transept, so moved by the near reality of the performance that I find it difficult to bring myself back to the 20th century.

I learn that since the coronation of Charles VII, there have been 25 more sacred royal kingships conferred here. In point of fact, it became a traditional ritual for several centuries when a new king arrived on the scene. As we know, we all adore our rituals. Well, in France a part of the planning for coronations began to include a festival that blossomed larger and larger over the years. Looking back, Reims, in Roman times was the third largest city in the Empire. Apparently not all roads led to Rome. Reims became a thriving, commercial center with a population of about 150,000. At coronation time, the city swelled with religious leaders, royal entourages, general travelers and curious revelers arriving from distant parts. Having witnessed the influx of tourists for the high holiday at Santiago in Spain, I would surmise that Reims took on a similar celebratory atmosphere at each crowning. The thrill of witnessing the soon-to-be-crowned dauphin, Charles VII, led by Jeanne d'Arc in her suit of armor astride her war horse, was undoubtedly a big draw. In 1429, after years of battles, some lost and some won, the relief of tension must have been great in France, knowing that Jeanne had finally realized her goal at Reims. Naturally there must have been dissenters who booed her, who favored the side of the British and judged Jeanne a fake, but all this fervor would have led up to a large crowd assembling at the open square in front of the Cathedral.

Cathedral of Saint-Denis, French Royal Necropolis

After a deeply moving sojourn in Reims, I head for west of Paris where I shall visit the famous cathedral mentioned above. Brimming with history, the Cathedral of Saint-Denis, is the largest, necropolis of France's Kings and Queens. Many of France's royals were buried here from the 5th to the 18th centuries. The medieval Cathedral of Saint-Denis is now referred to as a Basilica because it is connected to an abbey.

Hoping to find the tombs of some of the royals spoken of in this book, I pick up a map and brochure. To begin, there are incredible numbers buried here: 42 kings, 32 queens and 63 princes and princesses. This is indeed a ROYAL NECROPOLIS! The earliest dated tomb is that of King Clovis I (466-511). He was an early Christian king of the Franks (baptized in what is now the undercroft of Reims Cathedral in 508; see above) in the Merovingian period. Continuing on, through the list of sovereigns buried here, a student of French history can brush up against tomb after tomb on the main floor and in the crypt, rushing through roughly 1300 years, and ending abruptly with the tombs of King Louis XVI and Marie Antoinette in 1793. During the French Revolution, many resting places were rudely opened and desecrated. Marie Antoinette's and Louis XVI's most assuredly were disturbed.

It is heartening to find the 'gisant' (recumbent sculpture lying on a tomb) of my ancestor, Charles Martel (676-741), grandfather of Charlemagne. He was the King of the Franks with a moniker, 'The Hammer', that fit him well. Am accomplished warrior, he is best known for halting the advance of the Muslims and the spread of Islam at the Battle of Tours in 732. In this amazing battle against a mighty foe, he prevented the spread of Islam in Christian Europe.

Well in advance of this visit, I know that some of the sovereigns in my maternal genealogical upline on the French side are not to be found here, namely Queen Aliénor d'Aquitaine, and the tombs of her second husband, English King Henry II, and their offspring. I may have found Aliénor's first husband here, Louis VII, but cannot be sure.

I am most curious about the many French royals mentioned in this book, for instance King François I as well as Henri II of France and his Queen, Catherine de Médici. Soon I find myself standing in front of the tombs of Henri d. 1559 and Catherine d. 1589. Theirs are rather unattractive, oversize sepulchers – 'large in life and large in death'. Their children are interred here too. I look in vain for the tomb of Charles VII d. 1461, crowned at Reims with help of Jeanne d'Arc. I know he is here with his parents, but do not lay eyes on his vault. I also search for the vaults of Marie Antoinette and her husband, Louis XVI. Many of those who met their end at the Guillotine during the French Revolution may not lie under the stones bearing their names; so many unlabeled bodies were thrown into mass graves. I read their names and recall the many biographies I have devoured about the unfortunate, ill-prepared Queen Marie Antoinette from far-away Austria and her husband, King Louis XVI who aided America unstintingly during our fight for independence. I wonder where their earthly remains really are. In the cool, subterranean crypt I cannot dismiss the shudders I feel regarding their tragic deaths.

The church of Saint-Denis had its origin in the early days of pre-Christian Gaul. According to a 9th century abbot, Hilduin, around 250, a bishop missionary, Denis, was buried here after a horrific death in Montmartre, Paris. That is, he was supposed to have been beheaded and then walked to this spot carrying his own head. He was finally put to rest here and later made a saint; thus, the name Saint-Denis. The history of this place of worship continued with the Merovingian (mid 5[th]c - 8th c) and the Carolingian (beginning 9th c.) dynasties.

Abbot Suger, King Louis's right-hand man and trusted advisor, began work on the building of the cathedral as we know it. Although he was not able to complete his plan (he died in 1151), the church was, over time, finished and made a name for itself as the first Gothic cathedral.

Although I spend most of my time here in the undercroft searching for ancient tombs, I am appropriately awed by the grandiose size of the main floor interior space. Full orchestras give concerts here and music festivals take advantage of the excellent acoustics.

Jeanne d'Arc Bathed in Gold

Next, on another quest, I leave Saint-Denis to look for the impressive statue of Jeanne d'Arc, Maid of Orléans, in Paris. I find her mounted on her mighty palfrey, carrying a flag. The heavily gilded bronze statue rests on a tall plinth above the small city square named Place des Pyramides, near where Jeanne was wounded in a failed attempt to retake Paris from the English. (Also note that there is a copy of this statue in Philadelphia across from the Philadelphia Museum of Art at 25th Street and Kelly Drive. There is also a reduced copy inside the museum.) The statues of Jeanne in Orléans and Reims are just as inspirational as the Paris version, only it is not glowing with gold. In Orléans Jeanne is looking skyward, thanking God for his aid and gesturing with her sword as she sits astride a prancing horse. These statues are but a smattering of those built to commemorate Jeanne and her march to her demise in Rouen.

The following day I head back to Tours. By suppertime I arrive for a communal meal in Mado's blooming garden. I shall spend several delicious halcyon days exploring more specialties of the Loire Valley. Without skipping a beat, I find my place at the table, with introductions to students from around the world.

Bashmet at Saint Saturin, Tours

Wonder of wonders, there is a Bashmet concert this week. I am not finished with Bashmet yet! In fact, I arranged for the tickets before leaving Connecticut. Who says I do not do my homework? The concert is titled: 'Soirée autour d'Altos' (An evening of violas). Naturally Yuri will be conducting his Soloists de Moscow featuring his viola, his usual pianist, Mikial Muntian, a mezzo soprano, a clarinet, and a contra-tenor. I anticipate an amazing musical evening. The venue is the Church of Saint Saturnin, overlooking the river Loire, built in 1473 with the aid of King Louis XI.

The day of the concert has arrived. Tonight's program includes Turina's "Serenade d'Andalousie"; a piece by Alexandre Tchaikovsky, Mournful Pavaane for five violas, an extract from the "Suite Bashmet"; a Mozart; a Kantcheli; and Jacob's

"Suite for Eight Violas" in memory of Lionel Tertis. All these pieces feature the viola. After the breathtaking concert, I approach Yuri once again to tell him how much I appreciate his performance. The music is beyond words. How nice it is that he remembers me still.

A Taste of Vouvray and Chinon Wines

The Loire Valley is a center of production of fine wines. For example, across the river from Tours is the town of Vouvray; their vintners export delicious wines to America. One cannot miss Vouvray when in local restaurants or the Renaud home. The climate and geography of the region play an important role in the development of the Vouvray grapes. Because of the location of the vineyards on top of a plateau on the southern aspect of the right bank of the Loire: in years of cooler climate, the wine tends to be drier, like the sparkling Vouvray; in years of warmer temperatures, the wine production tends toward a sweeter, dessert wine. I prefer the sparkling Vouvray and consider it to be a celebration wine. In the early 1990s I carried this Vouvray home with me on the plane or had it shipped.

As for a local red wine, I attended a tasting/reception with Mado and Lucien in Chinon where the famous Chinon red wine was paired with a fitting dinner. In 2015, Eric Asinov of the New York Times, calls Chinon "a red wine with an attitude" It is made from the Cabernet franc grape. Asinov claims: "Good wines raise questions and considering these questions, deepens the pleasure by adding dimension to a wide range of expression."

Tours and Charles Martel in 732

Still in Tours, I am reminded of the history of old Tours. I covered the city on foot for ten summers and know it well. After a while, one tends to take for granted the beauty of the old buildings and their long history, as one passes by on the way to the market or to buy an antiquarian book. This town's history harkens back to Gaul and the early Roman era. One of the greatest moments in the history of Tours was in 732 A.D., when a horde of Muslims on horseback invaded the mainland in Spain after conquering most of Northern Africa, including Egypt. They had marched some 311 miles North to the city of Tours, as I mentioned earlier. They were repulsed by Charles Martel in the Battle of Tours. After that, in the 800s, Tours was invaded by the Vikings and then the Romans. When do the wars ever stop? Think of the wars with which we are most familiar that took place in France in the 20th century.

When I visited the old Château of Tours, the guide pointed out that, after the Roman era, there were sections of the fortification built in the 4th c. and onward to the 19th c. Included in that span of time, in the 11th c. the castle became the residence of the Counts of Anjou (also part of my ancestral tree). I make note of these ancestral findings as I go. There is also the Guise tower with its machicolations and pepper pot roof, 13th - 15th c. (time of Catherine de Medici). The pepper pot roof, or conical roof, functioned to direct rainwater away from the building. The point side up; the fat side down. These upside-down dunce caps were most often covered with slate tiles and are often seen on castles of the Loire Valley.

The city of Tours is strategically placed between the Loire River and its tributary, the Cher. As such, it has long been a center of trade and commerce. When the river was deep and navigable, it was at its zenith. Today merchant ships can no longer ply their trade via the river that has grown shallow and filled in with sand.

There is a story that Lucien told me over the dinner table one night about the river Loire. I had mentioned that I thought it strange that no one was swimming in the Loire. He said that one time a death was averted by a strange flow of the Loire waters. A man, who knew that the waters were dangerous, went in for a swim anyway. Suddenly, he was drawn under by a strong current that pulled him deeper and deeper below the surface. He could do nothing but go with the flow. At one point he was surprised but fortunate to be able to get a few breaths of air as the water passed through an underground air pocket. Again, he was drawn under and pushed under by the current for a long time, during which he was just able to hold his breath until the swift current brought him up to the surface down river, quite far from his original dunking. This is how the people of Tours discovered the Loire has two levels of running water, one below the other. Therefore, no locals swim here anymore. I was still confused, as I had not seen signs along the river warning of danger. Lucien has no answer to this. I am still befuddled. This is one of the many wonders of the Loire Valley!

St. Gatiens' Gargoyles

Gatiens was the first Bishop of Tours in the 3rd c. He was made a saint; thus, the cathedral is named for him. The twin-spired Gothic Cathedral was built between 1170 and 1547. Since there are no Protestant churches in Tours, I began to attend Sunday services at St. Gatiens as it is in walking distance from Mado's. In the first couple of years, I walked over with my classmate, a fellow French teacher, Rita. It was always a lovely way to start the day together. After church, we would stop at our favorite 'pâtisserie' (pastry shop) for a devastating sweet with 'café au lait' (coffee with cream) and walk back through the gardens by the 'Musée des Beaux Arts' (Museum of Fine Arts) and the "Jardin des Plantes" (flower garden).

We knew that one day we would find time to take the guided tour of St. Gatiens. On a rainy day that cleared in the afternoon, we strolled over to the church for their afternoon tour. The best part was climbing up to the roof to get a closer look at the 'gargoyles' (drainpipes that catch the rainwater on the roof and spew it out of their goblin-shaped mouths.) Gargoyles are also thought to ward off evil spirits. From our perspective near the top of the church spire, we could see the water from the morning's storm, still dripping from the gargoyles onto the pavement below. From this height it was an impressive sight, not only looking down over the vast structure of the church, but also admiring the broad view of the city. Our climb gave me a better sense of the expanse of Tours and the grand Loire that spans the city.

Tours is the second largest city in Touraine, after Orléans. It is known to students and professors of the French language as the area where the purist French is spoken. Voilà, the reason Rita and I chose Tours to continue our grad study French. Tours remains a major stop on the pilgrimage route to Santiago de Compostela.

St. Martin of Tours and the Body-Snatchers

Here is one of the reasons: St. Martin was the 2nd Bishop of Tours (316-397). Each day on our way to class we pass by the "Basilique de St. Martin". One afternoon after classes, Rita and I visit the "Basilique" (basilica) that bears his name, to see the spot below the altar where the remains of the saint are placed as relics. Churches of yore were eager to possess the relics of a saint, even better a martyred saint, to encourage support for their church, as well as to put their church on the map to speak – the map of pilgrims en route to Santiago. Saint Martin died nearby in the small town of Candes. Rita and I have been there too as we want to understand the full story of St. Martin's death. It happened is near the confluence of the Vienne and Loire Rivers.

When St. Martin died there, the locals, rapacious to preserve his corpse for the future fame of their city, made plans to secret the corpse away in the dead of night for their benefit. Unbeknownst to them, there was an opposing plan afoot by the people of Tours. After all, Martin was their Bishop. In the night, a band of men crept into Candes and stole the body for themselves and ferried it by boat back to Tours where it still lies. Candes is now called Candes-Saint-Martin. They will always be connected to St. Martin, even without his bones!

'Place Plume', Medieval Entertainment with Crepes

Later that evening, following our leisurely stroll through Tours, Rita and I meet Maryse and her friends at "Place Plumereau", the center square of the 'old city' where the late-night revelers congregate. The square is surrounded by fine, four and five story 15th c. residences built of stone and timber. Looking back a few years to the time when I was in the midst of my grad studies in Tours, when homework was done, around 10:30 each night, my roommate, Rita, and I used to walk over to 'Place Plume' (local lingo), to our favorite resto. Then, as tonight, the late-night tables are arranged outside, in the square that is bustling with activity. There are street entertainers in true medieval fashion. Then, as tonight, we order, Grand Marnier-laced crêpes with vanilla ice cream smothered in homemade, rich melting, chocolate sauce. What a way to end the day!

Château de Villandry in Loire Valley and Chez Moi

The next day I am off to visit a château that I only mentioned briefly in my chapter on Château-Hopping, Villandry. It deserves a big mention here as I love sharing it beauty with armchair tourists. The Valley of the Loire is often called the' Garden of France'. Let me show you one of its most extraordinary gardens. As I approach the château, there are cyclists pedaling along scenic bike paths emanating from Tours to visit this château and others in the neighborhood. It is a fine way to tour the Valley of the Loire.

In 1169 King Henry II of England (my forebear) and Philippe-Auguste, King of France met here to conclude the Peace of Colombières, after which Henry, in poor health, returned to Castle Chinon where he died a few days later. The château was acquired in 1532 by King François I's Secretary of State, Jean le Breton. Castle Colombières was re-built as a rectangle with two three-story wings and an inner courtyard, all surrounded by a substantial moat.

In the early 17thc the last member of the Le Breton family re-named the Château Villandry. By the 18thc the new owner made renovations and additions. By 1906 Dr. Joachim Cavallo and Ann Coleman acquired the estate and initiated research leading to its restoration and installation of extensive gardens to metamorphose the property into a tourist attraction of the 20th and 21st century.

The gardens here are planted in what is referred to as the old Renaissance way; in other words, only flowers or vegetables, not a mixture. The primary source for this information is Androuet du Cerceau, whose patron was Cathérine de Médici. This is a wonderful legacy she left to us.

Now, for a description of the interior of the Château de Villandry that I have toured at least twice: It is beautiful in every way. Each salon is exquisitely appointed. The colors used in the rooms are very appealing, so much so, that I could move right in. This estate, more like a home, holds a special place in my heart; the first time I made the interior tour, I fell in love with the newly painted 18th c. dining room accented with a graceful fountain-in-a-niche at one end. The walls are salmon pink. The entire ensemble of the dining room has enchanted me for years and has drawn me back again and again.

A few years ago, when my husband and I were redecorating a room in our house as a library, I chose the Villandry salmon pink for the area not occupied by bookcases and pale green with understated 'fleurs de lys' for the rest. I feel uplifted as I sit at my computer in this room, writing as I do most days. I believe that I have appropriated a small portion of the Château de Villandry for my personal use and enjoyment. Little did I know at the time of my first visit when I incorporated the salmon pink as a part of my being, that the dining room at Villandry had been classified specifically as an 'Historical Monument' since 1934.

The Villandry gardens are arranged on three levels, each one a beauty to behold. The top-level features "a water terrace; directly below is a level of box hedges, clipped yews, and flowers arranged 'en broderie' (like an embroidery pattern). At the lowest level occurs a still more intricately designed terrace, but organized into a geometric shape, all framed and outlined by trimmed hedges, paths and canals. Vines climb over trellises while yews stand like sentinels on either side of entrances and at intersections. The whole effect is as brilliant as stained glass and as abstractly decorative as a Persian carpet." I quote this description from an ancient article.

The present owner, Henri Cavallo, continues to add beauty and historic purity to the Villandry property by restoring the gardens to their Renaissance state. Although I have visited several times, always bringing friends, I never grow weary of walking through, up and around this immensely creative and elaborate garden. It is an inspiration to gardeners from all over the world.

Pilgrimage to Ste. Anne d'Auray, Brittany

After my Villandry trip, my son, Rusty, who knows his way around France quite well, meets me in Tours at Mado's for the rest of our summer together.

We shall make the trip into Brittany in pursuit of some Quimper pieces for my daughter's wedding next June. Naturally we start our time together at Mado's house, our hub. The plan is to make a couple of stops on the way to Quimper, located near the Point du Raz on the Atlantic coast. We will pass near the town of Sainte Anne d'Auray where I made a memorable visit last year. Below follows my experience at Ste. Anne for the high feast day that is celebrated there each summer.

Since I am a modern-day pilgrim of sorts, Mado always fills me in on places of historic interest where pilgrims gather. She tells me that Sainte Anne (Anna), the mother of Jesus' mother, Mary, is the patron saint of Brittany and that her day of celebration is July 26. This falls one day after the high holy feast day of St. James, July 25, in Spain. It would have been impossible to celebrate the two Holy Feast Days in one pilgrimage; thus, the journey Rusty and I made in 1993, is already covered in a separate chapter. Anna was also the name of a Celtic deity, worshipped in Brittany. So, the history of both extends for thousands of years.

When I made my pilgrimage to Ste. Anne d'Auray it was a hot July weekend. The crowds were large as expected, but nothing like in Santiago. Before the church procession began, I had plenty of time to roam the streets by the church to enjoy the tables of wares offered by the local ladies. I tasted the typical Breton crêpes, their breads in all shapes, and their pastries, of course.

I was most intrigued by the women in their local dress from long ago who were everywhere in town. They were characterized by their tall white 'coiffes' (heavily starched white lace head dresses) that stand many inches high in the shape of pillars on top of their pinned-up hair. The ladies are clad totally in black except for their headdress. I find that each region of Brittany has its own particular shape 'coiffe.' This is a wonderful welcome to Brittany.

This annual feast day celebrated at Auray is called a 'Pardon' (time of repentance and forgiveness). Later on, as the sun dipped below the horizon, the procession began in candlelight and paraded to a platform by the church. The beautiful notes of the Bretons singing were like heavenly music. I stood by a tree alone amidst the crowd. I could not hear the words spoken by the priest or bishop but was moved to think of my mother. She had been born with the Annah that she later changed to simply Anne. My mother passed away about 10 years prior to this evening, this night of memories, this moving ceremony in Auray. I was feeling very close to my mother at that time; sad that she could not come with me to this place that celebrated her name.

In Love with Pont Aven

While driving, I shared the impact of this event with Rusty. I give thanks to God for these hours of travel together in our rented car that give us ample time to recount and remember family members long gone from our midst. We continue to our intended stopover in the small town of Pont Aven. By veering off the main road to Quimper, we will have the opportunity to explore the place made famous by painter, Paul Gauguin. He was born here and later painted multiple canvases depicting the charming town of Pont Aven with his school of artists. Although first classified as an Impressionist, his style evolved into a more Symbolist way of expression. Gauguin began, over time, to apply larger sections of single colors and to avoid the layering of hues on the canvas. His early paintings are reminiscent of Pont Aven, in that he depicts the women of his Breton town in their familiar 'coiffes'.

After leaving Pont Aven, Gauguin settled in faraway Tahiti. He had been a close friend of Vincent van Gogh. It was after their stormy separation in the south of France, that he made this momentous move to Tahiti, and Van Gogh, eventually moved to Auvers-sur-Oise, near Paris. For Gauguin, the environment in Tahiti was different in every way from the stolid ways of Brittany. Instead of painting Breton women in black from head to toe, in tight stand-up 'coiffes' (head dresses), he was drawn to the beautiful dark-skinned nearly naked women of that Pacific island who were far from uptight about their bodies.

Rusty and I are staying overnight at a fine inn with a gourmet menu that comes highly recommended. It is the Moulin De Rosmadec. It is a perfect setting with an outdoor terrace restaurant where the breeze coming from the river is welcome after the heat of the day.

We take a leisurely walk around the town that is divided by the flow of the Aven River. Shakespeare lived by the Avon, but Gauguin lived by the Aven. Similar town names with slight difference in pronunciation. Both are inspirational places to live and be creative, in my opinion. I have visited both, but, as much as I love Shakespeare and the swans that flourish on his Avon, I am 'over the moon' for Gauguin and this sweet town, swans or not.

Content with our day so far, my son and I change and dine on the terrace at a lovely round table with a sparkling white tablecloth, lavishly decorated with flowers all around, and we take a look at their menu 'qui donne l'eau à la bouche' (makes my mouth water). I know this is oyster country and that they are famous for local oysters. For starters we have a choice of 'foie gras frais de canard maison' (fresh duck livers) or '9 huîtres plates de Belon #2' (9 Belon flat oysters number 2). Rusty takes the foie gras and I, the Belon oysters. One needs to know at this point that the flat Belon oysters are praised as the best in the world by those with the taste buds to know.

These French oysters, although harvested all over France, are then 'finished' as they call it, in the brackish waters of the Belon River in walled ponds. Apparently, the great variety of minerals, phytoplankton and rich marine nutrients give the oysters the desired 'ocean taste' that make them famous. Fortunately for us tonight, the Belon River is only three miles south of Pont Aven, so our oysters are the freshest they can be! My oyster craving is sated for the time being. Reluctantly, I share my oysters with my son.

For our main course, Rusty chooses the 'homard grillé Rosmadec' (grilled lobster), and I take the 'Pigeon farcie au foie gras' (pigeon stuffed with duck liver). We are spoiled in this restaurant, and the service goes hand-in-hand with the chef's culinary expertise. For dessert, Rusty orders the 'Soufflé chaud au Grand Marnier' (warm Grand Marnier soufflé) and I, 'Les crêpes soufflés au citron coullis muroise' (airy French pancakes with a lemon sauce). Crêpes are on all menus in Brittany. We turn down the cheese plate but do partake of the salad course. We both quietly sip a cup of coffee 'déca' (decaffeinated), mulling over our day of delights. The hotel and the chef live up to and beyond expectation.

The next morning, we cover more of the town on foot, with seaside hydrangeas in bloom and dear little bridges to linger on watching the slow-moving stream meandering by ancient stone homes on its way to the sea. I tell my son that if we must go from this enchanting place, he will have to drag me bodily away. I want to put down roots and be planted to thrive here. Never mind the call of Tahiti. It never enters my mind.

Quimper to Purchase a Wedding Gift

It is only a short drive to Quimper. Much as I demur at the thought of departure from Pont Aven, I finally give in. We are on a quest in Quimper today after all. We are looking for gifts of Quimper Faïence to have shipped to us at home. Lots of Americans collect Quimper ware, either entire sets, the plates or the cereal bowls, or specialty gift items such as figurines, tiles, even jewelry. Henriot Quimper is a protected brand name and is sold in very few locations in America. We could have driven to the Quimper store on the Eastern shore of Connecticut, but we have chosen to take the longer, but direct route to the source, since we can.

We find the store just outside town at the Quimper Faïence (earthenware) factory where the attractive hand-painted pottery is made. I have had this store in Quimper on my bucket list for years. I finally made it. In a matter of one-half hour looking around the storerooms filled with dishes of all sizes, I settle on a room filled with plates.

I know just what I want. While Rusty looks for the wedding gift for his sister, a covered tureen and matching tray that it sits upon, I plunk myself on the floor and start to sort through the stacks of plates. For my daughter, Amy, I will choose the pattern that is predominantly yellow 'Soleil' (sun) with a man and woman in the center; for myself, I choose the more familiar style and color. This one is a 'Mistral Bleu' (the name of a famous wind that blows in Provence) with a man and woman a featured in the center of each plate. I love all things blue and white. My kitchen is decorated with hand-painted blue and white English tiles and the voluminous draperies, a blue 'toile' (early French fabric design).

The shop girl tells me that I can sort through the stacks of plates and other dishes to my heart's content, until I find as many as I want. So, we seat ourselves on the floor for easy picking. The clue is that each item is hand-painted, so I want to find ones that match more or less in color and design. After an enjoyable search for just the perfect items, we have found our pieces and ask them to ship our purchases to our home address. They say that they do this daily. Not to worry about breakage. It is rare and fully insured in case it happens. Mission accomplished! Daughters Heather and Amy will be thrilled to receive our picks.

Intriguing Menhirs and Dolmens

Curious about Point du Raz, Rusty takes the wheel of our car, and we head to the end of a short peninsula called Razor Sharp in English. It is supposed to jut out into the Bay of Biscay (or Atlantic) the farthest on this side of Brittany. Also, this section of Brittany is called 'Finisterre' (end of earth), another name for the last bit of dry land before you get wet. We stand as close to the last bit of solid ground we can find without getting our feet wet and stare out over the endless stretch of sea with the wind in our faces. It is a good feeling. We are at peace.

Now we drive back unencumbered (that is, no large, bulky packages to carry back home from Quimper, since they were kindly mailed for us), toward Nantes from whence we entered Brittany. We check the map for a stop at Carnac. Meanwhile, back on the road, we keep an eye out for something uniquely Breton, signs along the route indicating either a 'menhir' or a 'dolmen'. We begin to recognize the small signs posted like street signs in the towns. If you have traveled in Brittany, you may not have noticed these unobtrusive signposts, but since Rusty and I like all things historic, we take up the trail of these signs. It goes like this: We search for a sign with the image of a 'menhir' or a 'dolmen', and we turn off the road post haste to find it. The stones can be hidden in someone's backyard, behind their stone wall or in a field like the one we are searching for now in a 'colza' (rape seed) field. They may also occur in large groups of standing stones, the likes of which we intend not to miss in Carnac.

Surely you are wondering what are these mysterious old 'items' that we are so eager to see. I am keeping you in suspense until you cannot stand not knowing! They come in two forms: the 'menhirs' (formed like immense tables) and the 'dolmens' (huge, tall, standing megalithic stones). These stones date back to 4500 BC.

Whoa! We spot the symbol for 'menhir' at a corner. We make a quick decision to satisfy our curiosity for the table-like stone. We are in a quiet neighborhood here, dotted with houses and small farms. The next sign points straight ahead across a well-mowed field. We park and walk over. The menhir is under a hump of ground with an opening, like the entrance to a cave. We duck down and walk in to see an enormous stone, one piece of which seems to go on forever. There is a large boulder supporting it at each end. The guidebook I carry relates that originally the 'menhir' could have been a burial place and was filled in with small stones until it was completely hidden. Over time, the small stones have been removed, leaving just the part we see, the 'menhir' or table. So, what we see as a table is nothing of the sort, but a fancy burial place, covered completely with earth and grass, seen only as a huge, strange lump thousands of years later. The person buried here must have been important, warranting such a large stone to be imported from across land and water to this spot. We keep our eyes posted to look for more.

Today we are rewarded with another sign, this time for a dolmen, and we leave our route to search for the second sign that marks the spot where the dolmen may be found, most likely on private property. We go back and forth, retracing our route on a back road and on my map. All we can see was a driveway into a private farm with a farmhouse of stone. It has to be here on this property, but we cannot see it from the road. We take a chance, enter the driveway and stop by the house. We get out to look for someone who can solve our dilemma. At last a woman appears. I guess she is used to being 'invaded' by tourists. Hopefully she will be welcoming. She is not.

Rusty politely implores her to let us see the dolmen that she admits is in the middle of her fully-grown colza field. Finally, she assents, points her arm toward the unforgiving field of tightly packed colza. We promise not to step on any plants, and we set out to find our way to the 'dolmen'. At this point, we are even more curious as to the shape and height of this 'dolmen'. We have not seen the 'dolmens' at Carnac yet, so have no measure of the size of this hidden dolmen. Rusty takes the lead and I follow. We pick our way as straight as possible between two tall, healthy, tightly-packed rows crowned with yellow flowers until we spot a tiny shack virtually surrounded by the tall plants that stand guard there.

Then we see it. It is a lot taller than Rusty with his arms stretched upward. It is as broad around as four men fingertip to fingertip. Okay, it is much larger than what we expected. I can see why the farmer's wife does not want to admit or advertise that she has such an ancient landmark in her backyard.

Photos are hard to take as we are so close to the giant stone. But circumvent it, we must. After our precarious way here, we need to have proof we found this thing called a 'dolmen'. Fully impressed, we backtrack and emerge unscathed from the colza field, thanking the woman for her patience. We drive on to Carnac.

The sight of the mown grass field dotted with scattered upright standing stones is amazing to see. In some cases, we see them standing is long straight rows. We find more and more 'dolmens' at Carnac. The sight is reminiscent of Stonehenge but on a much smaller scale.

It certainly is well worth the drive, as here at Carnac there are over 3,000 standing stones before us here. One simply drives up and looks, or gets out to walk around them, trying to fathom who placed them here and for what reason so long ago. The colza dolmen is more of a mystery since it is so much larger and therefore so much heavier than these. Try to remember that the size of a 'dolmen' is hard to judge, as much of the stone may be buried below ground. The Carnac stones are placed in long, straight rows, like so many soldiers waiting for orders to march. There seem to be circles at each end of the lines. Also, it is not easy to determine how much of each stone is buried, making it more difficult to gauge the actual height of each stone. Some say that the sorcerer, Merlin, cast the soldiers of Arthur into stone. In reality, no one really knows.

It is believed that these stones were brought here on boats from far away. The reason scientists know this is that they have made analyses of the rocks and found they are not consistent with the rock forms on this side of the Gulf of Morbihan.

Cruising the Gulf of Mobihan

That brings up another venture we propose to enjoy, spur of the moment, in this coastal section of Brittany. We drive down to the water's edge and find there is a mail boat that makes a circle tour here. The brochure says there are 365 islands in the Gulf of Morbihan, and lo and behold, there is a similar number in Casco Bay. I say, let's go. We have time today before going back to our hub at Tours tomorrow. Morbihan is connected to the Bay of Quiberon by a narrow passage with many shoals. I am ready for a short cruise. I don my large hat and my shades.

It feels good to be out on the water for a change. There are a moderate number of passengers, mostly local I am sure, who get off and on the boat at the many stops. This is not a tour boat, so no description of the islands we pass. We do have many questions about the next island where we cannot stop as it is <u>a sinking island</u>. Extraordinary! I can see there are standing stones half submerged on the island, they appear to be standing in a circle. It looks very strange indeed. This is the last place I expected to see 'dolmens'. I look it up later to find that this island has been sinking for a very long time and was once connected to a mainland peninsula. The stones are five to six thousand years old, but most tourists have no idea they are here. Well this is a nice surprise.

From the boat, we catch a glimpse of small harbors, quaint houses and boats with sails of many colors. There are sandy beaches and rocky outcroppings and much natural beauty as we pass silently past uninhabited islands. We are nearing the end of our Brittany visit. Our short lunch was the typical whole wheat crêpes just before the highway heading back to Mado's house.

I wonder what Mado has in store for us. She is waiting for us tonight (Friday) to join her family who is putting on a Greek dinner. Mado and Maryse have just returned from a trip to Greece, while we were in Brittany. It is their habit, and a nice one at that, to bring back ideas and props for a garden party. Many of their family members will attend as well as local friends, some of whom we know. Mado and Maryse are a great mother and daughter pair who really know how to put on a party with lots of atmosphere and good food. As it is close to the party time, we enter through their gate and can hear the Greek music wafting out of the house. There are lights strung on wires all through the garden. It looks magical.

La Vendée and le Puy du Fou

It is a marvelous evening. Including the extended family, there must have been at least 30 guests. We all have stories to tell of our different trips of the last week. However, our weekend is not over until Sunday, when our lively hostess and her husband, Lucien, treat us to a grand performance of the "Puy du Fou" (literally: crazy man's mountain). Sounds wild I know, but I trust Mado and her choice of what she proclaims a 'must see' for us. Sorry that Rusty will not join us this time.

It is quite a drive to the 'la Vendée' area to the west of the Loire that stretches along the Atlantic coast with beautiful sandy beaches. The name is taken from the Vendée River that flows through the territory. The history of the Vendée is one not often included in history books. The Vendéen Wars were fought during the period just following the death of King Louis XVI in 1793 and extended to the end of the century (1799). The Republican government of France decided to prohibit the Catholics from public worship. This sparked brutal fighting on both sides. There was confiscation of property, raising of taxes, and barring of traditional priests. In most of France, there was little opposition, but in the Vendée almost all rebelled. The Vendée was made up of four sections during the rebellion: the Armies of Anjou, the Marais, the Centre, and the Poitou, all of which were embraced by the Loire and the Vendée Rivers.

In 1793, well-funded Government forces marched from Paris into the Vendée with some 115,000 soldiers (by comparison Napoléon fought at Waterloo but with 60,000 soldiers). The Vendéens fought bravely for the first part of the battle and then lost ground and had to retreat. They waited for British ships that came too late. By December 1793 the rebels were defeated near Le Mans. The Republican Army of Paris was given orders to "leave nothing and nobody alive". The wars continued into 1799 with no religious freedom for the Vendéens. The rebels were severely weakened. In November of 1799 Napoléon took over with a welcome change in policy. He showed respect to the beleaguered rebels of the Vendée. He restored full rights to the Catholic Church in all of France. It was not until a couple of years after this night at the "Puy du Fou" in the Vendée that I began to comprehend what the Vendéens really experienced in those bygone days. I have noted that Mado conveys a sense of reverence when speaking of the persecuted Vendéens. I agree with her on that. I see a similarity between the persecuted Vendéens and the Cathars in a previous chapter. Neither group is mentioned in much depth in the history books.

The "Puy du Fou" performance Mado and Lucien are sharing with me tonight will not begin until nearly dark, so we set out in the mid-afternoon in the family car. I shall try to explain this enormous historical theme park as best I can. It brings periods of history to life through performances of epic proportion. To quote their literature: "By day one can watch gladiators fight for their lives, musketeers engage in swashbuckling sword fighting and Vikings rise out of the lake on ships to ransack a village before your eyes. But, here at the spectacle of "Puy du Fou" it is by night that the show comes alive behind the ruined castle to depict 700 years of history in one evening! All this with award-winning pyrotechnics and exquisite choreography. More than 1,000 actors, including children and live animals perform this show on a massive outdoor stage that boasts being the largest in the world.

We are here for the evening performance. From our seats we can see the lake bordered by a forest. As the extravaganza opens, we see more white horses than we can count, cantering in from each side of the woods along the lake. They canter up to the center of the huge outdoor stage in front of the château set. The show is beyond imagination (almost) and beautifully acted with supporting music, choreography, and lighting. It is a cultural, artistic trip into the past of the Vendée 'département' (like a county in the US) of France. During the French Revolution the Vendéens harbored anti-revolutionary sentiment. This set them apart from the rest of France and is at the heart of the story that unfolds tonight.

As the evening falls into total darkness, more special lighting effects enliven the ever-changing scenes. Hundreds of costumed actors enter and leave the outdoor stage as the story progresses and swells to a final crescendo back-lighted with a finale of fireworks. Our drive back home is peppered with my praise for the performance but most of all, my grateful thanks to Mado and Lucien for the grandeur of the outing.

Following the Loire to Sancerre for a Wine Tasting

I have but one more day with the Renaud family. I promised Maryse to drive to Sancerre for a wine tasting. En route we drive through towns of interest: Orléans, the town made famous by Joan of Arc where she routed the English, and Gien where the fine faience that I admire so much is made, decorated and fired. I have a few pieces and cherish them all the more now that I have visited this quaint town. Our drive today follows the semi-circular flow of the grand Loire to our destination, Sancerre. When we arrive at the winery where Maryse is greeted with open arms by the vintner/owner. We have a short tour and a long taste of the famous Sancerre wine.

Maryse has known the vintner in Sancerre for decades. We find him in his tasting cellar surrounded by vats of that much sought-after wine. Sancerre is a new one for me. Although I have tasted French wines from most corners of the country, I am not familiar with this one. I do know it is becoming more popular in the US.

I am ready to learn. First, Sancerre, according to my research, is located in the Centre area of France that has favored the resistance of the last hundreds of years. It was a pocket of succor during the Huguenots during the Protestant Reformation when they were eventually chased out of the country. Later, during the French Revolution, Sancerre village sheltered the anti-revolutionists who wanted to preserve the Monarchy from the Guilloutine. And again, during World War II Sancerre served as the center of command for the French Resistance movement. Therefore, I humbly assume that Sancerre has proven herself "sincere" and true once she decides to take sides in an unequal fight. So much for that angle, let us examine the Sancerre wines and how they are grown here and what makes them superior to taste buds around the world.

Mind you, I need help in describing the taste, flavor and bouquet of wine since I am not a connoisseur. I do know that the Sauvignon Blanc and Pinot Noir are their best sellers. The first is a white wine, the latter is a red. There is something about the makeup of the land that influences the taste. Sancerre is considered to be flinty and savory. I can only guess that 'flinty' refers to the limestone in the soil and savory due to the influence of the herbs and spices like chervil, savory, thyme, basil and tarragon that pair well with these wines.

Sancerre is the most recognizable appellation for French Sauvignon Blanc in the Loire Valley. All of the above make up the vine that grows in the semi-continental climate of Centre France, along with the "ripe gooseberry aromas and bracing acidity of the soil in which it thrives." If I can find it, I plan to buy some Sauvignon Blanc when I return to Connecticut. I like Maryse's choice of white wine the most.

After quite some time tasting wines and enjoying the spirited conversation around the wine barrels, we head back to Tours, stopping for a picnic by the River Loire. Maryse is seated on the grass. The setting seems peaceful, but across the river from us are the fat stacks of a nuclear power plant, the kind that provides most of the electricity for France. I was more than a bit uncomfortable there whereas, Maryse was cool as a bug on waving wheat, never giving it a second thought.

Now I turn my thoughts toward next summer and the new adventures I am planning with my long-time friend, Antoinette. We expect to walk in the footsteps of the Impressionists, a passion for us both. Our direction will be Normandy. Antoinette has a mission at the World War II beaches while I look into discovering how my ancestors lived and died much earlier in Normandy. It is sure we shall dine well and enjoy local wines wherever we roam.

Chapter Ten

Where the Seine River Leads:
Chantilly, Vaux-le- Vicomte and Chef Vatel

MY GOOD FRIEND, ANTOINETTE, AND I are happily en route from Paris into Normandy. We are full of anticipation. I am undertaking a fully new perspective on the work of the French Impressionists as we drive, looking for the small town of Auvers-sur-Oise. It is a beautiful day for a drive in the countryside, away from the bustle of Paris and the suburbs.

As we drive along at a good pace, I look to the right and am amazed to see a huge château perched on the far side of a good-sized body of water. It is quite a sight, and we are not sure what it is. I grab the "Green Guide" to find out. I read that it is the Château de Chantilly in the town of Chantilly. I know Chantilly for its lace, and it is the pattern of my silverware. All that aside, the château has a curious history. It is striking to look at. As we pass from a distance, it commands one's attention and appears to float over the water.

The Château Chantilly is made up of two edifices attached like a double string of pearls counting its reflection. The older side dates from 1560, and the other side, destroyed during the French Revolution, was rebuilt in the 1870s. In 1632, the Château Chantilly was inherited by the Grand Prince de Condé. Oh, yes, wait a minute. His name rings a bell for me. My husband, John, and I have just watched the film, "Vatel", that takes place here. Before revealing the horrifying happening at Chantilly, portrayed so well in the film, by

Gérard Depardieu, let me furnish you, reader, with the details of an earlier unexpected event with roots seeded at Château Vaux-le-Vicomte. Both Vaux-le-Vicomte and Chantilly accounts involved the chef, François Vatel (b. 1631 and d. 1671) and King Louis XIV (b.1638-d. 1715). Viewing Château Chantilly today in all its glory is unplanned and adds daytime fireworks to our trip. I recount the story to Antoinette as we ride along. Thankfully, she is driving.

Oh, my goodness, what a story revolves around these two castles. To understand the sequence, I turn first to Vaux-le-Vicomte and François Vatel, the most famous chef of his era. The event was the christening of this beautiful castle and grounds. His master at the time, Nicolas Fouquet, invited King Louis XIV along with roughly 2000 guests, for a visit to inaugurate the completion of his new château, about three hours from Chantilly, on the east side of Paris. Fouquet was the Finance Minister for King Louis XIV. N.B. No king, especially Louis XIV, would ever be bested nor outdone! In truth Fouquet had surpassed the King in all aspects of his glorious new château, namely architecture, interior design, and landscaping. To make matters worse, Fouquet had the gall, varnished pride, impertinence, stupidity or all of the above, to invite the king and his entourage to show off his precious jewel of a palace.

The aftermath of the huge blast meant 'curtains' for Fouquet, for he had committed the 'faux pas' of the century! King Louis surprised Fouquet in Britanny a few weeks after the party, captured him and swiftly swept him off to prison from which he was never released. Fouquet was imprisoned from 1661 until his death in 1680.

When Louis saw Fouquet's lavish new abode and all the splendors inside and out, he knew he had been bested by his Finance Minister; perhaps, most likely even, Fouquet had embezzled the funds to produce such magnificence. After the sumptuous reception at Vaux-le-Vicomte, the King returned to his comparatively simple abode, Versailles, in a rage. Only a hunting lodge at that point in time, Versailles was yet to be enlarged and beautified. Surely the story was frightening for Vatel who was on the premises as chief chef in charge of the grand fête.

So, a decade later, as portrayed in the film, "Vatel", Chef Vatel, was once again cooking for King Louis. This time Vatel was in the midst of enormous preparations for the last day's crowning meal at Chantilly. It had been several days of detailed planning, decorating and organizing an enormous crew of workers for his new master, the Prince de Condé. All was proceeding according to plan until, King Louis XIV and Prince Condé played a hand of cards. On the King's insistence, the two men placed a bet on the last hand of cards. They bet on who would own Vatel! Condé or King Louis!

The King had desired the services of Vatel after seeing the wonders he produced at Vaux-le-Vicomte lo, those many years ago and now again at Chantilly. Naturally the King won. The King *always* wins, n'est-ce pas? Vatel was told that the count had lost *him* at cards. Vatel felt deceived and betrayed by 'HIS Prince. Also, shortly after the card game, Vatel received the news that the order of fresh fish would not arrive in time for the dinner. The news hit him like a double blow to the stomach. It was more than Vatel could bear. He went into the kitchen, locked the door and took his life, either by a swift sword or poison. He died on the spot. Just at that moment, the fish wagons arrived! Alas, the irony of it all for poor Vatel.

So, here is the Chantilly of the Vatel story before our eyes. Shocking beyond Belief, the manner in which Louis XIV displayed his jealousy. Moral of the Fouquet debacle: Never outdo the King. Moral of Prince Condé fiasco: Never play cards with the King. And for Vatel?

Van Gogh at Auvers-sur-Oise, First visit

Onward to Auvers-sur-Oise commencing our quest to follow Vincent Van Gogh in his last months (1890). Antoinette and I both have a penchant for his work, and we want to be where he painted, see the environment that fired his inspiration.

We find his famous painting of the church of Notre-Dame-de l'Assomption d'Auvers-sur-Oise. In a way I think I prefer his painting to the real church. One cannot miss the elegant cobalt blue of the afternoon sky contrasting with the yellows in the foreground. They say that conditions today are much the same as when Van Gogh chose to paint here on a summer afternoon. Even the shadow at the left of the front entrance is clear before us, but with his highlights. He has truly transformed this tiny church from drab stone gray to vibrant colors. I saw the original painting by Van Gogh at the Musée d'Orsay in Paris a couple of years ago. But, hey, we are here now to view it up close and personal.

The village church is an example of 13th century early Gothic style and is flanked by two Romanesque chapels. We find it nestled in a copse of trees, giving it shade and a restful aura. Slowly we get a feel for the space as we walk around the tiny church that Van Gogh put on the map. It gives me a thrill to step into an impressionist painting.

Antoinette looks at me as if to say, we need more time in this town in order to know our artist more intimately. We have not allowed ample time here. We have a tight schedule today, so we shall complete our study of Van Gogh on our return trip to Paris. In this way we can allow the time we need to Follow our Dutch-born artist through his tempestuous last months of painting as he sinks slowly into the darkness of mental illness once more. The more we learn of his last days the more compelled to spend unhurried time in Auvers. Like MacArthur, we shall return!

On a brighter note, we follow the River Seine as it twists and turns, wending its way from Paris to the Atlantic Ocean. We choose a delightful place to spend the night: Château de la Corniche in Rolleboise. The Château was built by King Leopold II of Belgium (1835-1909) for his sixteen-year-old mistress, Blanche, Baroness Vaughan (1883-1948) and is situated high atop a corniche or tall hill with broad views of the twisting Seine River below. It is a four-star 'domaine' (property) with all amenities. From our room in the central section château we can see the boats peacefully plying the Seine westward to Le Havre. We can see great distances from here across the flat plains leading into Normandy.

Monet's Giverny includes a Trip to the Emergency Room and The Museum of American Impressionism

After a splendid breakfast, we navigate our way for the short distance of 20 miles to nearby Giverny, and Monet's famous garden and home. Claude Monet lived here from 1886 -1926 when he died. Being here is a dream come true for Antoinette and me. Everyone who loves impressionism loves Monet, his Japanese-inspired garden and his house. Both are carefully restored. The house is painted a comforting pink with green outlines around windows and door find the interior enchanting. The colors touch me readily. I am drawn to the blue and white kitchen with a theme that is played out in the hand painted tiles that surround the room, the blue and white check curtains. There is a collection of copper utensils and bowls and the old-style soapstone sink. I would love to live, cook and entertain in this kitchen.

The dining room is attractive as well with yellows, whites and pale greens. Yellow is the predominant hue and is seen on the walls, the wooden cabinet, chairs and table for 8-10 people. The table is set with yellow and white dishes with blue rims. The wooden, fan-back chairs are made comfortable with green and white check cushions. The ceiling is yellow and the floor, a pattern of ochre and white tiles. Using the complimentary colors to the ideal in this room, the walls are hung with blue and white plates.

Pale green vases march along the fireplace mantel, and hand-painted blue and white tiles surround the firebox opening. Don't you just love this color scheme? I believe it resembles the original plan put together by Monet and his wife. I am certain, it has inspired many a decorator and homemaker, like myself, to emulate Monet's interior decor. I have used some of the same color combinations in my home too! I never tire of blue and white with yellow accents. Monet was the master both inside and in the garden. He replanted and re-worked his world-famous water gardens over the years until they reached perfection.

The day that Antoinette and I arrive here is midsummer, the peak of Monet's beautiful gardens and, lest, we forget, also, the tourist season. We complete the house and garden tour and are about to spend time in the fabulous gift shop when Antoinette, my friend of many years, a professional teaching nurse, surprises me by saying that she has to sit down and does not feel well at all. We sit by the rounded bridge over the water lilies while she rests. In fact, she does not revive much, and she tells me she feels VERY ill. I ask her advice, since she is the health expert. She says she wants me to call for an ambulance to take her to the hospital. I do so with the help of the garden manager.

Within minutes, even though we are in the country, not that close to a town, the ambulance arrives, and I drive our car behind to the hospital. We are ushered into a curtained room. The doctor arrives immediately. I can see that Antoinette is very pale and weak. He, the doctor, has her rest on an examining table in a sitting position while he makes a quick assessment of her condition. He asks the nurse to fetch a glass of orange juice and a piece of French (of course) bread that Antoinette is to eat. No pills. Just some food. And within a short time, she regains her strength and seem normal again. Was it a hypoglycemic attack?

Well, with Antoinette's scare behind us, we have a nice restorative lunch and drive down the road to the next object of our interest — the American Impressionist Museum, a few hops from Monet's garden. I am so happy for Antoinette that her momentary crash health wise has a good outcome. We can continue our touring, but do not push to do much this afternoon.

The "Museum of American Art in Giverny" was founded in 1992 by American art collector, Daniel J. Terra. It is worth a mention here since I had recently heard of it through an art collector in new Haven, CT. I hoped that since we would be in Giverny, we should pay the new museum a visit. It is well worth it. The entrance is inviting with overflowing bushy mounds of blooming lavender. Today we see only the beginnings of the new museum's goal of showcasing American Impressionists.

Since then the museum has changed its name to "Giverny Museum of Impressionism" and added many paintings and offered special exhibits. I must say that creating this new art venue so near Monet's gardens was a capital plan. And like the Claude Monet's destination, Terra, the new museum's founder, has combined art and gardens to the zenith. Plus, it has a café, so lovers of art can feed their stomachs while feeding their souls at this double destination. Antoinette and I conclude our afternoon on a high note.

Rouen: Monet's Cathedral
King Richard's Heart
Jeanne d'Arc's Demise

We have secured a hotel in Rouen for one night. As it turns out, there were only two rooms available in the specific area we chose in town. It is directly across from the Cathedral of Rouen made famous in the paintings of Impressionist Claude Monet. Apparently, Monet set up a sort of temporary studio across the street from the Cathedral where he concentrated on this subject. Of course, I find it thrilling to spend even one night in this place, so important to the Impressionist period. As far as I am concerned, I have made it.

I open my hotel window and peer out at the cathedral during roughly eight hours of sunlight at best, counting late afternoon and early morning light. I know that in Monet's cathedral series, like his haystacks and others, he set up his easel at different times of day to capture the varying hues of the color spectrum that he sees on the church façade.

Monet even set up several easels at once, each canvas depicting the effect of light or the stone facade at differing times of day. He moved from one to the next as the light changed throughout the day. I saw some of these finished paintings at the Musée d'Orsay in Paris. Monet morphed the shadows and the splotches of light as he went along, even in different seasons. Here I am squinting to see even a shade or hint of lavender or yellow in the church portal. Did he have cataracts that caused him to see as he did, or is it the 'je ne sais quoi (That I do not know what) that makes an artist a true artist?

So, Antoinette and I have a perfect vantage point before Rouen cathedral. We use our imagination, and I frankly admit I cannot see the hues that Monet saw of the West façade of the cathedral, but since I have viewed several of these paintings, I can but marvel at his ability to sort out and transfer to canvas, the lovely blues and the multitude of colors he used in this large series focusing on one subject. Think for a moment how exciting it would be to create a "Son et Lumière" ("Sound and Light") performance here on the façade of the Rouen Cathedral, switching from one to the next of the many color adaptations Monet saw here.

Years later when I look up the Monet cathedral series online, I find many more examples of Monet's canvases on this subject than I ever imagined he had the patience to complete. More than thirty in all, painted in the 1890s. He used virtually all the colors of the palette in these renderings of the same church. He was indeed a master of his medium. I appreciate his talent more than ever before as a result of my trip to Rouen.

After some scouring around in my notes, I discovered a long, lost scrap of information about my forebear, Richard I, Lionheart, King of England, that is fitting to mention here as I gaze across the street at the Rouen Cathedral. After my dear Richard Lionheart was so brutally murdered in Chalus, France, whether on purpose or by chance, he was then interred alongside his father and mother at Fontevraud, the family burial place or royal necropolis. Now comes the new tidbit that I never knew until now, long after my time in Rouen. I found that after his death, Richard's entrails were buried at Chalus and his heart was buried in the Rouen Cathedral! And here also to mark the spot is a full-size recumbent figure of Richard. I was aware that it was not unusual for a king to request that his heart be buried in a specific location and his body, in another. But it did not occur to me to find the place where Richard's heart was buried, reasoning that this minuscule fact would never impact my travels. Wrong! This is why history is so exciting. It is full of discoveries. And this is one of the most curious.

Wait, for there is more Plantagenet history here in the bowels of Rouen Cathedral. Richard's elder brother, Henry, first in line of Richard's siblings to be made king, died young and is interred here. The young Henry was called the King Designate. When he passed away as a youth many of the hopes of his parents died with him. Fortunately, his parents, Henry and Aliénor, were blessed with many more offspring. Young Henry's tomb is another feature of the Rouen Cathedral, one of the oldest and most beautiful Gothic Cathedrals in France.

We are not content for Monet and King Richard to be the last word in Rouen. Remember I said we would follow Jeanne d'Arc's journey to the end point in Normandy? After the highs we still feel in our hearts while trying to get into the eye, hand and head of Monet in Rouen, we now turn the corner to find ourselves standing on the spot at the Old Market Place where Jeanne d'Arc breathed her last. We are not prepared for the sadness we feel as we stand on the ground where they took her to be burned alive. It is certainly a travesty from my 21st century point of view to contemplate such torture for a young girl who had won the heart of her King, Charles VII, only to lose his guardianship and be cast into prison. If you recall, in Chapter One of this book I closed the "Day in the Life of a Student" with the Opera, "Jeanne au Bûcher" (Joan at the Stake). It was not my plan to return to Jeanne near the close of my journeys in France, but here we are. Her profound effect on her country could not be avoided. You heard of her death in the music of Honegger; here we stand, mute after the long trek from Château Loches that night to Rouen today. Jeanne (1412-14-31) was cruelly tortured during a year in captivity. She finally relented and signed a confession saying that she never received divine guidance. Several days later she donned men's clothing, for which the court had severely chastised her. The court signed her death warrant, and on the morning of May 20, 1431, at age 19, she was handed over to be burned alive at the stake by her English captors with the complicity of her own French countrymen who had turned against her.

In her lifetime, Jeanne made the much longer journey than ours from her home town of Donrémy-'la-Pucelle' (the maid) in Eastern France (where she first heard her 'voices'), to Château Chinon where she recognized the disguised Crown Prince, Charles, in a crowd, then to Orléans where she led the French Army in defeat of the English (thus she was named the Maid of Orléans), to the Cathedral of Reims where she led the Dauphin to be rightfully crowned King Charles VII and finally to ruin in Rouen.

We have been at Jeanne's side along most of this route. The Jeanne d'Arc statue in Rouen depicts her in a long robe and full-length cape with hands clasped at her neck in prayer and her head with short bobbed hair tilted skyward. Let us recall here the gleaming gold statue of triumphal Jeanne in Paris. In truth, I was never surprised to see her venerated in statues as Sainte Jeanne in the smallest villages. It was not until 1920 that she was proclaimed a Saint of the Catholic church and canonized by Pope Benedict XV. The Maid of Orléans is the Patron Saint of France. She is not forgotten.

One footnote here as we prepare to quit Rouen: The Jeanne d 'Arc Monument we see here today, is not inviting, not heartfelt. And as I understand, over the years the information center to her life is now a huge unidentifiable glob of a monument comprised of a series of long straight lines in cold stone and steel, all constructed on the very place of her sad demise. Granted, a monstrous thing happened to her, but did they have to build a monstrosity to commemorate it? It is difficult to empathize with her life story, the teenage maiden of the 15th century who sacrificed her life to God, in this uninspired space.

Normandy Beaches:
British and American

With heavy hearts, Antoinette and I press on to new horizons along the River Seine this summer of 1995. We plan to hop over to the

Normandy coast beginning with the beaches of World War II. Then we shall work our way back along the Seine Valley as promised. Mado, always helpful in making my travel plans, suggested we find a hotel in Arromanches, a small seaside town in the section of Calvados. It is farther west than the mouth of the Seine, so we have departed from the Seine Valley for a detour. Right now, we need a rest and find a small B & B run by M. et Mme. Paumelle in a nearby village. Their 'Gite' (rooms for rent) is a charming thatched roof home with a garden of tall hollyhocks and window boxes of pink geraniums. Their rose of Sharon trees are full of pink and white blooms. There is a huge flat field of rapeseed in bloom across the road. The seeds are processed to make Canola oil. We are cheered by the warmth of the welcome we receive here.

The next day we drive over to the beach. This entire string of beaches harkens back to the Normandy Invasion of June 6, 1944. It seems that the all-important secret joint plan of American General Dwight D. Eisenhower and British Prime Minister Winston Churchill was to take the German occupying forces in France off guard by launching an early morning invasion of Normandy following a late night shindig during which the Germans felt safe attending a birthday celebration some distance inland. Following a night when the inclement weather was closing in on the English Channel and Northern Normandy, the Allies took to the sea and to the air. By morning when the German officer in charge awoke with a hangover, it was their worst fear realized.

The British were assigned to land at Arromanches beach. For two years they had been forming a method of approaching the shore. I am standing on the beach with Antoinette looking out onto the harbor imagining how it must have been. I can see full size remnants of the artificial port constructed by the Brits. They mapped out a landing strategy that was unique. Farthest out into the water are the cement breakwaters that form a ring around the bay. I can still see the remainders of these barriers. They are huge, rectangular, stationary cement blocks anchored in the sea floor. The next ring is made up of two long pier frames that rise and fall, floating with the tide. The frames and the under-water portion must have deteriorated over time. And closest in toward shore were floating metal piers that have also disappeared. All the same, what is left for me to see is real and a not so subtle reminder of that pivotal day in history, June 6, 1944, the Normandy landing of The Allied Forces, British and American).

My friend and I have a seafood supper at a small restaurant on the beach tonight, talking over our plan for tomorrow. Antoinette is looking for the grave of her uncle who is buried in the American cemetery high atop the bluff at Omaha Beach. We check our map and it is not far from Aromanches.

When we arrive at Omaha Beach, and find a parking spot we are facing the massive cemetery of soldiers who gave their lives here in World War II. They made the ultimate sacrifice for God and Country after many years of fighting against Hitler and his Third Reich. My eye scans the horizon to find the end of the identical white stones that mark each and every grave, all the same. All these soldiers are here resting in a final peace after anything but peace welcomed them on French soil. They were the brave ones who faced almost certain death as they disembarked from their PT Boats into the water carrying their rifles high above their heads. The German soldiers rained down a barrage of bullets on them before they had a chance to think. The water and the beach were soon bathed in their blood.

We owe much to these thousands of men who gave their lives to protect the liberty of the free world. They did not die in vain. This we know. Our hearts go out to them. I empathize with my friend as she looks over the shining white marble gravestones, each in the shape of a cross, (with tears in her eyes); I do not have a relative here. My Uncle Frank Aulls flew in just after D-Day to help to clear the way forward across France, pushing the enemy back across the Rhine River into Germany.

In a few minutes we find the information office. A female American officer greets us. Antoinette gives the officer her uncle's name and rank, and we wait for the location of his grave. We stand tense for the time it takes the officer to search for one man among so many. Finally, with the information and a map in hand, we count the rows to the right and the rows heading to the rear of the designated section of the cemetery until we come to his marker. It is under a spreading shade tree. We both feel a deep sense of tragedy and relief to have found Antoinette's dear uncle so far from home. Like countless others, he was never brought home to be with his forebears, nor laid to rest in the family plot.

Lo, these many years later many family survivors, like Antoinette, have made the trip to this cemetery to see where their loved one rests. I remember when President Reagan was in office. He came to the Ranger Monument at Pointe du Hoc, France, on June 6, 1984 for the fortieth D-Day ceremony held to remember our American young men who never made it back home after that fateful day on the beaches of France. He said, "We're here to mark that day in history when the Allied Armies joined in battle to reclaim this continent to liberty." Also, on that day the President paid a visit to Omaha Beach where I stand today eleven years later. He spoke: This is "a place where men bled and died". He added: "Every man that set foot on this beach was a hero." It was a hard-fought battle, but freedom prevailed.

Together Antoinette and I walk to the edge of the bluff to peer over the all but inviolable precipice to the beach far below. We want to get a feel for the place of which we have heard for fifty-one years. We do not say much to each other as we imagine that horrible day in 1944. It was a day of hope, but a day of terrible loss as well. Then we walk farther along the cliffs to inspect one of the German bunkers dug into the hillside with the opening high over the English Channel. On that June 6th, so this bunker was crammed with German soldiers loading, firing, and re-loading heavy artillery, all aimed at the wide sand beach and the shallow water below. It is dark inside the bunker today and looks foreboding. We do not spend much time near the German gun post. There are many of these along the coast. Silent now.

Guillaume le Conquérant:
Invasion of Britain 1066
Bayeux Tapestry 1070s
White Ship Disaster, Barfleur 1120
Monet's Honfleur 1890s

In the afternoon sun we drive to our next destination, Bayeux, the home of the Bayeux Tapestry. On this early afternoon we transcend several centuries back in time to the Norman Conquést of England in 1066. This is a date we all learned in grammar school. Yes, we are still in Normandy, but this time the battle we seek is not taken to the Norman coast, but is taken from Normandy across the English Channel in the opposite direction to England. Guillaume le Conquérant was about to sear his name in the history books. It was September 12 when William embarked for England with 500,000 knights and soldiers on 696 ships plus a multitude of small sailing skiffs. William, who was not about to be bested by anyone, was jealous of Harold who had just crowned himself King of England.

Up to this point Normandy had been a Dukedom. On the 14th of October that Year (1066), the battle was joined at Hastings between William, Duke of Normandy, and Harold, King of England. All the damage was done on one day. Harold was defeated and killed, leaving William as Conquéror and King of England. This battle has significance for me, no matter how remote the era, as William and I carry the same blood in our veins. (what little of his is left that is). The impact of the Normans on England is lasting. They built churches and abbeys, roads and castles that still stand. After the Battle of Hastings when the Duke of Normandy became King of England, Guillaume's dukedom became a part of England. Important to note: as a result, from thenceforth, the Normans, who were native French speakers, exported their language to England. Ever wonder why the English language has so many words of pure French and of French derivation? We have Guillaume to thank for this lovely blending of French and English vocabularies.

This leads me to another of my quests this summer, to follow in the footsteps of Guillaume as well as tracing his 'down line' (genealogical term with a new slant into the future) in France, before colliding with that of his descendant, King of the English, Richard Lionheart, the son of Queen Aliénor, d'Aquitaine. We placed him in the valley of the Loire at Chalus where he died and at the royal Abbaye of Fontevraud where he is buried. We shall meet with Richard again soon as we to follow the Seine River Valley back to Paris at the close of this summer. But today we make a stop in Guillaume le Conquérant's territory at the town of Bayeux near the Atlantic seacoast. We locate the Bayeux Museum, also known as the Museum of Art and History, that houses the amazing "Bayeux Tapestry" depicting the Norman invasion of England. Most likely the tapestry was commissioned in England by Bishop Odo, Guillaume's half-brother, a few years after the 1066 invasion. Odo, in turn, had it hand stitched by Anglo Saxon women on a long length of linen with many colors of woolen embroidery yarn. It was discovered in the Bayeux Cathedral, built by Odo in the 1070s. He may have wanted to feature it in his new Cathedral.

In 1995 we make our way inside to see the world-famous embroidery kept in a semi-dark room at the Bayeux Museum. One must stand in line to examine it up close, behind glass of course. The work is 230 feet long and 20 inches high and is exquisite, especially for an artifact so ancient. Incredibly it remains intact. The scenes represented on the piece are a pictorial account of events leading up to Guillaume crossing the English Channel and culminates with the Battle of Hastings. Depicted are knights, horses, and weapons in action in great detail. It is a one-of-a-kind masterpiece equal in some ways, to one of the wonders of the world, having lasted longer than some of the so-called wonders of the world.

Guillaume le Conquérant departed from the small Normandy fishing village of Barfluer en route to fight the Battle of Hastings. We must visit Barfleur before turning back to our trip along the Seine. It is a pivot point for some exciting moments in French/English history in more ways than just this one. Surely the departure of Guillaume le Conquérant in 1066 must have stirred up the neighborhood around Barfleur as did the departure of General Rochambeau from Brest for America in 1780. In both cases hordes of knights, their steeds, their equipment and war materiel were amassed in this place and likewise in the port of Brest further south along the coast of France before setting sail for two battles that changed history. In both cases England was defeated with lasting effects for centuries.

There was another setting sail sequence from Barfleur that made history on alert. It was the evening of November 25, 1120 and is worth recalling for history lovers as well as for those of us who are directly descended from the Dukes Normandy and Anjou (forerunners of the Plantagenets). Yes, this genealogical delving behind the veils of time to almost 60 years after the Norman Conquést reveals an event of shocking proportion. As I stand on the wall of the 'quai' (wharf) at Barfleur, looking toward the sea, I pull my mind back all those years to a night of frolic and revelry that preceded a terrible disaster not far from where I stand. It was under the reign of King Henry 1st, Guillaume's fourth son. He was a great ruler, well-educated and effective; he strengthened the crown's executive power by setting limits on royal authority and modernizing his administration. He enjoyed a long and peaceful reign of some 35 years. His greatest achievement was reuniting England and Normandy. It was said in those days that "Henry was a man against whom no man could prevail except God himself." In other words, he always got his way. Right? Not so on the day that had begun so perfectly right here in Barfleur.

King Henry I had just witnessed the knighting of his only legitimate son, William Adelin, who at age 17, was already accomplished and wealthy. It was a cold, blustery day. A few weeks earlier William, the King-to-be, had demonstrated his obeisance to Louis VI, King of France, and had been named Duke of Normandy, relieving his father of the title in preparation for becoming the future king. It had been a wonderful time of riding alongside his father for nearly a year touring

Normandy, learning as he went. Beyond all that great fortune, young William had Recently wed Mathilde, of the Foulke family, the Dukes of Anjou, thus uniting the Angevin and Norman families.

Together in Barfleur Henry the King, and William his son, as well as the latter's new wife, Mathilde, along with nobles, knights, and all the brightest and best upcoming stars of Normandy and England partied until late, until too late in fact. The King had borrowed a good-sized sea-going vessel called the White Ship, to ferry the crowd of elite young people from Barfleur to the south of England.

There would be as many as 200 passengers and 50 oarsmen plus the rest of the crew, another 50 men, to handle the sails aboard for the nighttime crossing. Due to the excessive reveling onshore, the hour for departure grew later. In fact, the passengers and crew were all drunk. There was no other word for it. They had partied and drunk too much for they could do so. They were high-spirited and feeling no sense of urgency to get underway. The royals and their friends with guards and many attendants, a judge and several cousins were young and well-heeled with a golden future ahead of them. In effect, an entire generation of Henry's family and friends were clustered onto the ship, unaware of impending disaster until it struck.

Before departure the King arranged for a sacred water blessing of the ship at which time Henry cautioned the captain to take the best care of this ship as she held his most precious loved ones in his charge as cargo. The ship had been "excellently fitted out and readied for royal service." Unfortunately, the crew and the passengers were not in such fine shape as the ship.

It is important to point out that the ship's rudder was not in the center as most are, but on the starboard (right) side. As a result, the man at the rudder, perhaps the Captain, was at times blinded to the port side by the sail. The King assumed that the Captain was well aware of the lay of the land to his port and to his starboard on the route away from the harbor. There were shoals and jutting rocks to avoid. The White Ship weighed anchor around midnight. Within a few minutes after setting sail over the choppy waters on that late fall eve, still at the mouth of the harbor, the ship crashed into a rocky outcropping that pierced a large hole in her hull. The ship took on water quickly. Passengers were thrown into the icy sea. Their heavy, layered silk clothing would have pulled them downward into the murky depths before anyone could reach the wreck to save them. Prince William was put into a lifeboat with a few others. Hearing his sister, Mathilde, crying for help, the small skiff headed toward her but desperate people in the area saw rescuers arriving and scrambled to climb into the small boat, capsizing it, leaving them all to succumb.

As a result, William the King designate, and his sister, Mathilde, were both drowned. Please note that young Prince William had three Mathilde's in his life – his mother, his sister and his wife. That night both he and his sister drowned. One man survived the disaster. He was a butcher from Rouen who was on board for business reasons. He made it through the night in the freezing water and climbed onshore in the morning of the next day. The butcher was the only one to relate the woeful tale of the accident: the night of drinking, the carelessness of all involved, the sinking of the ship and the skiff and worst of all the drowning of the King's son along with two of his siblings and cousins. The King had sailed to a different port in England and did not know the news for several days. It was an incident beyond belief, sudden, deadly and final. It was as unexpected as the death of English Princess Diana in a Paris car crash in 1997. The tragedy at Barfleur was worse, multiplied by hundreds of drowned innocents.

Antoinette and I experience life's highs and lows at every turn. We expect this by now and learn to take it in stride. We have known each other since 1961 and have encouraged each other as we traveled through the slings and arrows of 34 years. All highs would not be realistic. The same goes for the lows. We accept with relish whatever history and tourism bring. We are here together to explore and to learn. So onward and upward we go. Excelsior!

As we head back to the Seine River, our travel today leads us through resort beach towns with familiar names such as Deauville and Trouville. We drive along the shore roads wherever possible to see the wide beaches and the elegant hotels and homes. Our plan is to stop at Honfleur. We find a spot to park here, so we may stroll in the harbor made famous by Monet's paintings. The boats, gently bouncing up and down with the waves, are colorful, with hulls painted in a myriad of greens and blues. The old buildings that line the boat basin stretch around the curved flow of the water beside a wide cobble stone sidewalk. It is a beautiful sight to behold. We are entering Monet country again. I can feel it in my bones as I feast my eyes on the soothing colors surrounding us.

Monet's Étretat

We anticipate our next destination as we cross the mouth of the Seine at Le Havre driving north. It is 'Étretat'. (The last 't' is silent.) Why are we chasing down this small beach town that is not a household word for most unless one is a Monet devotée? Well, Antoinette and I fall into that devotee category. We want more Monet. Quite simple. Again, we are following the Normandy coast. As we pull up by Étretat beach and start across to the water's edge. Our first surprise is what is underfoot. Instead of the expected soft sand we have seen so far in Normandy, we are glad we kept our shoes on, for the beach is made up of fist size knots of stone from one side to the other. It is not the place to lie down under an umbrella! Ouch!

"Wait a minute. Look over there. There it is!" I say to my traveling companion, as I look up and to my left to see the 'Falaises d'Aval' (The Aval Cliff). It is unmistakable. We have all seen it in Monet's famous paintings. Undeterred by winter winds and cold temperatures, the determined artist spent most of February 1883 in Étretat. I like my creature comforts, and even as a former cross-country ski instructor cannot 'picture' myself here on this wind-shorn beach in winter. Indeed. This is where Monet spent days trying to paint the light just right on the cliff, the sea and sky. I feel a chill run up and down my spine to find myself here in this place of such creativity. How often do we admire an artist's work and even contemplate making the effort to put our feet where the artist planted his or hers?

This trip has been like that. It was here in this stony waterfront that the sun poured out its rays and reflections before Monet's all-seeing orbs. He painted from the cliffs; he painted from sea level, and all the while he saw colors the normal eye can never fathom. Still, here we are testing ourselves to see as he did over a century ago. It brings to mind Monet's multitude of essays to portray his object at different times of day. For instance: the facade of the cathedral in Rouen, the falaise at Étretat, his water lilies at Giverny, his haystacks. Like moths attracted by the light, we have traced Monet's footsteps all over Normandy to capture the light he saw. It is ever elusive.

Yes, we have been able to stand before some of the objects upon which he fixated: Rouen Cathedral and Étretat and found them unchanged over the years since Monet brought his easel to rest before them. As for his water lilies at Giverny, we have been able to see the objects of his interest in their re-blooming state, appearing much as they did in Monet's day. On the contrary, his haystacks, have totally disappeared, never to be viewed again in the rural fields of France.

In 1959 when I was traveling throughout France for the second time, my mother and I were drawn to a comparison of, you guessed it, 'haystacks'! We took photos, stopped to admire them in different shapes from one end of the country to the other, even watched the farmers forking their newly dried hay onto their personal haystacks. So, I have a pretty comprehensive view on 'haystacks' over the last nearly 60 years. Lastly, I admit that when feeling Monet-deprived, in less than 45 minutes I can plant myself before one of Monet's 'haystack' paintings in Farmington, Connecticut, at the Hill-Stead museum. All this said, we are here in France following the progression of Impressionism and finding it most thought provoking! Many mercis to the Rouen Cathedral, the Giverny water lilies pond, and the failaise cliff at Étretat for remaining unchanged over time.

In the early years of Impressionism, both Monet and his friend, Auguste Renoir were living hand-to-mouth even though the latter was living with his parents. They barely had enough to purchase oils and canvas. Monet would paint until the last drop of oil paint was squeezed from the tubes. Then he would keep busy sketching his next scenes until he had some cash, mostly borrowed, or until he managed to sell a painting and start all over again. It was a vicious circle as they struggled to survive to paint and vice versa.

Claude Monet ventured out to Étretat on the recommendation of other French painters, Delacroix and Courbet, who had painted here. When Monet arrived, it was midwinter of 1883, cold and windy most of the time. The weather was so forbidding that much of the time he was confined to his hotel room but managed with some difficulty to work from his window overlooking the sea. He completed his 'Stormy Sea at Étretat' with windswept high surf being observed by fishermen and their beached boats. Courbet's and Boudin's renderings were similar but were painted in calm weather. Étretat was a drawing card for so many aspiring artists at one time or another. It was a challenge any time of year and the superb light always appealing to the Impressionist painter.

Monet and Renoir 'en plein air'
Renoir's "Luncheon of the Boating
Party" at Chatou on the Seine

In 1869, Monet and Renoir decided to set up their easels side by side at the "La Grenouillère" (The Frog Pond) on the Seine at Bougival, not far from Chatou, to paint the same scene in their own styles. The scene includes a restaurant where their friends often gathered on the water. The two artists were fascinated with the reflection of the light on the gentle ripples of the pond and the mixing of social classes, their fashions of the day and the sense of a carefree atmosphere. They agreed that it was time to get out of their 'ateliers' (studios) to paint the world as it is in the natural light of day. This was the birth of Impressionism.

Luncheon of the Boating Party, Pierre-Auguste Renoir 1881. I visited Chatou, in Renoir's day, a village on the Seine River at the outskirts of Paris. One of Renoir's largest works at 4'3 x 5'8", I delved into the story behind its creation.

As followers of Monet and Renoir's group of Impressionists, Antoinette and I keep in mind that they showed a preference for working 'en pleine air' (outdoors), often near water: the Seine or the English Channel, but always in pursuit of that ever-elusive factor, light. We follow the Seine, crisscrossing it between the Châteaux of Malmaison and Saint–Germaine-en-Laye from Paris right into Renoir land. Recently I read a book about Renoir's experience as he made explicit plans and finally painted his oversize 'chef d'oeuvre' (masterpiece), "Luncheon of the Boating Party". American Novelist Susan Vreeland (1946-2017) was a New York Times Bestseller who combined historical fiction and art. She boldly titles her book on Renoir the same as Pierre-Auguste Renoir titled his prize-winning painting of 1881. To view it in person as I have done, the large canvas resides in the Phillips Collection, Washington, DC.

I mention Vreeland's book for several reasons: the action takes place in the small town of Chatou along the Seine only seven miles from Paris center. Also, since Antoinette and I are tracing the early

Impressionists who made the daring decision over 140 years ago to paint outdoors rather than in a studio, seeking the beauty of natural light, it is appropriate that Vreeland's subject, Renoir's painting, is all about an outdoor scene. And the book is a remarkable story, very readable, about the Impressionists, their daily lives together, along with their successes and bitter failures, personal and professional. Vreeland sheds light on the ongoing difficulty of hiring models and of selling paintings while trying to make ends meet. Although some of the boating party models lived nearby, others had to take the train from Paris to arrive at Renoir's appointed time for the interminable Sunday sittings while he sketched and finally painted them. They rendezvoused at one of their favorite haunts, the upstairs balcony restaurant of the "Maison Fournaise" in Chatou on an island in the Seine. It all sounds so enchanting. Vreeland reveals the credible backstory that goes along with the painting.

Interestingly, Auguste Renoir's famous 'boating party' was anything but spontaneous. The project was staged by the artist so he could paint in a convivial place where he knew the restauranteur. The 'faux luncheon' (fake luncheon) or luncheons were contrived to happen, not once, but as often as necessary until the work was deemed finished by Renoir. I say fake because at the moment of Renoir's snapshot they were not partaking in the meal but have in fact finished eating several times.

It is the clever enticement of the artist to tempt his fourteen models with a Sunday midday meal to be sure his sitters showed up. So, what were they eating? In truth they had ingested not lunch as the title infers but a full course dinner as is the habit of the French who eat so well and take the time to do so. For this memorable luncheon the participants gathered around the tight tables on the tiny balcony over the Seine. For Renoir, it was a bit like herding cats as the models were hard to please and did not always follow direction. On the other hand, the sun cooperated nicely and beamed in from under the awning lighting up the scene to Renoir's delight.

As for the meal, the varied subjects of Renoir's painting-to-be may have enjoyed: a fried fish first course since they are on the banks of the

Seine, and why not eat the fruits of her waters? Then they may have been served a 'poulet sauté aux artichauts' (chicken with artichokes); the usual green salad; for dessert a 'tarte Normande aux pommes' (custard apple pie) laced with Calvados; fresh fruits of the season (grapes are visible on Renoir's board); accompanied by a requisite cheese plate; and punctuated with local wines chosen by Madame Fournaise. The gracious meal served as an alluring treat, 'grace à' (thanks to) the artist, Auguste.

The "Maison Fournaise" still exists for the followers of Renoir. It looks very much like it did in his day. From a distance we stand to admire the scene and to fill in the tables and faces that once occupied Auguste, using our imaginations. I add that Chatou and La Grenouillère are worth a trip.

King Richard Lionheart's Château Gaiullard
Memoires of his mother, Aliénor d' Aquitaine

'Certes' (certainly), it is not easy, but my traveling pal and I must pull ourselves away from Renoir's world to continue snaking our route along the Seine's course while talking of kings, a ship of two prows and a field of crows. Let's start with the English king, King Richard I, and his double-prowed ship, leaving the crows for last. We pick up the denouement of Richard's life as it pertains to the meandering ribbon of the Seine, the major thread in our Normandy 'sejour' (journey).

Antoinette and I share the driving as usual and head toward our next Norman quest. The visit to Château-Gaillard (sometimes referred to as a double-ended ship) is one of revelation to me, a 28th generation descendant of Richard Lionheart, Duke of Normandy and King of the English. On this clear, summer's day, we learn that, upon his return from the Third Crusade, his imprisonment and ransom, he built the largest and perhaps the last 'château fort' (fortified castle) in France. And it is perched high above the Seine River. Following is an excerpt from my play, "Conversations with Queen Aliénor of Aquitaine", summarizing the king's life just prior to the construction of Château- Gaillard:

"After freeing her son, King Richard, Queen Aliénor returned to l'Abbaye Royuale de Fontevraud (A convent in the Loie Valley favored by their family) for rest and relaxation. Richard wrested lost sections of Normandy and in particular, the Vexin, from his younger brother, John, who had supposedly been guarding them for him while he was in the Holy Land. Upon Richard's release from prison, John agreed to return to the Angevin family tent and to no longer side with French King Philippe-Auguste Capet."

To start, the Vexin is the area north of the Seine through which we have been traveling, with Rouen the most important city. The 'Vexin Normand' (Duke of Normandy's possession) extends almost to Paris. For this reason, the King of France, Philippe-Auguste (1165-1223), son of Aliénor's first husband, Louis VII, King of France, wanted desperately to control the Vexin as it gave access to the English Channel. While away, Richard's younger brother, John, ceded it by name only, to the family enemy, Philippe-Auguste. Will no ruler ever be content with what he or she has? "While the cat is away the mice will play"; the old saying fits here. At this point in Richard's life as King of England, he must once again wrest the Vexin from Philippe and return it to his side of the game board. Building Château-Gaillard is a strategic step in Richard's plan to keep the Vexin. It is the ongoing saga of the second generation being in direct opposition to their parents.

As an important stopping off point along our Seine trip in Normandy, I chose Gaillard for us to explore today, but my ancestor, Richard, chose it first with his keen intelligence for its unique location concerning his warfare strategy at the close of the 12th century. I compliment him! This is my first time here, having held Château-Gaillard in my mind's eye until now.

Queen Aliénor's immediate family, or what remained of it by 1198, struggled to maintain the tradition of gathering the clan at Christmastime. They called it the Christmas Court. Aliénor hoped that, once built, she would join her loved ones here to celebrate the Christmas fête. But that was not to be. It never happened. Thus, even

Aliénor, Richard's aging mother, was left to imagine the magnificence of her son's creation. We have just arrived at the summit of the castle mount. It was a steep, twisting, stony path, but we made it. From our vantage point 'she' (the château), even in her sad state of disrepair, resembles a true ship of state. We stand near what would have been the ship's forward prow, high above the river Seine. The warm air rises from the moving currents below and catches my hair, billows the broad sleeves of my protective sun shirt.

In King Richard's day, we would not have been admitted into the gates without facial recognition or a pass from the King. Once inside the drawbridge, having successfully passed beneath Richard's innovative machicolis through which huge boulders and boiling oil would have rained down on us, we would have had to cross inner moats and ditches as well as high narrow bridges, to reach the upper level. We would have had to gain entrance to heavily bolted doors through tall, five-meter-thick, stone walls and then even more tall, triple concentric stone walls to reach the inner bailey and finally the keep. The highest part of the château was the keep with slit windows on all sides, where the royal family would have been safely installed when in residence.

For added protection against assault, Richard incorporated stone columns into the same thick walls, not only at the corners but at even distances between corners. His Gaillard was built to be impregnable. It was constructed and completed in record time…less than one year, still another amazing feat in those days. It was to be the largest fortification ever built in what we call France today. Back then, Normandy was, as you know, a part of England. It was all these things during Richard's lifetime.

It is documented that King Richard, on the one-year anniversary of the Gaillard accomplishment, pronounced: "She is my fine yearling daughter." So, Gaillard was female to her creator. It was as if this ship/château were placed here overlooking the mighty Seine as a guardian of Richard's kingdom. From here, whether at the bow or the stern, one could survey upstream and downstream and in all directions to easily forecast the arrival of an invading army.

Gaillard was strategically placed along the busy ingress from the sea to the French seat of government, Paris, and conversely, as a bulwark to prevent egress from France proper into Normandy. Richard, Duke of Normandy, would preserve his Vexin territory from Philippe-Auguste. The Lionheart realized his dream by installing the military stopgap he needed against Philippe's never-ceasing aggression. Richard was indeed King of the Mountain and ruler of all he could see. He would safeguard his people and his parents' holdings with this 'Ship of State'. King Philippe must have been severely rankled and totally stymied by this grand building project. In fact, we do know how the King of France reacted upon hearing of or sighting this mighty fortress from afar. Quote from Philippe Auguste: "If the walls were made of iron yet would I take them!" And Richard retorted: "By God's throat, if the walls were made of butter, yet would I hold them against Philippe!"

To Antoinette, I intone: "Let's stand here at the imaginary prow of Gaillard facing into the west wind and looking toward the sea that lies just beyond our view." Following is another quote from my play, "Conversations with Queen Aliénor": I say to Aliénor: "Do you feel the strong westerly breeze swirling up from the brackish river flow? It is not that far from full saltwater. Let's stand together facing into the wind as did the stars of the film, "Titanic" with the music swelling. Imagine that we are the stars, Kate Winslet and Leonard DiCaprio on the bow of the Titanic with our arms widespread facing into the wind, hair flying, high above the Atlantic. The only difference is that we are leaning into the wind at the bow of Château-Gaillard high above the right bank of the Seine River. I love it! Don't mind me. I often fall right into the trap created by the film writers and find myself transported by sight and sound into the story. Can you feel the connection? The similarity? The thrill?"

We both lean into the wind and agree that the view and the feeling are breathtaking! I cannot help thinking that some 800 years ago my ancestor, King Richard, might well have stood here on the precipice just as I am today, surveying his land and sensing pride in accomplishing such a feat as Gaillard.

While I am standing in the breeze over the mighty Seine, I recall a framed portrait of my son, Rusty, on the summit of Race Mountain. He is stretching out his arms in triumph after a long, difficult climb, and the wind is blowing through his red hair while rippling his shirt. That is precisely the image I have now of King Richard. More's the pity that photos were not possible in those days. How Aliénor would have reveled in his achievement.

With mixed emotions, I muse to myself, standing on the promontory 100 meters above the river, that Aliénor was never able to visit her son here during her lifetime. But, once again in my play, "Conversations with Queen Aliénor", through the magic of the written word, the impossible happens as Aliénor and I come into each other's presence in this very place. So, in a sense I have been here before. And in a matter of speaking, Aliénor did finally accomplish one of the last things she had hoped to do in her life: to visit Gaillard. For this I am pleased. In my play, Aliénor and I meet in several locations, mostly in France where we reminisce about events in both our lives. Despite the difference in our stations in life, we find much to share, for each location is meaningful to us both.

Aliénor, Antoinette, and I, high above Le Petit Andely and Saint Saveur, are enclosed in a ring of fog

From our vantage point high above Gaillard, I can see a slender, church spire. I tell Antoinette it is the church of Saint-Sauveur in the town of Le Petit Andely. During construction of Gaillard, King Richard performed a kindly act for his 3,000 workers. He observed that his hired hands, working far from home in most cases, would need a church to attend on Sundays. As if the main building site was not challenge enough, he added the church of Saint-Sauveur to an already ambitious goal.

After making the complete self-guided tour of the ruins, Antoinette tells me she feels a little chilly, so we put on our sweaters and consider leaving this magical place. We had just opened our map to check our next destination and had not realized that the afternoon was coming to a close. If you will, let me interject another excerpt from my 'Conversations with Queen Aliénor'. It includes part of the conversation I had with Queen Aliénor at the close of our visit to Gaillard on a late afternoon much like this one. N.B.: At this point I address Aliénor as 'Nanna' the familiar term I used for my maternal Grandmother, Marguerite Aulls. In the play: 'J' is Jini speaking, and 'A' is Aliénor.

"JINI: (Putting the map away) I am beginning to feel a little chilly. I see that the late afternoon fog is slowly rolling in. Look, Nanna, while we were talking the fog crept in on cats' feet and we have not even been aware of it.

ALIÉNOR: (She walks toward the edge of the castle mount nearest them, to look around.) Really? I see it now. It is just as you say. There are billows of fluffy white moving in below us on this side.

ALIÉNOR: Here, may I take your arm? Let's look over the opposite side closer to the river. I am curious to see if we are being surrounded by a magical white mist. (The two women, being careful not to stumble over the loose stones, walk across the top of the outer bailey to the other side)

JINI: Aha. Just as I thought. The fog is closing in on this side as well. It is beautiful isn't it? We are almost encircled with ethereal white fog.

ALIÉNOR: The best part is that we are high enough way up here to be in the clear. It is beginning to look like an elegant white fox collar snuggling up to keep us warm. My sweet child, isn't this fun?

JINI: My goodness yes, and the sun is still visible in the sky above. What an amazing sensation.

ALIÉNOR: We are truly favored to be together in this beautiful place today. I wonder if my son, King Richard, ever experienced this phenomenon when he was in residence at Gaillard? If so, he must have thought he was close to God, even blessed by God. Oui, 'certes'! (of course) I feel that way now myself in your presence here at Gaillard."

Back on terra firma in the Seine Valley, we are nearing the end of our most edifying journey through Normandy, Antoinette and I drive through Caen, to view more of the territory of Guillaume le Conquérant. He died in 1087. Here we give one last nod to him at the place of his burial in the 'Abbaye aux Hommes' (Abbey for men). My journey following in his footsteps has now reached closure as we bid farewell to Guillaume. So much history to follow in Normandy and always more to learn!

An encouraging piece of news since our visit is that renovations have begun on a total reconstruction of Château- Gaillard and will in time restore her to her original glory. My friend, Antoinette and I shall keep up with the improvements online. How nice we can do that when at home in the peace and quiet of our workspaces.

Van Gogh's Last Days at Auvers-sur-Oise
Final day of Seine trip

Now we do an about face to return to Auvers-sur-Oise as promised, to pick up the final thread of Van Gogh's life. This charming town has more to offer in the way of art history than meets the eye. There is something larger here that beckons us back to Vincent van Gogh. We must see it to its conclusion.

This chapter began with Vincent and will close with him. Van Gogh was a Post-Impressionist. He was at once a painter who evokes interest and yet sends signals of warning in a way unlike any other. His style was unlike any other as well. He suffered from mental instability most of his life and spent time in an institution with questionable results.

Some of his final works are frightening and dark. Still, through all this he continued to paint beautiful flowers and fine portraits.

Antoinette and I resume our study of Vincent Van Gogh after his discharge from the Institution in St. Rémy in the south of France. We learn from our knowledgeable guide in Auvers that Van Gogh's friend, painter Camille Pissarro, who had also transitioned into Post Impressionism, recommended the move to Auvers. It is known that as a result of the Franco-Prussian War 1870-71, some 1500 of Pissarro's paintings were lost when he fled to London. This devastating development undoubtedly discussed between the two hard-working, barely recognized artists could have cast a pall over fragile Van Gogh's psyche. With his health in mind, Pissarro put Van Gogh in touch with Dr. Gachet in Auvers. The physician would keep an eye on him. In due time Vincent painted his doctor's portrait: Yet, another painting that Van Gogh's brother, Theo, would have difficulty selling. Much later it sold in 1990 for 82.5 million dollars! Vincent arrived in Auvers on May 20, 1890. He found a room for rent in the Auberge (Inn) Ravoux, now an historic landmark, where we are exploring his final habitat. Several other artists lived here as well. It seemed like a good fit for the troubled Vincent after leaving the Asylum in the south of France. He was feeling more stable and was discharged from the institution. Here at Ravoux, Vincent would be in the company of artists who shared the same difficulties as he in barely affording to buy painting supplies and very rarely finding buyers for their work.

Tragically, Vincent sold only one painting during his lifetime. His many failures over time, had added heavily to his life of rejection by his family and the girl he loved. He failed in his study to become a preacher, as well as his in work as a Protestant Evangelist. More recently he also lost his friend, Paul Gauguin. Events like these had been the theme of his life.

That being said, we learn that following his arrival at Auvers, Vincent became a regular around town, getting to know the locals, even painting their likenesses. He appeared to be stalwart, healthy and energetic. During this period, he painted some of his most familiar scenes: "Crows over the Wheat Field", painted with his back to the quiet Church of Notre Dame that we viewed at the start of our trip. His "Starry Night", not painted here, but not long before leaving the Asylum in St.-Rémy-de-Provence. It was sketched from his room and finished outside in another wheat field with Cyprus trees. He made at least 20 sketches and paintings of this scene from behind his barred window.

During his short stay at Auvers, he completed 77 paintings and 50 sketches between his arrival on May 20 and his sad demise on July 29 at age 37. Two days prior he had ventured into a field and shot himself in the chest. He managed with difficulty to return to the 'Auberge' where he fell into bed and following two days of suffering, died. Such a sad, sad, story of a great painter whom we love and revere to this day. I was fortunate to see his "Starry Night" as part of a complete retrospective of his work, at the Museum of Modern Art in New York City when I worked just across the street.

While touring the Auberge Ravoux, I am saddened to see Vincent's second floor room, more like a cell, furnished with the most simple, single cot, a chair and a built-in bureau and one window. The floor is bare wood. It was here that he kept all his beautiful paintings, probably just leaned upright against the wall. Here he lived out his last two months and died in agony and despair. I believe he was the last one to occupy this room. It is now a part of the museum. During our visit today, there is music playing in the background. Not sure if they are still doing it. The music is sung by American opera singer, Jesseye Norman, who sang "La Marseillaise" finale at the Paris parade on July 14, 1989 celebrating the Bicentennial of the French Revolution (See chapter three). Vincent and devoted brother, Theo, are buried nearby in twin graves.

Though downhearted, my friend and I are compelled to follow Vincent's traces downstairs to the dining room where it is said he dined on a regular basis. We descend the stairs just as Vincent used to do and are seated in the unpretentious dining room. Surely a good, hot meal will do much to cheer us today. I understand that the menu is much as it was in Vincent's day over one hundred years ago. So, we order a dish he preferred, so they say, 'terrine de lapin aux lentils' (rabbit terrine with lentils).

The word 'terrine' refers not only to the dish in which it is baked, but also to the preparation of the meat without bones, flavored and pressed into the oval shape of the baking dish, topped with pastry and served warm or cold. We are not disappointed. Another day beyond compare to be savored in our study of artists who painted their hearts out for the pain and love of it all. It has been a splendid in-depth tour of Normandy, wending our way along the Seine River during which we followed several threads of French art, French architecture along with French/English/American history dating as far back as Guillaume le Conquérant. We wanted to stand in the shoes of the Impressionists and those of my Norman, French/English ancestors and in each instance, we found even more in the way of little-known history than we could have predicted.

Au Revoir Paris; We Encounter a Bomb!

We have but one day in Paris to repack and repair to De Gaulle Airport for our non-stop flight to New York. We are staying at my favorite small hotel, Esmeralda, on the left bank of the Seine directly across from Notre Dame Cathedral and two steps from St.-Julien-le-Pauvre Church (the oldest church in Paris). I have had some memorable visits to this charming, old world Hotel Esmeralda. It is fitting that we should spend our last night on the Seine in the heart of Paris! I am so happy to be here again. Once, when I visited here, I was with my son, Rusty, and Rita, a classmate at the University. We had a suite of rooms that time with a balcony that faced Notre Dame. Today we have a nice double room with a similar view. No complaints, except that we have little time left in the City of Light.

We seem to have endless energy, so we make our way to the Luxembourg Gardens to do some errands in that direction. When we finish, we sit in iron chairs by the pond to watch the children float their wooden boats of all sizes and shapes. It is relaxing after being on our feet most of the day. We are going to have dinner at the Explorateur Restaurant, only two short blocks from the Esmeralda. Now we begin to feel droopy and have to admit we are too tired to walk all the way back. We hail a taxi. We simply want to have a good dinner with a glass of wine, then retire early.

On the way back in the cab, we are surprised to be told by a policeman to halt suddenly behind a line of traffic, also being stopped for some reason. There are crowds of pedestrians on either side of us. We ask the driver what the problem is. He has no idea, and he tells us to sit tight until he can find out. People are scurrying past us by then; some are running! What could be the hold up? At last the driver gets out of the taxi, walks forward to inquire of the 'agent de police'. When he finally returns, he has the answer. There has been an explosion almost directly beneath where we sit. The 'Métro' runs below us. Just under us a terrorist has set off a bomb minutes ago. Not good news to hear any day anywhere! We look at each other in shock. The traffic will not be going anywhere. We quickly determine that much.

After some minutes of indecision, seeing no sign of injuries and having not heard the noise of a bomb, we decide that for now there is nothing in our immediate area above ground to fear, so we pay the driver and climb out of the cab heading toward the Explorateur Restaurant on foot. It is about six blocks. Fortunately, we know the way. So off we go. Our adventures are ending on a sour note, but we shall make the best of it. After all, we are going to a restaurant we know well and will have a relaxing meal. We will pick up a paper in the morning to learn the details. We are more than thankful we were in the right place at the time and NOT in the Métro where we could so easily have been with our sore feet!

When we arrive at the hotel we are welcomed by the owner and her black cat. We are home safe on the Seine where we started. The more I think about it, this tome is really a tale of two rivers: The Loire and the Seine. Before boarding our return on Air France plane home, I give

Mado a call to tell her of the success of our trip along the Seine. Speaking for myself, my mind is awash with the light and spellbinding hues of the Impressionists. I am filled to overflowing with new information in my favorite fields of art, architecture, cuisine and history, all of which nourish my hungry soul.

Chapter Eleven

Chopin and Sand: Chasing Rainbows.
Frederic Chopin and George Sand at Nohant

ALWAYS CURIOUS, I TURN TO a new adventure where history and music are intertwined. It is the bittersweet story of Frédéric Chopin and George Sand.

One of my favorite composers is Frédéric Chopin. My childhood music teacher, Miss Cadogan, in Hornell, New York, introduced me to his music. So, this summer, move over, Bashmet, as Chopin takes center stage. This weekend happened while I was still studying in France. In fact, I am taking a long weekend away from Tours to indulge myself in Chopin's music. How does a Polish composer figure in my summer plans? Bear with me. I will weave the fascinating story of the last years of his life spent in France as they are revealed to me. The next four days I plan to immerse myself in his music. I am making a side trip away from the Loire Valley to the actual "Centre" (a Department) of the nation I love, to drive to the region known as the "Le Berry" (former province of France). My quest: Chasing Rainbows, following my beating heart to discover the heretofore little-known pulsating core of Chopin's last years in France.

Per my winter reading of French newspapers, an article about Chopin caught my eye. I mentioned it to Mado when I arrived in Tours, and she said: "You are in luck. The famous 'Festival Chopin' is in full swing from the end of June into July in the town of Nohant only a few hours' drive from Tours." There are two locations in France proper where

Chopin spent time. One is Paris and the other is the small country town of Nohant in the "Centre Département". Mado added that the festival is well worth a trip from anywhere if you love Chopin. I do; so, with that recommendation in mind, I ask a couple of friends at the Institut to join me in trip to Nohant, but no one is interested. "So", said the little red hen, "I shall do it myself." And I did.

I may not be able to stoke the fire in anyone else's belly, nor can I dowse it in my own! I am off on this extraordinarily sweltering weekend alone. I make a hotel reservation in Nohant and rent a car without air conditioning (those with A/C were taken for the weekend). Off I go with my map and directions from Mado spread across my knees to mitigate the heat from the ever–scorching sun that tries to broil my legs. I am venturing into a region of France of which I knew next to nothing. What I do know is that Chopin composed beautiful music, and I am making a beeline for it, intending to get my fill.

Frédéric Chopin was born in Warsaw, Poland on February 22, 1810 (some believe this is the date of his baptism). During his youth he was a celebrated child prodigy, and his piano concerts featuring his music were in demand. He composed mostly for the piano: études, sonatas, mazurkas, balades, nocturnes, polonaises, preludes, rondos, scherzos, waltzes and impromptus. Some of the themes are so sweet and unforgettable that we music-lovers tend to hum them without even thinking they are Chopin's. I am referring specifically to his 'Fantasie Impromptu' No. 4, Opus 66 in C sharp minor that he wrote it in 1834 as a piano solo while living in Paris. The tune is light, rapid and enchanting. It tugs at your heartstrings and once heard, resides there. It is optimistic; it soars; it transcends earthly bonds.

I read that Chopin did not want to have it published, not even posthumously. His agent went ahead and handed the manuscript over to the publisher anyway, happily for the rest of the world that has come to know it so well.

I call my trip to Nohant: "Chasing Rainbows" in honor of Chopin and this particular melody because of dear Chopin's hummable tune that has come to be known also as "I'm always chasing rainbows, watching clouds drifting by..." Most everyone knows it. Chopin's unforgettable "Impromptu" theme was adapted into a song for the first time by Harry Carroll; lyrics by Joseph McCarthy and recorded by singer Harry Fox (April 1918) on Columbia records. It was also sung by "The Dolly Sisters" in the Broadway musical comedy called "Oh Look!" the same year. Judy Garland also sang Chopin's "Impromptu" theme in the movie, "Ziegfield Girl". And again, without so much as a reference to Chopin, it was the leading song in the Twentieth Century Fox 1945 film "The Dolly Sisters" starring Betty Grable and June Haver. I played it on the piano beginning in the late 1940s. I saved the sheet music of the second song from "The Dolly Sisters" ("I can't begin to tell you") to illustrate the American venue where Chopin's music thrilled audiences in the form of a popular hit song. Who knew? Certainly not the composer.

While on the subject of Chopin's 'Impromptu', I often make tangential references to films and books that relate to my adventures in France. This time I wish to tell you the reader, about a 1991 film titled: "Impromptu", about George Sand (played by Judy Davis) and Frédéric Chopin (played by Hugh Grant), concerning the time they spend together at Sand's French country home in Nohant. The film takes place here. It is often wild, strays from the truth, depicts the couple with their Parisian comrades as unconventional. The film presents a glimpse of the couple's life in Paris as well as her country residence in Nohant in central France where I have visited more than once. Chopin and Sand received artists, writers, and composer for weekend house parties. Franz Liszt (played by Julian Sands - a descendant of George?) who is portrayed perhaps reliably as incorrigibly indecent to his erstwhile long-suffering lover, Marie, (played by Bernadette Peters).

In the film, there is a duel, quite fashionable at the time and sometimes led to horrifying results, even death. The duel, the type of which may have occurred in real life, between Sand's two lovers and which spotlights Chopin as weak and most assuredly, not up to the task of keeping up with his love interest: Aurore Dudevant/aka George Sand, who sports trousers, top hat, and smokes a cigar. She is thrust to the forefront of the slow-moving feminist movement that does not flower until women win the right to vote. Sand is way ahead of her time.

Back to earth in Nohant, I settle into my room and walk to a nearby bank to cash some travelers' checks. While standing in line, I overhear the couple behind me speaking English with an American accent. Aha! I turn around to address them tourist-to-tourist and find that they are also here for the Chopin Festival. Upon further prodding I discover that they know some good friends of mine in Watertown, CT. Now, that is really a surprise, since I find myself in what I call 'way off the beaten path' here. The couple are a part of a tour group following in Chopin's traces from Poland to Majorca (Spain), to France, including Nohant, and Chopin's burial place at Père Lachaise cemetery in Paris. I love running across like-minded travelers. One has but to strike up a conversation and voilà, the serendipitous surprises dance into my path; they serve to broaden my horizons.

My new American acquaintances are more than gracious. I am pleased that they speak English, and they are thrilled that I speak French as they have questions to ask me about Nohant and the schedule of musical events. Fortunately, I happen to have connected with a group of "Chopinistes" (lovers of Chopin) as I call them. They graciously invite me to dine with them in a fine restaurant that night. I accept with pleasure.

At Nohant, this weekend I will hear Chopin's "Impromptu" played by Halina Czerny-Stefaska, who is an expert in concertizing uniquely Chopin's compositions. This is her life's work. Now, as I write this memoir, I see that she passed away shortly after the turn of the second millennium. All the concerts this weekend are presented by masters of Chopin on the piano, exhibiting his compositions as only a master can. I can hardly contain my excitement to be surrounded by such talent.

It is the 'bon moment' (a good time) to fill in some background on George Sand as we are tourists in her hometown. Since I have studied French literature for many years, I feel comfortable blending with my new friends on their Chopin/Sand focus study here in the center of France. George Sand was born July 1, 1804 and named Amantine-Lucille-Aurore Dupin. Although born in Paris, she spent most of her childhood in Nohant, carefree, loving nature and riding horseback astride, free as the wind. At the age of fourteen, she lost her father and was sent to Paris to a convent where she, as many Christians, was in direct communication with God through prayer. Before long, her grandfather brought her back home to Nohant, fearful that a form of mysticism becoming popular at the time, might influence Aurore.

Following a failed marriage to Casmir Dudevant, she returned to Paris leaving her daughter, Solange, and son, Maurice, behind. Seeking her independence, she began to write, adopting a 'nom de plume' (pen name), George Sand. The reason was simple. In the writing world of her day she would have a far better chance of being published if she were perceived to be a man. Not only did she sign her books as George Sand, but she dressed in her long black riding trousers with a jaunty matching jacket, and she sported cropped hair. With her persona forming anew, still in her late twenties, she went on to become one of the most prolific and most successful female novelists of her era.

Chopin and Sand were regulars in Paris social circles. They both knew and were known by many of the notable artists of the era. It was, therefore, not a surprise they would cross paths. It happened, pre-arranged or by chance, on the evening of October 24, 1836 in the salon of pianist /composer Franz Liszt's paramour, Maria D'Agoult. Although details of the personal relationship between Chopin and Sand that grew from that meeting, will never be known, the handsome composer (Chopin) and the successful writer (Sand) became the "beautiful couple" of the century. All the same, they were surrounded by difficulties and triumphs in their individual fields and in their personal lives. Theirs is the kind of enigmatic love story that fascinates for centuries.

Being an erstwhile writer and music aficionado, I am swept up in their struggle to find real love and to nurture it as a gift. I hope, in walking through the home they shared here in Nohant and listening to Chopin's music, that I may draw closer to them both. This is to be a weekend of discovery for me. I feel it in my bones.

I purchase a ticket for every concert given and will attend as many master classes as possible. It had not occurred to me to sit in on master classes before I arrived, but I learn from my American friends that to attend master classes is to know Chopin more intimately. I want to be surrounded by this unlikely love duo: her writing about the people who lived in this rural community 150 years ago; his composing, most likely inspired by Sand. I will listen attentively to his famous "Imporptu" melody and chase the ever-elusive rainbows Chopin must have sought. The two artists were the epitome of the romantic period they sired.

The guided tour of Sand's country home is enchanting, in some ways like Monet's at Giverny. I love to see the rooms where the food of life is prepared and then consumed in their respective dining rooms over intimate family meals and candlelight party gatherings. Both dining rooms sing to me with blues and whites — my colors too. The dining table is set for a meal and beckons the diners to the table. It is as though we, too, are invited for a meal with George, Frédéric, and 'companie' comrades). Theirs is a large oval table surrounded by white painted wooden chairs with upholstered backs, seats and arms, all exquisitely done in a lovely sea blue with white stripes. I am taken in at a glance. Oh, my goodness. Each setting has a place card. It feels as if it was prepared with a flourish just before our arrival! I stroll slowly around the table to see who is invited for supper with me. I note:

George Sand 'mais, certainement' (of course), at the head of the table.

Gustave Flaubert (novelist)

Ivan Turgenev (Russian writer)

Alexandre Duma, fils (playwright)

Eurgene Delacroix (artist)

Pauline Viadot (mezzo soprano)

Frédéric Chopin at the foot.

Such an intimate group of friends, most of whom I know, if briefly. I have studied Sand, Flaubert, Dumas and long admired paintings of Delacroix. Turgenev and Viadot are new to me.

Upstairs in the gracious home are the bedrooms and giving off from a long hall is Sand's writing room. The author preferred to write late at night and often not stopping much before dawn. This is so much like my habit of awaking in the middle of night and creeping down to my library to pound the keys until nearly light. It is such a perfect atmosphere in which to think and to create at will without interruption of life's little foibles.

Sand's lifestyle must have left little time for rest as the house was often filled with their Parisian acquaintances. Franz Liszt (composer/pianist) and his lover, Maria D'Agoult, were favorites on the guest list here with their growing family. Late night 'soirees' left little time for Sand to grab a few hours' sleep, night or day. This group of friends loved to have a good time together and, being creative, they were never at a loss for ideas. Sand built a theatre in the house. I thought it was very well-integrated to the size of the dwelling. In fact, our tour takes us to see it. We descend to the lower level below the main floor. The theatre has a raised stage, small, but perfect for portraying portions of Sand's novels set in the countryside near Nohant.

Let it be noted that Chopin was very productive during his seven summers spent with Sand in the country. He composed three quarters of his entire 'oeuvre' (life's work) right here. What does this say about these two lovers? They possessed a necessary depth of urgency to create plus a continued renewal of inspiration urging them on from within. Imagine trying to write or compose music with activities going on all around, people coming and going, and do not forget Maria's baby crying. Chopin did not have inexhaustible energy due partly to the fact that he was plagued with tuberculosis and a weak constitution. He must have had that certain 'je ne sais quoi' (I know not what), in his mind and heart to keep up with Sand's frenetic pace.

Just briefly, Sand was super prolific in her writings: 2 autobiographies and a shorter one on their trip to Majorca; ca. 60 novels between 1831-67; and 14 plays. Chopin, as I mentioned, was prolific in his work as well. He composed in all the genres of piano music, so numerous I could not count them all.

Beyond all this work, Sand was his caregiver and his light, his true inspiration. She did everything in her power to make him comfortable and to love him through difficult periods. She took him to the island of Majorca for the sun and the clean air to improve his health. Although the humidity may have aggravated his tuberculosis, overall, the trip may have extended his life.

Along with their God-given talent hey were a couple of opposites; she was a true aristocratic blue blood and he, not so much. She was a liberal free thinker who followed her heart and did not always think things through but acted impulsively. He was more conservative. She was an activist. He, not so much. She had many lovers before and after him. For example, some of her lovers: Jules Sandeau (she borrowed part of his last name for herself and her 'nom de plume' (pen name) and had it notarized); Alfred de Musset, poet/ dramatist; and Prosper Merimée, author of "Carmen". Chopin, not so much. He was monogamous. He was fleeing from a failed affair when he came to Paris and met George. At their first meeting, she was impulsive and did not wait for an introduction. She planted a kiss full on his lips before he had time to utter a word.

Sand and Chopin were caught up in the romanticism of the era, both in their writing and composing and in their personal lives. Even living closely together they followed their separate paths as artists in their own fields and both displayed genius in their separate fields, of which there is no doubt. Living together under one roof as they did, was an amazing feat. She did her best to not be burdened with his illness but found numerous ways to help him as best she could. It must have been depressing at times when they both knew he would die young. She loved him unreservedly. That was her way; to do something fervently from her heart, I can only surmise…that is all I can do from the distance of time. It has been posited that we should be thankful to Sand for loving him as she did. It certainly granted Chopin a longer life than he might have had without her.

Here at the 'Festival Chopin' the musical programs are beautifully presented in a variety of venues. I would say that the piano soloists were names well known to close followers of Chopin. I admit I am not familiar with many of them but intend to follow up when I return home. Most of the pianists have been playing Chopin for decades and play with perfection. Most are European. Many, of course, are Polish and not often seen in the northeastern United States. I buy a collection of Chopin's music on CD's with six individual CDs including his best compositions. I spend each morning at master classes. This is a new experience for me. Each class is conducted under the tutelage of a master on the piano who devotes his time to one composer, in this case, Chopin, thus instructing a worthy and industrious student to become a true master of the subject. Each master works with one student at a time in a small room.

I enter with my American friends and find a seat to observe the teaching and the learning process in the allotted two-hour session. During this time the master sets the program, usually working with one particular Chopin composition. The student then plays the piece but expects to be halted whenever the master makes a comment or a correction. It is a most interesting process to witness. Through the progress of the class we can see how the student gradually improves his or her technique while playing and re-playing passages of Chopin's demanding style and challenging pace.

On the last day I return to Sand's home to review the area, if not the exact room where Chopin worked and wrote his music. He left Sand and Nohant after a falling out in 1847. He barely put pen to paper after their rupture. It is sad to contemplate his lingering illness without the woman he had loved. Chopin died in Paris in 1849 and is buried in the famous Père Lachaise cemetery in Paris. I have not visited the cemetery where so many famous men and women are buried. It is not as special to me as Saint-Denis that I described earlier, nor Fontevraud with which I close this final chapter, but auspicious, nonetheless.

Before driving back to Tours, I savor some precious moments walking through Sand's gardens, pausing at the large flat stone that marks her grave. The long weekend has plucked my heartstrings for the star-crossed lovers who once romped in these gardens 150 years ago on moonlit, dewy grass.

So, dear reader, this is where my rainbow-chasing ends. The "pot of gold" is the books and music Sand and Chopin left behind for us to enjoy.

Chapter Twelve
Now I Lay Them Down to Sleep

EARLIER I WROTE ABOUT A royal necropolis, Saint Denis, in Paris where many of the French royal families and their progeny are interred. Today I am visiting the Abbaye Royale de Fontevraud, another royal necropolis, where my deceased warrior ancestors have lain sheltered for over 800 years. The Abbaye is the central feature of this charming, medieval town of the same name. So, I am off again on a visit of discovery in my rental car.

I have often referred to my forbears, namely King Henry II and his wife, Queen Aliénor and their son, Richard Lionheart, in this collection of summer adventures. it seems appropriate now, as I near the end of my decade of summers spent in France, that I should allow my ancestors the peace they deserve. In a matter of speaking, I shall lay them down to rest at last within the walls of the Abbaye Royale de Fontevraud.

Today, I am making my second trip to the 'Abbaye' (abbey). Founded by Priest Robert of Arbrissel ca. 1101, it was planned and built as the perfect monastic city. It remains the largest group of monastic buildings in France. It is on the borders of Anjou, Touraine and Poitou, near the town of Chinon, site of the favorite castle of the Plantagenets. There is much to explore here, especially for me, as I have taken it upon myself to learn as much as I can about my great grandmother Queen Aliénor of Aquitaine. As you know, to learn more about her life story has been one of my most important quests throughout these ten summers. Today, to further my knowledge, I have requested an appointment with the

Keeper of the Abaye's archives, M. Souverain. I tote my genealogical upline in a book published by a cousin. His research is an easy read starting with me, my parents and maternal grandparents dating back, name by name, in a straight line to Aliénor, so I may prove my interest is legitimate.

I tuck my notebook under my arm and am ready to delve as deeply as I can into their books and papers in the time I have allotted for this serious research visit. M. Souverain searches for some items for me to commence. They are the oldest documents I have ever seen. Of course, they are written in 'olde' French from the early medieval period (12th century). I am not fluent in the tongue of that time, (Occitan), but I have read some songs, poems and short histories from that early time in my graduate studies. I am truly thankful for that preparation.

Suffice it to say, I find that holding these precious documents and reading what I can, to be an honor. I take notes and ask for a few copies to be made for me. The librarian and others are most accommodating. It does not take long to discover that my study will be limited as I am not an accomplished medievalist. Nonetheless, they leave me alone in a carrel to go over the tomes for as long as I please. I am humbled by this experience.

Later I am ready for the tour of the Abbaye in order to learn about its beginnings. My colleague, Rita, also a French teacher in Connecticut, joins me for the tour. Now that I have gone well beyond preliminary studies of my forebears, Aliénor and her family, I want to see where she spent her last days.

Our guide tells us the Abbaye of Fontevraud was created as a mixed or double order of men and women from all levels of society, headed by a series of abbesses. Some of the sisters were of royal blood. Until 1792 it was a place of prayer, silence, abstinence and work. For all these reasons, it sheltered a unique monastic order, a treasured atmosphere in which to live, study and worship. The itinerant priest, Robert of Abrissel, Britanny, may indeed have founded a perfect city of peace and tranquility. It lasted for nearly 600 years. In 1792 the last abbess was sent packing by the Revolutionaries of the French

Revolution. One of the goals of the Revolution was to rid society of the two highest levels: nobles and priests. (abbesses and nuns fell into that category as well). By 1804 Napolélon ruled that the Abbay be transformed into a high security prison. During World War II it was an intermediary stop for prisoners of Third Reich en route to prison camps in Germany. Some were executed here.

We pass through the well-clipped hedges, the recently flowered fruit trees and gardens in the French mode of perfectly balanced flower beds. The entire complex covers over 32 acres.

The tall church steeple dominates the ensemble of edifices, whereas the spires of the Romanesque kitchens pique our curiosity the most. First, we enter the kitchens to view an unusual architectural style inside and out. From inside we are urged to look up to the ceiling to see the many openings once used to vent the ovens. The ceiling is still tinged with the black soot of all those fires over centuries of use. From the exterior, it looks like a sort of beehive, but a curious building style I have never seen before. The closest in shape and use in my opinion would be the American Indian tepee that had only one fire vent at the top. The purpose was the same in both cases, to expel the cooking smoke, odors and the excess heat. Just imagine the smoked turkey and smoked salmon that issued from here to the tables in the refectory. They grew most everything they needed on site; always the best way to control a healthy menu even today. To work with one's hands in the soil is said to be close to God.

We see the large, open refectory where residents took their meals; climb to the top floor to see the view over the town and the gardens. The cloisters are beautiful from any point of view with their rounded Romanesque archways marching in even cadence around the gardens. I recall as many as 10 or 12 arches on each of three sides. It was constructed on a grand scale. The walkway along the cloisters affords the visitor or resident a sense of order. When I look up there are lovely examples of vaulted ceilings. Bowing my head, I notice the renovated white marble floors with interspersed blue diamonds underfoot, as beautiful as the countless arches.

The last building to tour is the Abbaye church. It is an exquisite example of Romanesque architecture that spans the ninth to the twelfth centuries leading up to the Gothic period that we all recognize in Saint Denis, visited in chapter 11 and others. The outline of the base of the church on the ground conforms to the shape of the cross. Many Romanesque churches have two towers. Fontevraud has but one square one. The apse is very tall with clerestory windows along the upper walls. Fontevraud has the open transept, and there are no aisles. Chairs can be added or subtracted. At Fontevraud I see it generally without chairs. Typically, the supporting piers are in the form of broad columns with a multitude of stone moldings added for extra stability that lead to the ceiling for support of the heavy roof. Most important are the rounded archways throughout the edifice inside and out, above windows, cloisters, and walkways. In my opinion I find the interior much more breathtaking than the exterior as the former reveal a truer, even breathtaking continuity of style than the latter. The overall design here described is reminiscent of the "Abbaye de la Madeleine, Vezelay", where I stood with Aliénor at the 'Preaching of the Second Crusade' in my "Conversation'" play. That conversation occurred the summer I studied at the University of Bourgogne at Dijon.

I adore this place as a whole but am partial to the Abbaye Church as this is where my grandmother, Aliénor, lies as a 'gisant' (recumbent figure) upon her sepulchre in perpetuity. I feel closer and closer to Aliénor with each visit. She must have found true peace here with none of the distractions of everyday life outside the cloister.

In truth Aliénor's quiet life here was interrupted on a couple of occasions when, without her intervention, the course of history would have been greatly altered. These were times Aliénor had to be consulted as there was no one else of her stature to confront the rising problems that she alone had to face. One such state crisis was when her son,

Richard, was returning from the Third Crusade and was captured by Leopold of Austria, then imprisoned by Emperor Heinrich of the Holy Roman Empire and held for more than two years in total (1192-1194). During that time Aliénor was worried when he did not return as planned. When she found out where he was being held, she was handed a note demanding a huge ransom or she might never see her son again.

It was 1193, and Aliénor was in her 71st year. Accordingly, she left the security of Fontevraud where she was residing at the time and began to raise the enormous sum required for her son's release. I recount the story around this history-making event in my play, "Conversations with Queen Aliénor". At length, after securing the gold, silver et al she made her way to Western Germany in severe weather with a small group of her protectors to hand it over to the stubborn Emperor. In time, after many detours and stand-offs with the Emperor, she was permitted to see her son and take him home. She had crossed the 'narrow sea' (English Channel), struggled over mountain passes and swollen, icy rivers in winter to free her son.

Aliénor then returned to Fontevraud, her place of refuge in her elder years, to reflect and to recover. The ransom journey was not the only challenge she would face in her golden years. Her priorities did not change simply because she was well into her third age. The long-term sustainability of her kingdom, even though ruled by her son, John, remained at the top of the list for this undaunted Queen of the English (former Queen of the French).

In 1199 at 77 years of age, at the command of her youngest son, King John, the elderly Queen undertook another long trip from her home in Poitiers, Anjou (Loire Valley), to Castile, Spain. Her mission was to choose one of her two granddaughters (children of Aliénor's daughter: Queen Eleanor of Castile, aka Eleanor of England, and Eleanor's husband, King Alphonso VIII of Castille), to eventually become the future wife of the future King of France, Louis VIII. To reach her goal, Aliénor crossed the Pyrenees and traveled to Castile either in a sedan chair or on horseback. Her trip took a similar route to the one Rusty and I followed en route to Santiago de Compostela in an earlier chapter. Although we sped there in our air-conditioned car, we could not help thinking of the travails of our great, great, grandmother as she faced extremes of heat and freezing temperatures crossing the mountains, undulating hills and flats of northern Spain.

Amazingly, Aliénor accomplished the first leg of her trip, reaching the residence of her daughter, probably in Burgos, in winter. While there, she chose ten-year old Princess Blanche. The young princess would live with her in-laws-to-be until ready for marriage; the consummation of which would not take place until the child bride was at least 15. This was the custom of royal families in those days.

For grandemaman, Aliénor, it was a difficult trip health wise, and as result she was encouraged to spend extra time with her daughter and family in Castile. This was a real pleasure as mother and daughter had not seen each other since Eleanor's wedding about seven years earlier. During this period of hiatus, Aliénor gathered her strength before attempting the strenuous return climb over the Pyrenees. As planned, Aliénor personally escorted Blanche and their combined retinues to Bordeaux where Aliénor paused to rest while Blanche was safely delivered to her uncle, King John, in Normandy. By late spring of 1200 Blanche was transferred to the royal household of French King Philippe-Auguste II, father of young Louis, her husband–to-be in France. Although the trip must have tried Aliénor's physical abilities to the extreme, she succeeded with Queenly aplomb.

Queen Aliénor is known today as the "Grandmother of Europe". Remember that she bore 10 children to two Kings. We are left to surmise, that once a queen, always a queen and that her work was not finished until she breathed her last breath. If you permit, I will again include an excerpt from my "Conversations with Queen Aliénor", so you may have it in the Queen's words (my fictitional adaptation):

"Aliénor: Looking back before my captivity, when Christmas rolled around each year, I was usually pregnant. Henry was not home all that often, but when he came to my bed, I conceived! It was like clockwork. I was either already pregnant at Christmas or became pregnant shortly after leaving the birthing bed around that time of year. I gave birth 8 times between our first son, William's, birth in 1153 and the birth of our last son, John, in 1166. And that is not counting my two daughters, Marie and Alix, born from my first marriage to Louis VII, King of France.

Jini: I am trying to catch my breath, thinking of all those pregnancies, all those royal babies in such a short time. And you retained your health! Incredible in those days with so many women dying in childbirth.

Aliénor: I give thanks for my enduring state of good health. I remember thinking during that period of my life, that my Christmas present each year from Henry was another child.

Jini: I know I am straying slightly from our subject of Christmas Courts, but I cannot help but think of the consequences of all those pregnancies...ten children born healthy. According to my calculations there were five girls and five boys, only one of whom died very young. That was William, your first child with Henry II, and he died at age three. How you must have mourned that early loss.

Aliénor: Indeed, I did. We pinned so many hopes on our first son. Please go on.

Jini: Let me see. Where was I? Oh yes, and 51 grandchildren! Quite a brood. My but, you were fertile. Your daughters, Matilda and Eleanor (knowns by her English name), surpassed even you in fecundity, each producing a dozen progeny. So many reasons to be proud.

Aliénor: There would have been more progeny if my husband, Henry, had stayed home. He traveled our lands constantly. Do not forget that in our time, as a Queen, it was my bounden duty to produce heirs: males to inherit the throne, and females to send off to foreign lands to wed into other royal families. What better way to placate enemies than to become relatives?

Jini: Sadly, the follow-up is that you lived to see eight of your ten children die, a fate any parent dreads. Only Joanna and John out lived you. In your day, boy babies often grew up to die in battle and girl babies often grew up to die in childbirth. It is still so today. Although modern medicine has conquered many of the childbearing dangers, we are still at war. We continue to send our sons and now even daughters, off to war. WOE to us as mothers who have no control over what battles we fight as a nation.

Aliénor: Not so fast, my dear. JOY is us! Do not forget how my progeny led me to you nor lest we forget what fun we have shared in comparing stories about our children. We both survived childbirth without problems and rejoice in our downlines. You are one of my children too! Now it is my turn. Let me count. From your two marriages you have three children and nine grandchildren, right? (Jini nods) Not bad either, I might say. I know you cherish each and every one. (Aliénor hesitates and looks pensive) Little do our children know how much we pray for every good thing to come to them in their lives and how much we worry about setbacks even when they become parents themselves."

Now, reader friend, you can readily see why Aliénor is named 'Grandmother of Europe' and that she overcame the insecurities of childbirth and left the statistics writers in the dust!

Returning to our tour agenda here at Fontevraud, there are rooms for conferences such as the one I visited my first time here in July 1989 for the celebration and study of the life of King Henry II on the occasion of the 800th anniversary since his death, July 6, 1189. Bless the historians of today who remember these dates. My visit here that day was occasioned by the unanticipated invitation of a French lady whom I literally ran into on the sidewalk in Chinon. She was attending the conference and was in Chinon to catch a quick lunch before returning for the afternoon session. She then drove me here to Fontevraud. Amazing, n'est ce pas? That day was my initial contact with others like myself who followed King Henry II and his family. What a great way to be introduced to the Fontevraud that Aliénor loved so much. I call it a "not by chance meeting", on the anniversary that marked the conference that brought me first to Fontevraud was the same anniversary that marked Aliénor's release from her over nearly two-decade incarceration in Salisbury tower, England. Her husband, Henry II, threw her in prison, condemning her for collusion with her sons against him; but he was King, and she, his subservient wife. Her story was quite the opposite. Nonetheless, she persevered and survived thankfully to be freed upon the day of his death! July 6, 1189 was a bad day for Henry and a good day for Aliénor. I just happened to be in the right place at the right time to latch onto the shoestrings of their legacy story.

That day when I was shown into the necropolis where Henry and Aliénor lie recumbent I found the Abbaye Church to be in a state of dishevelment. Apparently, the restoration of the nave was in the midst of change. The 'gisants' (recumbent sculptures) were scattered and, there was dust aplenty layered with the smell of new concrete in the air. Background on the restoration project: In 1975 the Abbaye was named the "Cultural Center of the West of France". To my knowledge, restorations have been in progress ever since. So, as the years drew on and I visited almost every summer beginning in 1989, I have witnessed much renovation along with obvious improvements. Eventually the 'gisants' were moved into their permanent positions behind guardrails and now may be viewed close-up. I feel so fortunate to have witnessed these changes.

This area is a beautiful space for concerts here at Fontevraud. The main Concert hall is not far from the 'gisants' and is the chamber from which float the strains of early music that I adore. My husband, John, and I attended one very fine concert of early baroque music of Spain. It was the Opera 'San Ignacio', said to be the lost opera of the

Jesuit missions of the Amazon. Why am I not surprised at the subject matter! I am mesmerized by the full orchestra of original instruments with musicians and singers in good number. The acoustics in the 'salle' (room) are astounding to say the least. I bought their CD that I am listening to as I write. What a grand way to bring back the memory of another aspect of Fontevraud.

My husband, John, and I had driven almost two hours to make the concert, and then had to return the same distance on our late-night return trip to Tours. It was worth the trip. Early music is readily available in Europe if you know where and how to find it. Some of the most wonderful musical evenings for me have been spent from one side of France to the other, enjoying these unveiled musical gems.

My friend, Rita, and I have saved the crème de crème for last in our tour of the Abbaye. It is the church nave and the 'gisants', of which I speak so often. They are placed in their proper locations, Top: left to right: Queen Aliénor and King Henry II. Bottom: left to right: Queen Isabella of Angoulême, (wife of King John of England, son of Aliénor and Henry II) and King Richard I Lionheart. To see them once again here, brings chills to my spine. I spend so much time in the presence of my grandmother, Aliénor, while writing at my computer keyboard that now, I relish yet another pass by her sleeping persona today. I enjoy sharing this moment with you, my reader, most likely my last chance to view all four 'gisants'. Of course, I cherish most, my time with Aliénor while recalling my 'off the cuff' "Conversations" with her, our 'repartée' (talk) holding nothing back between us for six scenes in my three-act play. For Aliénor it is a welcome, all too brief return to life, an escape from eternal recumbency, reading atop her hard, stone sarcophagus into eternity at Fontevraud. I know it is a stretch of the imagination, but are you with me?

Queen Aliénor d'Aquitaine reads atop her seplechure at the Abbaye de Fontevraud, France. I visited her frequently during my decade in the Valley of the Kings. As a result, I have written a 3 Act, 6 Scene play titled: Conversations with Queen Aliénor in which I meet with Aliénor (my 29th great grandmother), first in Connecticut, but mostly in Europe, in locations of mutual interest to the Queen and myself.

Back to my "Conversations" play: my grandmother, Queen Aliénor, and I are walking together through the Royale Necropolis (burial place of royals) of Fontevraud. I ask her what she is reading. It is the question I hear most frequently regarding Aliénor and the book she holds here. She answers that she is reading the steamy love story of her day: "Tristan and Isolde" (or is it her prayer book?). Even she does not recall. Or, she does not care to reveal the truth. Aliénor leaves it to us to fill in the blanks.

"(Aliénor and Jini move into the necropolis chamber where Aliénor's partial family grouping lies in effigy. They enter the large, cool nave of the Abbaye Church).

Aliénor: We are alone here. There is only the soft sound of our feet on the cool stones. Let us walk hand in hand beneath the immense multi-footed columns that surround the catafalques where my family and I lie frozen in stone for eternity. I am feeling cooler now too in this place. You too?

Jini: (Jini follows her lady grandmother toward the nearest figure) Oh, yes. I welcome the coolness here.

(The two women are alone in the royal burial chamber. They are as silent as the recumbent stone figures. Jini follows Aliénor as she circles the grouping of four family members. Since there is construction going on, there are no ropes cordoning off the sleeping figures. Aliénor trails her hand over the painted stone, now much faded, surrounding the first sarcophagus, that of Isabella d'Angoulême.

Out of reverence Aliénor and Jini fall silent, each descending into her thoughts of times past and of what is to come. Finally, Aliénor speaks.)

Aliénor: I have clouded feelings as I look upon my family in this way. I feel the distance that separates us now, yet still remain connected by the hip to each of them. I must say that I regret not being able to know Isabella as well as I would have wished. She joined the family too late for that. She was my son John's second wife as Queen Consort of England. They were wed in 1200 in a period of much upheaval. My son, Richard, and I had recently returned from his imprisonment by the Holy Roman Emperor; then, as you know, Richard built the grand Château Gaillard and died by 1199. John, who long wanted to be King, finally got his wish.

(Aliénor points to Isabella's effigy): My John married Isabella when she was very young. It was his second marriage, and she produced four children in their time together. John, my youngest, died in 1216 and Isabella in 1246. Of course, being much younger than John, she lived on to remarry and give birth to nine more children. My we were a fecund bunch, weren't we?

(Aliénor continues): Isabella is buried here because, in her last years she lived at Fontevraud much as I did. We both found refuge here. That much we shared. I have compassion for her as I know that the poor dear must have had a difficult life with my John. One thing for sure, we shared a dislike for the Philippe-Auguste II, King of France.

(Aliénor moves over to stand by Richard's recumbent figure. She stands by his feet peering up toward his face.): My Richard should have lived much longer, God be blessed, but for his gluttony for gold and other riches to finance his interminable battles against French King Philippe-Auguste II. I cannot help thinking that God finally put a stop to his overwhelming sense of pride. I know I should not judge him so harshly for I loved him the most of all my sons. As you see he is lying at the feet of his father, King Henry II. That was intentional. Richard wanted it so. I believe he had pangs of regret over having taken sides with his brothers against his own father. It must have weighed heavily on his heart toward the end. So, here he is paying obeisance to his father even in death.

(Aliénor moves to the last figure, that of her husband, Henry, who lies on her left. She is on his right, a not so subtle sign of her superiority over him in death if not in life.)

Aliénor: Of this foursome, Henry died first, and he had made it clear that he wished to be interred here. (With her left forefinger Aliénor gently traces the curve of Henry's cold, hard, chin and then slowly moves to cup his forehead with the same hand before stepping back to assess the royal foursome including her own sleeping figure. Aliénor and Jini maintain the reverent silence for a few long moments)

Jini: My heart is overflowing with love and adoration for you and yours, dearest Nanna. For you and OURS, that is. They are long gone, but not forgotten 800 years hence. With luck another 800 years will pass before interest in the Plantagenets who made such waves in the world, grows dim. Your Richard was shortsighted when he said that he would be surprised if he were to be remembered in 100 years.

This is indeed a tender moment that we share. I could never have dreamed when I was a research student at Fontevraud that I would someday stand here beside you, sharing as we are and talking of my uplines and your downlines. I barely find words to express my deep emotion.

(They step away from the dormant recumbents.)

Aliénor: I know the dear ones we see lying here are but earthly representations of what we all were in our lives, but I also believe that our souls have long since fled to our Heavenly Maker. May we rest in peace. (She crosses herself)."

Back on terra firma, I find myself in full reality lingering for a moment, not wanting to leave my dearest grandmother behind after spending such quality time together. I slowly back away, whispering my silent au revoir to Aliénor, praying that the Plantagenet family feuds have been forgiven. "Now I lay them down to sleep" at last in their beloved Fontevraud. I turn and take my leave.

Rita and I find our way back to Tours chez Mado and Lucien where a bountiful outdoor supper awaits us 'en plein jardin' (in the garden). Maryse has invited some friends to join us under their spreading banana tree. She greets us with her winning smile and a huge tray of Lucien's home-raised 'escargots en croûte' (snails baked in individual pastry covers), one of her specialties that the epicurean in me still relishes fondly, along with Kir Royale to celebrate 'le14 juillet (Bastille Day).' What could be better for two rapaciously hungry Francophiles returning to the fold?

About the Author

Jini Jones Vail is married to John Lester Vail, Sr. They reside in Watertown, Connecticut. Jini is the mother of Heather Woodring, Amy Dyer and Rusty Dyer and is the grandmother of nine. She was born in Hornell, New York, and is a graduate of Sweet Briar College with a BA in French Literature. She pursued graduate studies in the same field at the University of Touraine and the University of Bourgogne in France. As an historian, she is also a passionate writer of poetry, children's stores and family history, essays and the three-act, six-scene play, "Conversations with Queen Aliénor d'Aquitaine" in which she meets her 29th grandmother, Aliénor, in six locations of mutual interest, mostly in Europe.

Jini has combined her love of French and American history in a biography/military history:

"Rochambeau, Washington's Ideal Lieutenant, A French General's Role in the American Revolution".

(available on Amazon, iTunes, Kindle and Audible)

It is an in-depth account of General Rochambeau's life (1725-1807) and his American Campaign 1780-1783). Vail was a Commissioner on the Connecticut Governor's Commission on American and Francophone Cultural Affairs where she worked with Dr. Jacques Bossiere and Dr. Yolande Bosman to initiate the research and establishment of the Washington and Rochambeau Revolutionary Route (W3R) in the

1990s and early 2000s, now a National Historic Trail overseen by the National Park Service. This more than 700-mile route from Newport, RI to Yorktown, VA and returning through Connecticut into Boston to board their ships to France. The final battle of the American Revolution was the Battle of Yorktown, Virginia, where the French planned the siege and together with Washington and his Continental Army won the final pivotal battle of the American Revolution, October 19, 1781.

Vail is a member of Trumbull-Porter Chapter of the Daughters of the American Revolution and as a Francophile, is active in the Alliance Francaise of NW Connecticut. She is a presenter of French History, Rochambeau, with special interest in her family, church, cuisine, art, music, travel and all things French.

For more about the author, see her website: jinijonesvail.com and her history bites at: revolutionaryrochambeau.com.

WA